BEFORE THE SHOOTING BEGINS

Searching for Democracy in America's Culture War

James Davison Hunter

THE FREE PRESS

NEW YORK   LONDON   TORONTO   SYDNEY   TOKYO   SINGAPORE

The Free Press
A Division of Simon & Schuster Inc.
1230 Avenue of the Americas
New York, New York 10020

Printed in the United States of America

printing number

1 2 3 4 5 6 7 8 9 10

Library of Congress Cataloging-in-Publication Data

Hunter, James Davison
   Before the shooting begins : searching for democracy in America's culture war /
James Davison Hunter.
      p.   cm.
   Includes bibliographical references and index.
   ISBN 0–02–915501–0
   1. Abortion—United States. 2. Abortion—Moral and ethical
aspects. 3. Abortion—Political aspects—United States. 4. Culture
conflicts—United States. 5. Pluralism (Social sciences)—United
States. 6. United States—Social conditions.   I. Title.
HQ767.5.U5H86   1994
363.4'6'0973—dc20   93–42433
                                                               CIP

Some of the material in this book has been published in modified form elsewhere.
Much of the argument of Chapter 4 was published in *First Things*
(July 1992), and the section on the press, in Chapter 6, was published
in the *Columbia Journalism Review* (June/July 1993).

To my brother, Whitney
and my sister, Kati

CONTENTS

v

PREFACE

Some would say the shooting has already begun. Pro-choice activists, for example, point to the shooting of abortion providers, David Gunn in Pensacola, Florida, and George Tiller in Wichita, Kansas, not to mention the vandalizing of abortion clinics; pro-life activists point to the violence done to millions of pre-born children. The point is taken. Yet America is still some way off from large-scale civil strife and open violence. The real question, of course, is how well does our democracy mediate disagreement that is seemingly, if not in fact, incommensurable and unreconcilable. It is to the end of exploring this question that this project was undertaken. This book, then, should be seen as a companion and follow-up to my earlier work, *Culture Wars: The Struggle to Define America* (Basic Books, 1991).

I would like to emphasize straight away (what some reviewers of the earlier book missed) that the culture war of which I speak cannot be explained in terms of ordinary people's attitudes about public issues. Contemporary cultural conflict has at its core, competing moral visions. These moral visions are often enough reflected (imperfectly) in the world views of individuals, but by virtue of the way they are institutionalized and articulated in public life, these moral visions acquire something of a life of their own. It is at this level that the term culture war—with the implications of stridency, polarization, the mobilization of resources, etc.—takes on its greatest conceptual force.

Needless to say, democracy is an institution that also has a life of its own—normative ideals, ritual practices, a history, and so on. At the animating center of democratic experience, of course, is free and open public discourse. There is no democracy without it; it is the very stuff by which disagreement and controversy are mediated. At its heart, then, this book is an inquiry into the way we reflect upon and talk about our deepest differences in public life. Of public words there is no end, but is it the kind of substantive reflection and argument necessary to sustain democratic life?

In this book, as in *Culture Wars,* I have worked very hard to keep my own opinions about the issues of contemporary public dispute to myself. Probably the last thing public discussion needs at this time is the voice of one more activist committed to this or that program of change. Given the nature and significance of the contemporary culture war, it is enough to see clearly. This book aspires to that more modest end.

Nevertheless, position-taking is the reigning ontology of public life. One does not quite exist in public if one cannot be identified ideologically in the never-ending, ever-changing struggle for power. Though I have made every effort to be neutral in my analysis of particular issues and fair in understanding all sides (with both liberal and conservative colleagues holding me accountable), some will undoubtedly read this book with the chief purpose of linking it with the agenda of one social movement or another. So be it. But those who focus on this will miss the book's central concern: the possibilities of (and problems facing) substantive democracy in our historical moment. Democracy is a fragile enough institution that none of us can ever be complacent about its practical out-working—and especially in the context of deep and abiding cultural fragmentation. The danger of power politics (and its attending tyrannies) may be more immediate than we care to imagine. While never losing sight of the details of particular cases, it is my hope that this book will provoke the reader to reflect mainly about these larger matters.

I am indebted to numerous people for their help in writing this book. Carl Bowman of Bridgewater College not only co-authored Chapter Four but provided helpful commentary at every level of the analysis and interpretation. I am very thankful for his colleagueship and friendship. I am deeply indebted to Carol Sargeant and Beth Eck who helped me with the mechanics of the project at all stages: in conducting interviews, in library research, and in editing parts of the manuscript. I am also grateful to Rebecca Goodwin, Kimon Sargeant, Leslie Gunning, James Hawdon, John Fries, and Daniel Stuhlsatz who stepped in at strategic moments to lend assistance. Periodic conversations with Alissa Rubin, William Galston, Robert Wuthnow, Craig Dykstra, James Wind, Richard Horner, Ken Myers, Guy Condon, Clarke Forsythe, and Charles Allen were all enormously instructive. In addition a number of people read and commented on the manuscript as I neared completion and to them I am especially grateful for their observations and suggestions: Stephen Ainlay, Sarah Corse, Beth Eck, Os Guinness, Joseph Harder, James L. Nolan, John Seel, Garrett Sheldon, and Brad Wilcox. I would also like to express my gratitude to Susan Arellano of The Free Press for working with me on the ideas of this book from its inception to its completion. The grace, insight, and gentle prodding she offered was crucial to the completion of the book in its present form. Finally, and as always, I am grateful to my wife, Honey. The sojourn is infinitely richer and more bearable in her company.

— PART I —

Introduction

— Prologue —

Democracy and the Culture Wars

What Is at Stake

Every generation has its struggles. People being what they are, such struggles are inevitable. In this, of course, we are hardly immune. But in our time, a large region of public contention has opened up that is peculiar for both its moral character and its historical significance.

Think about it for a moment.

At the very center of contemporary cultural conflict in our society—the "culture war," as it has been called—are a cluster of public issues concerned, ironically, with the most private of all matters: the body. Controversies about abortion, sexual harassment, pornography, "vulgar" art or music, sex education, condom distribution, homosexuality, AIDS policy, or euthanasia and the "right to die" all trace back to the human body. Those issues that do not relate to the body deal, more often than not, with the social institutions that claim authority over the body (family, church, school, law and the like). The body, it would seem, is the underlying symbolic of the culture war. This being the case, the politics of the culture war is, in large part, a politics of the body.

3

But why the body?

Clearly the human body is more than just a biological organism. It also has social meaning and significance. In short, how we understand the body—its functioning, its representation, and its discipline—reveals a particular cultural understanding of nature, what the so-called natural order of things will allow or not allow, and human nature (what it means to *be* human). Indeed, as Michel Foucault has instructed us, the body is ultimately a reflection of, and a central metaphor for, the implicit order that prevails in a civilization.[1]

If the body is indeed a metaphor of the social order, then a conflict over our understanding of the body—latent within all of the issues just mentioned—signals a conflict about (if not a turning point in) the ordering of our social life, and perhaps civilization itself. This is why abortion, to mention the most prominent case, has been and remains so deeply contested. The controversy over abortion carries many layers of meaning, to be sure, but at root it signifies different propositions about what it means to be human. As such, the controversy contains within it a metaphor for two different civilizational ideals in conflict.

In this light we begin to see the significance of the contemporary culture war. Cumulatively, the various issues of cultural conflict point to a deeper struggle over the first principles of how we will order our lives together; a struggle to define the purpose of our major institutions, and in all of this, a struggle to shape the identity of the nation as a whole. In a broader historical perspective, however, this culture war may also mark an epoch-defining moment—although in what sense is still unclear. One thing, though, is certain: when cultural impulses this momentous vie against each other to dominate public life, tension, conflict, and perhaps even violence are inevitable.

Conflict and violence? This observation is not made lightly, if only because *culture wars always precede shooting wars*—otherwise, as Philip Rieff reminds us, the latter wars are utter madness: outbreaks of the most severe and suicidal efforts to escape the implications of any kind of normative order.[2] Indeed, the last time this country "debated" the issues of human life, personhood, liberty, and the rights of citizenship all together, the result was the bloodiest war ever to take place on this continent, the Civil War. There is little doubt that we are in the midst of a culture war of great social and historical consequence, and thus the possibility of conflict and violence should not surprise us. The memory of the shooting murder of abortion provider, Dr. David Gunn of Pensacola, Florida, in February 1993 should stick in our mind as a poignant symbol of just this.

The question this book takes up is whether American democracy can face up to conflict of this subtlety, significance, and potential volatility. Can democratic practice today mediate differences as deep as these in a manner that is in keeping with the ideals set forth in the founding documents of the American republic?[3] Or will one side, through the tactics of power politics, simply impose its vision on all others?

The question is not an idle one—for the simple reason that cultural conflict is inherently antidemocratic. It is antidemocratic first because the weapons of such warfare are reality definitions that presuppose from the outset the illegitimacy of the opposition and its claims. Sometimes this antidemocratic impulse is conscious and deliberate; this is seen when claims are posited as fundamental rights that *transcend* democratic process. The right to have an abortion and the right to life, for example, are both put forward as rights that transcend deliberation. Similarly opposing claims are made on behalf of gay rights, women's rights, the rights of the terminally ill, and so on.

More often than not, though, the antidemocratic impulse in cultural conflict is implicit in the way in which activists frame their positions on issues. This is what is meant by the popular phrase *political correctness*—a position is so "obviously superior", so "obviously correct", and its opposite is so "obviously out of bounds" that they are beyond serious discussion and debate. Indeed, to hold the "wrong" opinion, one must be either mentally imbalanced (phobic—as in *homophobic*—irrational, codependent, or similarly afflicted) or, more likely, evil. Needless to say, in a culture war, one finds different and opposing understandings of the politically correct view of the world.

Consider, by way of illustration, the way in which both sides of the cultural divide in America attempt to identify the other's agenda with the deadly authoritarianism of Germany's Third Reich. One is first tempted to dismiss such associations as the stuff of a cheap polemic merely intended to discredit one's opposition. But such associations are not only found in the purple prose of direct mail or in the sensationalism of demagogues. Below are two compelling statements made by serious intellectual players on—in this case—the issue of abortion. The first was made by novelist Walker Percy in a letter he wrote to the *New York Times* in 1988:

> Certain consequences, perhaps unforeseen, follow upon the acceptance of the principle of the destruction of human life for what may appear to be the most admirable social reasons.
>
> One does not have to look back very far in history for an example of such consequences. Take democratic Germany in the 1920s. Perhaps the most influential book published in German in the first quarter of this century was entitled *The Justification of the Destruction of Life Devoid of Value.* Its co-authors were the distinguished jurist Karl Binding and the prominent psychiatrist Alfred Hoche. Neither Binding nor Hoche had ever heard of Hitler or the Nazis. Nor, in all likelihood, did Hitler ever read the book. He didn't have to.
>
> The point is that the ideas expressed in the book and the policies advocated were the product not of Nazi ideology but rather of the best minds of the pre-Nazi Weimar Republic—physicians, social scientists, jurists, and the like, who with the best secular intentions wished to improve the lot, socially and genetically, of the German people—by getting rid of the unfit and the unwanted.
>
> It is hardly necessary to say what use the Nazis made of these ideas.
>
> I would not wish to be understood as implying that the respected American institutions I have named [the *New York Times,* the ACLU, NOW, and the Supreme Court] are similar to corresponding pre-Nazi institutions.
>
> But I do suggest that once the line is crossed, once the principle gains acceptance—juridically, medically, socially—innocent human life can be destroyed for whatever reason, for the most admirable socioeconomic, medical, or social reasons—then it does not take a prophet to predict what will happen next, or if not next, then sooner or later. At any rate, a warning is in order. Depending on the disposition of the majority and the opinion polls—now in favor of allowing

women to get rid of unborn and unwanted babies—it is not difficult to imagine an electorate or a court ten years, fifty years from now, who would favor getting rid of useless old people, retarded children, anti-social blacks, illegal Hispanics, gypsies, Jews . . .

Why not?—if that is what is wanted by the majority, the polled opinion, the polity of the time.[4]

Consider now a second observation made by legal scholar Laurence Tribe:

The abortion policies of Nazi Germany best exemplify the potential evil of entrusting government with the power to say which pregnancies are to be terminated and which are not. Nazi social policy, like that of Romania, vigorously asserted the state's right to ensure population growth. But Nazi policy went even further. Following the maxim that "Your body does not belong to you," it proclaimed the utter absence of any individual right in the matter and made clear that abortion constituted a governmental tool for furthering Nazi theories of "Aryan" supremacy and genetic purity.

Nazi propaganda constantly emphasized the duty of "Aryans" to have large families. Family planning clinics were shut down, often on the ground of alleged ties with communism. The Third Reich made every effort to control contraception, ultimately banning the production and distribution of contraceptives in 1941. The state, largely at the behest of SS leader Heinrich Himmler, abandoned its commitment to "bourgeois" marriage and undertook to promote the "voluntary" impregnation of "suitable women." Allowances were paid to women, married or not, for having children.

Abortion and even its facilitation were, in general, serious criminal offenses in Nazi Germany; a network of spies and secret police sought out abortionists, and prosecutions were frequent. By 1943 the penalty for performing an abortion on a "genetically fit" woman was death; those on whose premises abortions were performed risked prison sentences.[5]

Clearly more is involved in these two statements than mere rhetorical posturing. Each passage conveys a deep and well-thought out suspicion that their opponents embrace an authoritarianism that can only exist at the cost of human liberty and ultimately, perhaps, human life. The perception and the fear of this kind of authoritarianism, reinforced by the quest of both sides to force a *political* solution to these controversies, may be a measure of the extent to which democratic practice has become a thin veneer for the competing "will to power."

Thus, on one side we hear a senior writer for *Christianity Today* "reluctantly praise" the "extremism" of the pro-life movement. Drawing wisdom from the abolitionist movement of the nineteenth century, he concludes that the Civil War (precipitated by the activism of the abolitionists) was ultimately justified because "the nation was redefined as one built on liberty and equality, not compromise."[6] Shall we do the same with abortion or, say, homosexuality? On the other side of the cultural divide we hear Andrew Sullivan of the *New Republic* come to a similar conclusion: "The fracturing of our culture is too deep and too advanced to be resolved by anything but coercion; and coercion . . . is not a democratic option."[7] Indeed!

To be sure, the exercise of state power, even if through conventional politics, can never provide any democratically sustainable solution to the culture war. We must come to terms with the underlying issues of these controversies at a deeper and more profound level. But in a vital democracy, the means to that end are serious public reflection, argument, and debate.

I have used the terms *discussion, debate,* and *argument* loosely in the past few pages to describe how much of the social conflict on the contemporary American scene takes shape. In fact, it would seem as though there is very little real discussion, debate, or argument taking place. Debate, of course, presupposes that people are talking *to* each other. A more apt description of Americans engaged in the contemporary culture war is that they only talk *at* or *past* each other. If it is true that antagonists in this cultural struggle operate out of fundamentally different worldviews, this would seem inevitable. Is it not impossible to speak *to* someone who does not share the same moral language? Gesture, maybe; pantomime, possibly. But the kind of communication that builds on mutual understanding of opposing and contradictory claims on the world? That would seem impossible. And then, too, there is not really much talking, even if it is only past one another. What is heard is rather more like a loud bellowing, in the clipped cadences of a shouting match.

The irony in the way we Americans contend over these issues is striking to say the least. America embodies the longest-standing and most powerful democracy in the world. The principles and ideals that sustain it, not to mention the very founding documents that articulate those ideals, are a source of national pride and a model that many nations around the world strive to imitate. Yet the actual manner in which democratic discussion and debate are carried out in this country has become something of a parody of those ideals: obnoxious, at the very least; dangerous at the worst. In short, the most important and consequential issues of the day are presented through (and all too often based upon) what amounts to slogan, cliché, and aphorism—observations and opinions rendered within a ten-second "sound bite" and manifestos published in the latest direct mail copy or in a paid political advertisement in the *New York Times*. To be honest one would have to admit that advocates on all sides of the issues contested are culpable. And so it is that grave social concerns about the status and role of women are fashioned as anti-family; ethical concerns about the act of abortion are labeled anti-choice; policies rooted in the desire to redress the agelong oppression of minorities are dismissed as quotas; people who are nervous about the social effects of affirmative action risk being called racist; the severe problems of the criminal justice system are represented by the pathos of a Willie Horton or Charles Manson; deep moral quandaries about homosexuality are reduced to pseudopsychoanalytic categories like homophobia; art that questions social mores is decried as smut or blasphemy; and the enduring work of generations of intellectuals and writers is dismissed as the sexist, racist, and heterosexist claptrap of dead white males. The cacophony that too often marks contemporary public "debate" skreighs on.

The problem is not that positions on complex issues are reduced to caricatures, even if the latter are ugly and slanderous. In political discourse this has long been a practice. Rather, the problem is that democracy in America has evolved in such a way that public debate now rarely seems to get beyond these caricatures. Democratic discourse becomes a trade in accusation, an exchange in vilification, and all of this occurs in a context where the first principles of our life together are at stake. The discord taking place in public life, then, goes beyond mere political disagreement following the collapse of consensus over these matters. It is very much a war to impose a new consensus by virtually any political and rhetorical means possible.

What of the average American in all of this? Ordinary Americans greet the bellowing of what now passes as public "discourse" with an attitude something akin to dread. Indeed, there is an exhaustion that characterizes the national spirit when the controversies recur. Surely the rhetoric of public debate is more polarized than we are as a people. And so it is that many Americans wish that these battles would just go away.

Private life, of course, can be a refuge for us. Heaven knows that between finding and keeping a job, making ends meet, holding a marriage together, raising kids, and the like, we have enough to oc-cupy our time and attention. But our biographies invariably inter-sect the skirmishes of the larger culture war. We are discriminated against in getting a job or in receiving a promotion, a teenage daughter becomes pregnant and pleads for an abortion, a nephew "comes out of the closet," a local group of citizens wants to remove the textbooks from the neighborhood school because they are not multicultural enough—and private life is no longer much of a refuge at all.

And so we find ourselves embroiled in controversy that we seem helpless to influence or change. The terms of the so-called debate have already been set for us by powers and processes over which we have no control. Thus, for all of the diversity of belief, opinion, and perspective that really does exist in America, diversity is not much represented in public debate. Rather than pluralism, democratic discourse tends to reflect the dualism of opposing extremes. Clearly most Americans do have opinions on the critical issues of our day, but most of the time those opinions conform to neither of the reign-ing positions. Indeed, the majority of voices that would dissent from either credo are for all practical purposes drowned out by the rhetoric of ideologues. Voices in the middle—of a perplexed or even a well-conceived ambivalence—are rarely if ever given a hearing. Here again, the life and spirit of democratic practice suffers.

There are those who say that the conflict of which I speak—the culture war—is not terribly important in the final analysis. Cultural issues, these critics say, are tangential to the "real" issues: labor law; the allocation of tax burdens and government expenditures; the struggle for limited resources in the workplace, in neighborhoods, and in schools; the emergence of a predominantly black underclass and its relation to welfare, crime, and illegitimacy; and so on. It is these more basic issues, they say, that really challenge democracy. Culture is epiphenomenal—a silly national sideshow.

No one would deny the importance of economics, labor, international finance, and the like, but is it not unwise and ultimately artificial to draw a line separating the "hard" issues of economics or the state from the "soft" issues of culture? (This is what Marx tried to do in his unfortunate distinction between economic "substructure" and the legal/political/cultural "superstructure.") Surely the way that we cope with these so-called hard issues is a function of our normative assumptions and ideals (and our interests, justified by these ideals). What issue is *not* filtered through an ideal grid of how things should be? It is these normative assumptions, principles, ideals, and interests—often unspoken and unaccounted for—that define us as a nation. It is these ideals that are in conflict, and it is for this reason that issues seemingly unrelated to those of the culture war are nevertheless affected by it.

Even some who recognize the significance of contemporary cultural conflict nevertheless say that the system for dealing with it is fine as it is. Those who take this position, in my opinion, are ignoring, not listening to—or, more likely, repressing—that which is counter to their own interests. It is the perspective of those sitting on top, like the industrialists of the past (and some even today) who ignored the voices of the workers they employed. Then, as now, there is a disenfranchisement that those in power refuse to acknowledge. As Rieff teaches us, such "repression is the Freudian word for lying to oneself without ever quite knowing it."[8]

Still others would contend that the conduct of democratic debate today may not be perfect, but it is certainly as robust as it ever has been in the past. This, too, misses the point. What haunts us about the character of contemporary public discourse is not so much a distant legacy of high democratic conduct deep within American experience. It is always a mistake to elevate the past as though it were some gilded age of life as it should be—an Edenic time from which we have fallen and that we now yearn to regain. The harsh details of the historical record insist that such a past never really existed. The memory that invokes this imagery is selective and fragmented; its effect is nostalgia, but its purpose is usually ideological. What haunts us, rather, is not a legacy of past experience but an ideal: the ideal that a just and democratic order that we all aspire to requires that somehow we do it a little bit better.

To realize fully the promise of the democratic ideal, of course, is a fantasy of utopian proportions. "Do not expect Plato's ideal republic," Marcus Aurelius said long ago, "be satisfied with even the smallest step forward, and consider this no small achievement."[9] The old Stoic's words chide us for any unwarranted idealism we might secretly cherish. His warning should indeed be the epigraph of this entire essay. Even so, one might think that with more than two hundred years of practice we would be wise to new problems that arise and how they might be addressed. If this is not an unreasonable assumption, then why does public discourse in the world's most powerful democracy continue to be so dangerously shallow at such a critical time in its history?

Struggle is inevitable, to be sure. Our predicament is that the stakes of the struggle we are in are so very high, while our ability to cope with the realities—not just the symbols—of that struggle is notably wanting. Let me be clear: democracy will not emerge phoenix-like from the ashes of the culture war. It will either be trivialized or revitalized. This book is a search for the common ground in American life where a more substantial and robust debate about the public good/goods can be engaged and sustained.

Why is such debate relevant? *If the culture war is really a war over first principles of how we will order our lives together, then the only just and democratic way beyond the culture war is through it— by facing up to the hard, tedious, perplexing, messy, and seemingly endless task of working through what kind of people we are and what kind of communities we will live in.* If we say the cleavages are too deep to resolve any other way, then it is time to choose sides and set up the barricades. If, however, we say they are not—if we choose to be democrats, pledging to face up to our deepest differences without harming each other, and to resolve them in a manner fitting the ideals of democratic governance—then it behooves us to look carefully not for the middle ground of compromise, but for common ground in which rational and moral suasion regarding the basic values and issues of society are our first and last means to engage each other. This is the democratic imperative.

The culture war will be with us for some time to come. Racial conflict, gays in the military (and in the rest of society), multiculturalism, text-book controversy, condom distribution to school-age children, arts funding, fetal tissue research, the tense relationship between church and state, reproduction technology, and the like all will be flash points in the coming years for this deeper conflict. Yet rather than deal with this larger matter through the entire range of controversies, I focus here on one controversy in particular—the one surrounding abortion—as a window into the relationship between democratic practice and the culture war as a whole. The special significance of the abortion controversy has been mentioned already. It not only mirrors the culture war as a whole, it has been a centerpiece of our postmodern politics (the politics of the body) for many years. Abortion remains the knottiest moral and political dilemma of the larger culture war, contested now for more than two decades with little hope of a satisfying resolution. Pitting the basic human concerns of life and liberty against each other, it brings home to most Americans the stakes of the entire cultural conflict. It is, then, an ideal case—a prism, if you will—through which to explore how democratic practice faces up to the larger challenges of our time. If the common ground of democratic argument can be found here, it can be found anywhere.

— 1 —

A Search for Common Ground
What Democracy Requires

We Americans generally want to think of ourselves as good people. That, in many respects, is where the trouble begins.

This predisposition to be good, or at least to see ourselves that way, is not just a personal preoccupation (though it certainly includes that). We want to think of ourselves in a public sense—say, as a people and as a nation—as good, too. Among other things, this means that we want our institutions—our families, our schools, our places of worship, our businesses, and the like—to reflect the standards of goodness that we hold: to be fair rather than unfair, just rather than unjust, true rather than duplicitous, and so on.

No where is this more true than in the body politic—the realm of law, public policy, and the affairs of state. Here especially we project our own ideals of the good life and of the common good and evaluate the workings of government accordingly. Indeed, while the legitimacy of a government depends upon the consent of those whose lives are ordered by it, that consent is based upon a popular conviction that law, public policy, and even the structure of government itself are generally responsive to an understanding and vision of the public good held by its citizens.

Competing Visions of the Good

The problem is that the culture war we are in at the end of the twentieth century posits opposing and, often enough, mutually exclusive visions of the public good. For instance, implicit in the contest over multiculturalism are fundamentally different meanings imputed to the ideals of pluralism, tolerance, and equity. Hidden within the controversy over moral education (values clarification, sex education, and the like) are different understandings of virtue into which children are to be socialized. Underneath the conflict over homosexuality in all of its public policy dimensions are, among other things, competing ideals of masculinity and femininity and of natural and appropriate sexual behavior. And so it goes throughout the range of disputes of the contemporary culture war. But these are abbreviations. Consider, then, how these moral visions get played out in greater detail in one particular conflict, the controversy over abortion.

As Kristin Luker has observed, the controversy over abortion contains competing symbols of the ways in which we understand the meaning of womanhood and motherhood in particular. Abortion, for pro-choice advocates, symbolizes a woman's control over her reproductive capabilities.[1] This control signals that a woman is no longer on unequal biological footing with a man; that she does not need to interrupt her career if she chooses not to, and thus she can achieve the same level of social and economic autonomy and power as a man.

For pro-life advocates, however, abortion symbolizes an affront to the high and holy calling of motherhood. Since only women can have children, motherhood is viewed as a responsibility dictated by nature for the perpetuation of the human race. To sacrifice the life of an innocent child for the sake of economic and social autonomy is a perversion of the natural order: to pursue a career is fine, say the pro-lifers, but not at the sacrifice of a child's life. The destruction of the fetus through abortion, then, sends the message that motherhood is just one commitment among many, and not even necessarily the most important one.

It follows from this that abortion signals competing ideas about the source of meaning in life. For a pro-life woman, being a wife and a mother in the private realm of the home is intrinsically meaningful; there she can control the pace and content of her work. Paid labor outside of the home, particularly if it is demanding and poorly compensated, is therefore "harsh, superficial and ultimately ruthless." It is a world that inverts higher moral values for base, utilitarian values. By contrast, for pro-choice women the traditional division of labor between men and women only relegates women to second-class citizenship. It is through productive labor in the public sphere, a social realm long denied her, that a woman can achieve genuine equality. Of course, most women who are not activists want career *and* motherhood (and insist they can have both), but their position in the controversy signals the priority they give to the issue of meaning in their lives.

Abortion further points to underlying ideas of what constitutes meaningful life and death in our society. Pro-choice advocates imply that life has meaning as long as it constitutes a conscious and rational existence; choice is the principal expression and political symbol of life. Since the fetus is neither conscious nor rational, it has no meaningful life—and therefore its "death," if one can use that term, is virtually meaningless. The majority of pro-life advocates, by contrast, contend that only God can give life, and if He gives it, it is meaningful by definition since humans at all stages of development reflect His image and purpose. Every unborn child is to be valued; every abortion means the destruction of providentially ordained life.

Not least, abortion implicitly symbolizes different ideas about what moral and social obligations we hold toward others. Pro-choice advocates insist that our primary obligations are to women, whose rights and needs have for too long been denied or suppressed. Certainly, they will say, our obligation to a living person is greater than our commitment to what is at most only a potential person. On the other hand, since the anti-abortion advocate begins with the assumption that the fetus is a human child, he or she comes to the conclusion that those who are pro-choice are self-centered. According to this logic, in matters of life and death, our obligations must extend first to those who are most defenseless. To come down on either side of this issue, then, is to make a statement about who is qualified for inclusion in the human community, and thus who is worthy of our care and protection.

By its very nature, then, the issue will strike a chord deep within us. The problem is that these underlying matters are rarely if ever debated explicitly or directly. Nevertheless, it is because of the fundamental ways in which we define ourselves through this issue—even if only implicitly—that the abortion controversy is so important to us personally and so decisive for the larger culture war.[2]

Not surprisingly, the competing ideas of the good extend to abortion law itself. Was the landmark 1973 Supreme Court decision *Roe v. Wade* good law or bad law? The answer, of course, depends upon what side you are on, but curiously, the controversy even extends to what *Roe* was. One side insists that *Roe* allows for abortion on demand for the full nine months of pregnancy, while the other insists that *Roe* is a decision hammered out of moderation and compromise. Even legal scholars argue back and forth with these alternative interpretations.[3] The same has been true of the *Casey v. Pennsylvania Planned Parenthood* decision of 1992, a decision that upheld the right to an abortion mandated by *Roe v. Wade* but yet also upheld the Pennsylvania law requiring informed consent, parental consent, and a twenty-four-hour waiting period under the new logic that regulations are acceptable as long as they do not impose any "undue burden" upon the woman seeking the abortion. Both pro-choice and pro-life activists reacted strongly to the decision: the former were upset that abortion was no longer defined as a fundamental right and thus, in principle, could be impeded by certain regulations that could in fact be burdensome; the latter that no legal protection was extended to the unborn.

But what are we to do about differences as rudimentary as these?

The Problem of Consensus

One of the more fashionable suggestions in contemporary political philosophy is that we try to ignore these differences by resigning ourselves to their utter incompatibility. Alas, proponents will say, you have your notions of the good life, and I have mine; so let us just agree not to argue over the matter. There can be no universal theory of the common good that we will all agree to, nor can there be any way to "fix" or "ground" objectively even a partial understanding of the common good,[4] so let us abandon the quest altogether and talk about something else.[5]

The suggestion sounds easy enough and, in many ways, is philosophically appealing. And yet at the same time it also shouts of sociological naïveté. The reason it is naïve is that there are institutional pressures at work in society that seem to drive us to fashion some kind of rough (if still general) uniformity in public culture. Those institutional dynamics are at work whether or not we like it or think it is a good thing.

There are, for one, pressures created by the practical need for a universal system of law and justice. These laws are not just formal rules telling us what we can and cannot do. Laws, if only implicitly, also contain a moral story that proclaims the ideals and principles of the people who live by them, and as such gives particular legal prescriptions their meaning and purpose.[6] They speak of a society's understanding of the common good.

Universal public education exerts other pressures toward finding and maintaining some kind of general agreement in public culture. It is not so much the particular skills children acquire in school as it is what they learn about the national heritage and culture, and the duties of civic life necessary to sustain that heritage. Plainly these are matters subject to different interpretations. So how will answers to these questions be framed for children? Which interpretations of national life and heritage will be passed on? What are the duties of public life and why should children, soon to be adults, be compelled to assume them? Questions concerning the common good naturally are implicit here, too. And then there is the need for policies to guide a nation's interaction with other nations. In matters of trade, immigration, and most prominently war, standards of justice and prudence are inescapably at play.

There are other institutional pressures as well, all forcing us to contend for the terms—the ideals, standards, and principles—by which we will conduct our lives together. Closing our eyes to these matters will not make them go away. All of this is to say, then, that the state cannot be neutral in matters pertaining to the public good.

In all of these areas the state makes binding decisions affecting the whole of society, in the name of society itself. To formulate law and policy, then, is to create and sustain a *particular nomos,* a normative universe that draws distinctions, discriminates, judges, excludes and includes—in short, takes sides on the matter of the public good.

The state's involvement on questions of the public good is not a trifling matter. Indeed, it should make us pause. After all, as Max Weber taught us long ago, the state is founded and maintained by violence. In enforcing compliance to law, it claims the sole legitimate use of violence.[7] Those who fundamentally disagree with the principles contained in law, refuse to submit to them, and work outside of established channels for changing them are therefore vulnerable to the exigencies of state-imposed violence. It matters a great deal, then, how the government formulates law and public policy in response to the controversies of the culture war.

In the end, philosophers may have the luxury of dismissing such matters as uninteresting, but citizens do not. The sociological and political exigencies of our society press for some kind of working consensus, irrespective of our wishes. For all citizens in a democracy and for the state that claims to represent them, coming to terms with the fundamental differences over the "common good" is perhaps the central question we face.

Where, though, do we find a working agreement on the common good in a public culture as fractured as ours? This is the question that provokes this book.

Consider how this plays out in the case already mentioned—the abortion controversy.

The Abortion Deadlock as Case Study

Abortion—the exasperation is nearly audible. If there is an exhaustion that has beset Americans over the issues of the culture war, it is truly deepest in response to the abortion controversy. Nearly everyone is weary of hearing the opposing arguments drone on about why we should or should not have legal abortions. Most wish that the issue would just go away, or that someone would just change the subject. From time to time, it is true, we are distracted by other issues: the fallout from the recession, the casualties of the drug war, or the politics of arts funding hold our attention for a time, but invariably the abortion conflict returns. Indeed, with every presidential election, every Supreme Court appointment or decision on the matter, and every anniversary protest rally, subterranean tensions flare with renewed intensity. Two decades have passed since *Roe v. Wade,* and the issue remains deeply entrenched, utterly deadlocked in a cycle of advantage and counteradvantage between opposing interests. Skeptics and activists on both sides mutter to themselves about when it will all end, but the truth is that it will not—at least, not in this lifetime.

Why the Abortion Controversy Will Not Go Away

Such pessimism stands in sharp contrast to the views of many. With the election of Bill Clinton to the presidency in 1992, many observers quickly came to the conclusion that the abortion controversy was for all practical purposes over. Charles Krauthammer, for instance, said that "one can reasonably declare a great national debate over when all three independently (s)elected branches of government come to the same position."[8] In 1992, the Supreme Court reaffirmed the central holding of *Roe v. Wade* in the *Casey* decision. Given this and an apparent majority of pro-choice votes in both houses of Congress, the new president-elect vowed to make good on his campaign pledge to pass the so-called Freedom of Choice Act (FOCA), the legislative equivalent of *Roe,* as a safeguard against any future challenges. Certainly there seemed to be grounds for such a claim.

These events, however, only ensure that the controversy will rage on as it has for decades, but through different political strategies.[9] One pro-life leader reflected about the political season this way:

Antislavery leaders must have shared a similar anxiety in March, 1857. After more than 25 years of unremitting toil, they saw—within the space of a week—President James Buchanan sworn into office as a proslavery Democrat and the Supreme Court issue its decision in *Dred Scott,* declaring a constitutional right to own slaves and stripping Congress of any power to limit the spread of slavery. The triumph of slavery seemed complete. But, of course, just three and a half years later, Lincoln was elected President, and, even without the Civil War, change would have come.[10]

Indeed, all three branches of government *did* share a consensus about slavery in 1857. In 1920 all three shared a consensus about prohibition, and in 1964 they shared a consensus about racial equality. In each case, consensus among the three branches of government did not bring to an end those great national debates. Far from it. To be sure, the pro-life movement remains one of the largest grass-roots movement in America, and media commentators make a significant miscalculation if they underestimate the resolve and commitment that fuel it.

At the national level, several strategies will be pursued. Pro-life organizations have vowed to challenge the constitutionality of FOCA in the courts. They have pledged to engage in offensive litigation and legislation to thwart efforts to expand the funding of abortion through the government and through national health insurance organizations. They will also challenge every effort to expand abortion referral and practice on military bases and other government institutions. Medical malpractice suits against physicians and clinics performing failed abortions will be pursued relentlessly. Pro-life groups will challenge the legitimacy of the Freedom of Access to Clinic Entrances Act (which affects protest groups like Operation Rescue). Challenging fetal experimentation and fetal tissue research will also be high on the docket for pro-life advocates.

At the state and local level, politicians with pro-life inclinations and commitments will continue to chisel away at the legal edifice surrounding access to abortion. In recent years, pro-life activists have made electoral gains and are poised to enact regulations that the Supreme Court has viewed as constitutional. Battles long waged at the national level thus will be reenacted around the country in state legislatures. At the grass-roots level, pro-life organizations will continue to mobilize their largely middle-class, churchgoing constituencies toward the restriction of abortion practice. Operation Rescue and other "rescue" organizations, in particular, will continue to create an environment where the private practice of abortion is stigmatized and actual access to an abortion is even more difficult.

In some respects, pro-life initiatives regarding access and provision of abortion services are already making the legal and political battles beside the point. As is often cited, 83 percent of the counties in America already do not have a single abortion provider. What is more, the number of obstetrical-gynecological residency programs training physicians to do first-trimester abortions has dwindled dramatically. In 1985, 25 percent of all such programs offered this training; in 1991, the figure had dropped to 12 percent.[11] Already it is clear that fewer young doctors are willing and available to replace older abortion providers as the latter prepare to retire. The stigma is great: the practice is low in prestige and fairly isolated from mainstream medicine, and the personal costs (particularly if the physician has children) make the specialization unattractive to say the least. In the end, the laws protecting a woman's access to abortion are of little use if the service is not available. Pro-choice activists, obviously, will not sit still for this. Motivated by their own high ideals, they will strive to find ways to compensate. Thus it is clear that the abortion controversy will not disappear but will continue to nag at the public spirit.

Some have suggested that the long-term solution to this controversy resides in technological advances that may somehow allow us to circumvent the conflicts altogether. But these hopes are probably naïve, too. The medical profession and the new diagnostic environments created by medical knowledge will continue to "medicalize the womb," as Jonathan Imber has put it, but every so-called advance will likely spawn new protest movements and countermovements.[12] The introduction of the abortifacient, RU486, for example, will generate controversy at every level—legal, legislative, and grass roots. (The lines are clearly drawn. Peg Yorkin of the Feminist Majority Foundation has said that the RU486 "genie" is "out of the bottle" and that to get it to American women, "we are prepared to do whatever we have to do."[13] Keith Tucci of Operation Rescue has countered, "When they invent new ways to kill children, we will invent new ways to save them."[14]) In the case of advanced genetics, "choice" will take on an entirely new cast: the choice will no longer be to have a child but rather to have a particular child with certain diagnosed qualities. Implied in these technological changes, then, will be a further transformation in the criteria for what constitutes "normal" human life. The implementation of these changes is likely to be contested as well.

Reproduction in its various facets will continue to be a major area of social and political conflict in the years to come, even as the specific points of conflict shift and change. Thus abortion-rights advocates are dreaming if they think that their opposition will just get tired some day and go away, as are anti-abortion advocates if they imagine that all will be well the moment abortion is outlawed. As with a perpetual check in the game of chess, moves and counter-moves create the impression of change, but the underlying disagreements remain unaddressed. A groping urgency for a deeper and sustainable resolution lingers.

False Promises

The importance of discovering a constructive way to move beyond the seemingly intractable realities of the culture war and the problems it creates for just governance is understood by many. This is particularly true with regard to the abortion controversy. But even well-intentioned proposals for coming to terms with the deadlock are not necessarily politically sound. For the purposes of illustration, consider three broad but concrete appeals with the avowed goal of facing squarely the problem of abortion. Each is distinctive for the high-minded purpose to which it aspires, but also for its failure to deliver what democratic practice requires. They contain a lesson for us about patterns and propensities that play out in the larger society.

Consider first the appeals and perspectives of Laurence Tribe, legal scholar at Harvard University Law School, and of writer/essayist, Roger Rosenblatt.

Tribe's book *Abortion: The Clash of Absolutes* is offered as a constructive reflection that may "lay the groundwork for moving on." "The face of the abortion argument," he writes, "need not remain frozen."[15] The endorsements for his book raise our hopes high: "wise and powerful . . . vibrant with ethical passion" says one reviewer; "rational and humane," says another. We wait with bated breath. Roger Rosenblatt, best known for his essays on public television's "MacNeil-Lehrer News Hour," makes a similar plea to move beyond the deadlock in his book *Life Itself: Abortion in the American Mind.*[16] Our expectations with this book are raised even higher than for Tribe's for on the front cover we are told that "Roger Rosenblatt answers the most bitterly divisive social question of our time." If one were somehow to overlook the singular accomplishment promised in that subtitle, one could read about it again in a Rosenblatt essay in the *New York Times Magazine* entitled "How to End the Abortion War."[17]

It is true that both of these books display a certain tone of sensitivity and compassion that one does not typically hear in the rhetoric of the activists. Both writers favor the effort to make our society more hospitable toward children, more supportive of motherhood, and more encouraging to child-raising families. Both view the fetus as more than mere human tissue, and as significant regardless of whether a woman imputes value to it. (Rosenblatt, in fact, says he is "ready to concede that a fetus is some form of person."[18]) Both also call for increased tolerance and humility on the part of all parties involved. And both finally conclude that America needs "to create social conditions in which the need for abortion is increasingly unnecessary."[19] As Tribe puts it, "We must strive for a society in which every child a woman conceives is wanted and in which every child born has someone to love and nurture it."[20] At least in tone, then, both call for a more humane and socially responsible social order in which abortion finally proves unnecessary.

But these ideas are, in themselves, unexceptional. No one, least of all pro-lifers, would disagree. The issue is, what do we do until then? The answer Rosenblatt and Tribe offer us is anything but ameliorating: no legal interference or deviation from the abortion rights granted by *Roe v. Wade.*[21] Rosenblatt, at least, is upfront about this in describing himself as "conventionally pro-choice."[22] His hope is "that *Roe v. Wade* remains intact or that Congress passes a law that expresses the same stipulations."[23] "Abortion," he insists, "must be preserved as an option."[24] Tribe's position does not vary from this but is put forward more defensively, if not tendentiously. For him, *Roe* is the compromise position that everyone would recognize if we only looked seriously at the history and content of the law.[25] Both books, then, are little more than apologias for maintaining, without any compromise whatsoever, a pro-choice resolution to the policy debate.

What is most interesting is not where these two commentators come out on the issue, but rather the way they envision the role of the democratic process in addressing this controversy.

Let us leave aside Rosenblatt's facile use of public opinion data,[26] his simplistic and often condescending stereotyping of pro-lifers[27] and nearly anyone who is religious,[28] and his superficial discussion of morality,[29] and move to the heart of his contribution toward resolving the conflict. In his own words, "The best ending to the entire controversy might be the eventual reinstatement of *Roe v. Wade* or the legislative equivalent terms of it, *but only after people had had the chance to hear what others thought and, more importantly, to discover what they themselves thought*" (emphasis added). The key here is not "to dismiss [abortion's] deep seriousness or to regard it merely as a routine convenience of modern life";[30] rather, we need to appreciate "its gravity."[31] To this end, people need to "struggl[e] to unearth [their] feelings," "mak[e] their feelings known," "express [their] doubts, concerns, or abhorrence."[32] Laws permitting abortion should convey "the range and complexity of feelings on the issue . . . acknowledging that abortion is the taking of life at some stage . . . [but] that the best antidote to abortion is to make it less necessary."[33] The emotional turmoil many Americans feel about abortion, Rosenblatt tells us, is acceptable as "but another of the many useful frictions of a democracy [*sic*] society."[34] In the end, it is our appreciation of the gravity of abortion (derived from getting in touch with our feelings, expressing those feelings, and listening intently to others do the same) that will make abortion rights acceptable to most Americans.[35] In sum, Rosenblatt contends that abortion is a legal expediency justified by our emotional engagement with what we are doing and a hope that someday, through better sex education and other community help, abortion will become progressively less necessary. To put it differently, Rosenblatt's answer to "the most bitterly divisive social question of our time"—the way "to end the abortion war"—is, in essence, to allow abortion in all circumstances but to feel bad about it. A therapeutic unburdening, for Rosenblatt, defines both the content and purpose of democratic discourse about abortion.[36]

In Tribe's case, the democratic process is rather beside the point, since he does not view either direct democratic referendum or legislative action as the proper arena for judging this issue.[37] The whole purpose of an independent judiciary, he contends, is to be anti-democratic so that the rights of a minority are not threatened by the will of the majority. Because Tribe views abortion as a fundamental and constitutionally guaranteed right, he believes it should be protected at all costs—even from the democratic process. Yet Tribe himself recognizes that any legal or political solution to this issue that bypasses the will of the people will eventually fall short. Pro-choice advocates should try to persuade their opposition "that theirs is indeed the better view" in order to legitimate the abortion right.

Here we come to the most troubling aspect of Tribe's view of persuasion. It is heard in a curious bit of advice he offers: "Polling data suggest that if the pro-choice movement is to maintain its momentum, it cannot let the pro-life side shift the debate to *why* a woman wants any given abortion. The movement's current popular appeal clearly depends on keeping the question focused on *who* will make the decision."[38] The passage is remarkable for its candor, but in the end it is a concrete illustration of a theme carried implicitly throughout the book. One might well ask Tribe's endorsers how "ethically passionate" or "rational and humane" the author can be if he obliterates the question of obligations from the debate. In making this statement, Tribe suggests that perhaps the central question posed by one side of the conflict be ruled out of court from the very start of the debate. Perhaps he hopes that if pro-life advocates are effectively silenced, they will simply disappear.

There is something similar to this in Tribe's tempered speculation (yet forthright hope) that technology might transcend the conflict altogether. He looks for these technologies in new forms of contraception for men and women, the approval and marketing of the RU486 "abortion pill," and even the future development of an artificial womb. Such technologies, he says, are hopeful but not without their problems:

> If a technology were developed that permitted resolution of the abortion question without the loss of life or liberty, society would have to deal with the trade-off between the increased risk to the pregnant woman (from requiring removal of the embryo or fetus) and the increased chance of the fetus's survival (from requiring its

placement in a surrogate mother or in an artificial womb). And society would also have to address the entire strategy of seeking to replicate, outside women, something that has always seemed special and indeed miraculous about womanhood. Some may well believe that the very notion is a perversion of how technology should be put to human use. Still, the prospect offers, at least in theory, one end run around the current clash of absolutes.[39]

His qualifications notwithstanding, the hope Tribe places in technology for circumventing the debate is probably unrealistic, for reasons already noted.[40] But more to the point, it gives him the luxury of basing the resolution on the development of processes that are largely independent from interaction with the human community. In this, our responsibility to debate seriously the terms by which people with fundamentally different commitments will live together is sidestepped altogether.

So much for a constructive response to the abortion conflict in the proposals of Rosenblatt and Tribe.

A third call for constructive thinking comes from R. C. Sproul, an individual largely unknown in secular intellectual circles but a theologian, minister, and teacher prominent among evangelical Christians. Here again, we are presented with promises to cut through the "strident slogans and impassioned rhetoric" to achieve a "clear, compelling, and most of all compassionate" view of the problem of abortion. Our expectations for resolution to this controversy are set no less high by this book than by those offered by Rosenblatt and Tribe; the front cover promises "A Rational Look at an Emotional Issue."[41]

The question, of course, is (as Alasdair MacIntyre puts it) whose rationality? The answer upon reading the book is clear from beginning to end—rationality from an orthodox evangelical perspective. Still, no such qualification is given beforehand; in fact, we are told that "both sides of the debate [are examined] in light of biblical law, civil law and natural law."[42] The appeal, then, is quite broad with something in it for almost every American.

Unlike Rosenblatt and Tribe, however, Sproul ends his "rational" examination of the issue with an uncompromising affirmation of the pro-life position. He is convinced "that abortion-on-demand is evil . . . against the law of God, against the laws of nature and against reason."[43] To make this case—and in the process explore such controversial questions as how sacred human life is; when life begins; whether abortion is murder; which right should have the greatest priority: the right to choose, the right to privacy, and the right to life and the nature of the relationship between church and state—is an audacious undertaking, to be sure. One might imagine a densely argued *summa theologica* of pro-life reasoning from this professor of systematic theology, but one gets only a 157-page chatty narrative replete with pro-life clichés, homespun anecdotes, summary bullets, and discussion questions.[44]

That an evangelical theologian finds the pro-life position the only rational one with regard to the controversy is no more surprising than secular libertarian intellectuals like Tribe and Rosenblatt discovering the only common ground to be in an unqualified pro-choice position. Not surprising and not terribly interesting. Again, what is more interesting is the way that Sproul relates democratic processes, and the tensions of pluralism they entail, to this controversy.

Though Sproul devotes an entire chapter to the government's relationship to abortion policy, the word *democracy* goes virtually unmentioned throughout the book, much less the particular realities and problems of democratic pluralism vis-à-vis this issue. The will of the people and even the popular legitimacy of the laws themselves are irrelevant to Sproul's argument. His concept of government is strictly generic, and the issue of its role in dealing with abortion is described (much like in Tribe's book) in a preemptive fashion. In Sproul's case, this is because he approaches the problem in the diction of theological absolutes: governments are instituted by God and are accountable to God for their actions; their proper role is to be on the side of good, not evil; it is their fundamental right to rule by force so long as it is exercised justly, that is, on the side of good; the protection of human life is at the heart of proper governmental concern; by denying the unborn the fundamental right to live through *Roe*, the state has reneged on its solemn duty before God; and therefore, the government must create laws that protect the unborn.[45] The central fallacy of Sproul's analysis, of course, is that he sees the government as something independent of and exercising command over the people. Democracy, however, is about *self-*government among people who very often make different and opposing claims about what their government should stand for. It is not necessary that Sproul, as a Christian theologian and pro-life apologist, accept the legitimacy of his opposition's claims, but these claims are not acknowledged except in caricatures.[46] He does not even recognize the circumstances out of which pro-choice claims are made; the matter of substantive public debate is not even a category in his thinking.

Should we laugh or cry? In the end, of course, however tempered these three arguments may seem, however empathetically concerned these authors may be with the experiences of women, however sincere their call for mutual respect—a "tone" of reasonableness and a "tone" of concern to constructively deal with this issue together do not constitute "ethical seriousness." Indeed, all three of these pleas for constructive reflection end by circumventing the intractable realities of pluralism and the hard and tedious task of figuring out how we live together amidst such deep and seemingly unresolvable differences. Rosenblatt proposes what is in fact a debased discourse rooted in a therapeutic purging of emotions, rather than an engagement over principles rooted in the convictions of conscience and life experience—all in a context in which the result is rigged from the outset. Tribe and Sproul, to different ends, propose to circumvent democratic discourse altogether. Thus, by failing to take serious and substantive account of the Other in this controversy (that is, to acknowledge the moral demands of the opposing worldview, collective experience, and claims), Tribe, Rosenblatt, and Sproul each offer little more than a recipe for a continuation, if not a further entrenchment, of the conflict in its present form.

A Note on the Problem of Legitimacy

The failure to address the knotty problem of Difference in these approaches dramatizes a peculiar bind the state finds itself in: the problem of sustaining its own legitimacy. The culture war, and the particular controversies that constitute the larger conflict, posit a

crisis of legitimacy. In practical terms, this means that people on opposing sides of the cultural divide operate with fundamentally different criteria of legitimacy: what one side regards as good law, the
other side regards as bad law, and vice versa. The state, then, is
caught in a zero-sum bind. Its legitimacy is contingent upon embracing what others reject as illegitimate, and rejecting what others
hold as fundamentally good.

In the case of abortion, certainly this was what was behind the
anger of feminists after the *Webster* decision in 1989 and their threat
to create a new political party for women. It has also been behind the
conservatives' long-standing cynicism toward the Supreme Court.
After twenty years, the effects of these polarizing tensions became
so prominent that the Court addressed it directly, even making it a
foundational part of the *Casey* decision to "retain and reaffirm" the
"essential holding of *Roe v. Wade*": "The Court's power lies," the majority opinion read, "in its legitimacy, a product of substance and perception that shows itself in the people's acceptance of the Judiciary
as fit to determine what the Nation's law means and to declare what
it demands."[47] Given this, continuity with previous practice is key:
"The legitimacy of the Court would fade with the frequency of its
vacillation."[48] To "surrender to political pressure," the Court reasoned, "would subvert the Court's legitimacy beyond any serious
question." To those who dissent from their judgment, therefore, they
announced it was time to call "the contending sides of [this] national
controversy to end their national division by accepting a common
mandate rooted in the Constitution."[49]

The issue at stake in the abortion controversy and the larger culture war, though, does not center on the legitimacy of the Court but
on that of the law itself. People will concede the former if they accept the latter. Thus rather than resolve the controversy, as it hoped
to, the logic of the *Casey* decision itself laid the foundation for intensifying it and possibly undermining further its own credibility (at
least in the eyes of pro-life Americans).[50]

The deadlock over abortion and the problems it has created for
the state in its claim to authority are repeated over and over again
within the various issues of the culture war. Some are obviously
more intense, enduring, and far-reaching than others. In each, no
matter what position the government takes, its authority will be

called into question by some. Cumulatively, then, the culture war posits a crisis of legitimacy for the modern state.

This is not the only source of jeopardy to the legitimation of the modern state. Some social scientists rightly point to significant declines in the confidence people have in various institutions of contemporary society to perform their tasks and the loss of public faith in their leaders to bring about any effective change.[51] The state is just one key institution affected by this. Others point to the crisis of legitimacy endemic to bureaucratic forms of political organization and administration.[52] The ever-expanding state is ever alienating to the public and increasingly unresponsive to the latter's needs and desires. Still others have shown that the capacity of the modern state to make plausible claims about its own legitimacy has been eroded by contradictory expectations placed upon it, especially as they relate to the modern economy.[53] These problems are not mutually exclusive or, in fact, unrelated to one another. Together, however, they do create problems with the state justifying its activity. The culture war, operating with its own fairly distinct sociological and historical dynamics, only intensifies this difficulty.

The Depth of Fragmentation

In a more traditional setting, a state facing crisis or conflict could invoke common values and ideals rooted in traditional religion or folk culture (or even nationalistic identity) as the means to maintain social integration and to buttress its own flagging authority. But these older cultural resources no longer resonate deeply in the collective consciousness of the nation; pluralism has rendered them weak. Instead the modern state has increasingly had to rely upon procedural norms concerned with the legality and constitutionality of decisions as its source of justification. The problem is that the legitimacy of the procedures themselves, not to mention the institutions established to put them into effect, are also vulnerable to public scrutiny, criticism, and cynicism.

The depth of fragmentation is a marker of the novelty of our situation. From its beginning, the institution of liberal democracy has implied an ethical ideal of the social order in which individual interests and the larger social good would be reconciled, if not synthesized. The early architects of this vision (including John Locke and the leading lights of the Scottish Enlightenment) and its actual builders on the American scene (Jefferson, Madison, Adams, and others) operated within a crudely synthetic moral framework that owed as much to biblical revelation as to Enlightenment reason. To be sure, there were differences among them; at root, though, they conceived of the world as a rational and transcendent moral order that embraced both public and private spheres equally. As such, it could allow for an infrastructure in which reasoned debate between competing interests could occur.

We know now just how unique and historically contingent this formulation was. In the context of the present culture war, that formulation has all but completely unraveled: deconstructed by postmodernist philosophy and social science, and rendered practically implausible by pluralism itself. To the extent that a moral center does exist, it has been effectively silenced by the acerbic rhetoric of the extremes. In the end, the older formulation is all but useless in constructing our notions of the social order.[54] In a culture war such as ours, the disagreements go all the way down.

Looking for a Sustainable Resolution: Shallow Versus Substantive Democracy

Again, the question is how some kind of working agreement on the common good can be forged among those for whom the very existence of the Other seems to represent an obscenity and an affront. One unfortunate option, alluded to already, is power politics.

Coercing Consent

In power politics, consent—that elusive agreement on the common good—is coerced. The very idea of a coerced consensus presupposes that the mere exercise of force is not enough. Even those predisposed toward a crude form of power politics recognize that to impose law or public policy without regard for the concerns and counterclaims of those opposing them is impractical. Voices of opposition will continue to criticize and thereby gnaw away at the legitimacy of imposed structures of authority. Those who support a given policy will therefore seek to undermine the credibility of the opposition so that newly asserted claims to legitimacy are passively received. Consensus must be coerced.

To coerce consensus in this situation involves a self-conscious imposition of a viewpoint with the ultimate goal of an unconscious acceptance. In other words, a means of understanding the world is imposed that makes a given configuration of legal and political prescriptions seem utterly reasonable. This is what some scholars have called "symbolic power" or "symbolic violence."[55] Though often discussed as merely one kind of power, in fact it is power in its most thorough and perhaps insidious expression.

Its exercise is seen in political/cultural activities oriented toward "the production of common sense."[56] The activities aim not only to frame particular positions as superior to all others, but also to make the reasons for that superiority seem "natural." The capacity of a social group or movement to make its particular preferences and practices seem natural is the key to its control; these particularities become standard throughout society while shrouded in a cloak of neutrality.[57] Reality then is redefined so completely that the very categories by which disagreement is organized are delegitimated from the outset. The very ground by which dissent could be put forward is ruled out of bounds.[58]

Ruling out particular topics of discussion a priori is, needless to say, a rather undemocratic use of power. Activist organizations on both sides of the cultural divide are naturally predisposed to precisely this kind of political strategy. It is seen in their efforts to monopolize symbols of political legitimacy, depicting themselves as defenders of the institutions and traditions of American life while depicting the opposition as the foes. Public discourse is weighted toward the negative side of this equation: *both* sides demonize their opposition as extremists who are outside of the American mainstream. It is the other side that is "militantly intolerant," "deceitful," "self-righteous," and ultimately "antidemocratic," and "totalitarian." As we have seen, this gets played out in more subtle ways in the commentaries of Tribe, Rosenblatt, and Sproul.

The essential elements of power politics are implicit in the high hopes that many (such as Tribe) place in technology to circumvent our difficulties. It is not the intentions of the scientist but the very form of scientific and technological thought that represents a systematic distortion to democratic discourse. The reason is that science is concerned only with manipulating the natural world; by the very nature of the enterprise, it excludes values from any consideration. As a consequence it undermines the communication necessary to achieve social solidarity and the attainment of consensus. As Jurgen Habermas put it, "Technological consciousness reflects not the sundering of an ethical situation but the repression of 'ethics' as such as a category of life."[59] The problem, of course, is that power politics expressed in these ways involves a denial of Difference and a disregard of the democratic imperative to argue and debate.

Generating Consent

The idea that in a democracy consent can be coerced through the mechanisms of power politics is hard to square at first take. It begins to make sense, though, when we distinguish between forms of government and forms of power. Democracy, like monarchy, is a form of government. But democracy can be despotic in the way it exercises power,[60] particularly when democratic processes becomes shallow rather than substantive, and thin and weak as opposed to strong. What I mean by substantive versus shallow democracy is illustrated by the way the two forms address the problem of conflict and the requirements of public discourse. Let us take the problem of conflict first.

When shallow, democracy tends to repress, minimize, or even ignore conflict altogether. Substantive democracy, by contrast, is not only consonant with the idea of conflict, it depends upon conflict and the frank recognition of the substantive differences it implies. The crucial premise to the substantive democratic option is that consensus or moral agreement should not necessarily be the first and most urgent priority of a social and political order, particularly if such consensus is achieved by compelling people to compromise their most passionately held beliefs and commitments. In principle, this is recognized in the constitutional insistence that matters of conscience are out of the reach of the state's authority.[61] This being the case, the idea that a political system, in the face of serious moral conflict, should quickly press toward a moral consensus—something akin to the arithmetic mean of what all Americans believe and value—would be as undesirable as it is ridiculous. At root, such a tactic only feigns acknowledgment of the sociological realities of pluralism. The priority in substantive democracy, then, is to find not the "middle ground" of fast moral compromise but rather a "common ground" where the particularities of people's beliefs are indeed recognized as sacred to the people who hold them (and, therefore, as nonnegotiable), but common problems can nevertheless be addressed.

This brings us to the requirements of public discourse in the face of such conflict. When democracy is weak and shallow, public speech becomes a language game that has the form of meaningful communication, but is in fact merely another form of aggression. Sound bites and direct mail, for example, require no accountability to the public and provide no possibility of a meaningful public response. In shallow democracy, then, public speech becomes a device for increasing power—a weapon facilitating the coercion of consensus.

By contrast, the heart of substantive democracy is a more palpable and robust public speech. As Benjamin Barber describes speech of this kind, it entails listening no less than speaking, is affective as well as cognitive, and is not cloistered in the domain of pure reflection but brought out into the world of action.[62] Needless to say, the nature and shape of this substantive idea of public discourse is hardly novel but "has been at the root of the Western idea of politics since Aristotle identified *logos* as the peculiarly human and peculiarly social faculty that divided the human species from animals.[63]

It is in a substantive view of conflict and of public discourse that common ground in democratic pluralism becomes possible. Let me be clear here; the common ground to which I refer is not "dialogue" in the vacuous sense often invoked by some ministers, marriage counselors, and conflict-resolution specialists. It is, rather, robust and passionate and utterly serious civil reflection and argument.[64] In this sense, it builds upon an agreement about how we should contend over our moral and political differences—a public agreement over how to disagree publicly. As George Weigel has put it, when an agreement is realized at this plane, genuine disagreement becomes an accomplishment, and authentic debate becomes a virtue.[65] Only in this context can there exist the possibility of forging politically sustainable solutions to the conflicts that divide us.

In the final analysis, *substantive argument is the one essential ingredient that can make the concept of democracy—and the consent it implies—meaningful.* This is true whether the form of democracy is representative or direct. It is the stuff essential to the species, if you will, in all its variations. Needless to say, though, the substantive democratic alternative to power politics is by its very nature a long-term and messy proposition, particularly when the cleavages in a nation become deep.

Searching for Substantive Democracy: Regions of Public Life to Be Explored

This book is an expedition of sorts, an empirical search into three main regions of social life today where this kind of serious public reflection and engagement might occur or be encouraged. The regions are explored in Part II, Part III, and Part IV of this book.

The Special Agenda Organizations

Part II examines the world of special agenda organizations (the National Organization for Women, Concerned Women for America, the American Civil Liberties Union, the National Right to Life, and so on).[66] One can think of the special agenda organizations of our generation as heirs of the political associations that were prominent in the early nineteenth century and about which Alexis de Tocqueville spoke so approvingly, saying that they "unite the energies of divergent minds and vigorously direct them toward a clearly indicated goal. . . . While they have no power to make law, they do have the power to attack existing laws and to formulate, by anticipation, laws which should take the place of present ones."[67] In Tocqueville's view, these associations were essential to the vitality of democracy, for they had the power "to hold back tyranny of whatever sort . . . either the despotism of parties or the arbitrary rule of a prince."[68]

On balance, special agenda organizations still play a vital, even essential role in American democracy. At their best they can function like the "small platoons" Edmund Burke observed in early democracies, with the potential to buffer the individual from the sometime oppressive power of the massive bureaucracies of government, big business, and labor. They are in many ways a measure of the amount of freedom that exists in our society. As James Madison put it, "Liberty is to faction what air is to fire."[69] For this reason, no one would ever want to see them disappear. But this does not mean that we should be satisfied with their performance or the kind of influence they wield.

While unable to anticipate the future, Tocqueville himself saw the possibility that these associations could create dangers to democracy; he believed that their excesses could turn "a fount of life into a cause of destruction."[70] Madison before him also warned of possible instability, a weakening of public leadership, and injustice. And indeed there is a certain ideological tyranny inherent in the politics of special interests, as we shall see. Where these organizations acquire a life of their own (an existence, power, and agenda independent of the people for whom they presumably speak), they become one more bureaucratic base of power and interest, claiming to speak on behalf of ordinary people but in fact oblivious to their concerns.

What is more, issues that already are difficult because of the deep moral nature of the disagreements become impossible to resolve in the hands of these organizations, for the very means and mechanisms of a just and democratic resolution—serious debate with the participation of many—have been rendered out of reach, if not obsolete. The new media technology and litigation, the principal places where such debates now take place, make it nigh impossible. To call the problem this creates a simple breakdown in communication is a wild understatement. Public debate under these conditions is "systematically distorted," as Habermas puts it, for the rhetoric used and the interests at play intensify polarities and make the rational exchange of opposing claims virtually impossible. The "distortions" in public debate run much deeper, as the reader will learn in Part II of this essay.

The Worlds of Ordinary Americans

As Thomas Jefferson argued, the strength of American democracy lies in "the affections, the opinions, and the suffrages of the people."[71] "The people themselves," he said elsewhere, "are [democracy's] only safe depository."[72] James Madison also believed that only an alert citizenry actively participating in public affairs could counter the consolidation of interests and power of those with direct access to the halls of government. He was deeply concerned that the electorate not take public affairs for granted, either by ignoring them or by tolerating the excesses of those individuals and organizations that were active.[73] But is the American public inclined or able to face up to its part in the democratic process? More practically, are we capable of pressing beyond the rhetorical polarities of the present culture war to a more inclusive, nuanced, reasoned, and (in Habermas's term) undistorted discussion of the underlying issues of national life and purpose? It is largely due to the kind of discourse engaged in by the special agenda organizations that so-called middle Americans are lost to the public debate.

So where do ordinary citizens *really* stand in the controversies of the culture war? For answers to these questions, my assistants and I carefully examined the most comprehensive public opinion survey ever conducted on the abortion issue. We also talked to dozens of people who are not activists on any side of the culture war but are nevertheless quite opinionated and eager to share their views:

- Lisa Rodriguez is currently (though perhaps permanently, by her decision) on maternity leave as an accountant for a small marketing firm in San Antonio, Texas, and "having a blast" raising Jason, her four-month-old son. Now forty (and married at thirty-five), she was "more than ready to start having kids." Her opinions about abortion are vaguely pro-life; she likes to think of them, however, as her own business. She has never walked in a pro-life march, never participated in a "rescue" ("Certainly not!"), and never contributed money to any pro-life groups. She is sympathetic to what these groups are doing, but it is "not her nature," as she puts it, to get involved.
- Marc Fielder lives in Manhattan Beach, California, one of the seaside towns in the greater Los Angeles area. He works as a sales manager for an airline shipping company and as a part-time actor. In his late thirties, he is single and sexually active. He says he does not think much about the abortion issue. It is only the business and the sports sections of the newspaper, he confesses, that

he really cares to read. He says he is pro-choice, but he looks at the activists on both sides in the abortion war with bemused contempt: "Don't these damned people have anything better to do with their time?" But in time he makes it clear that his offhanded cynicism covers a deep ambivalence that stems from an experience in which his current girlfriend had an abortion, mostly at his prompting.

- Robin Wysocki and Betsy McRae (who do not know each other) are both in their early thirties, single, college educated, and from middle-class backgrounds. Both had abortions when they were in their twenties. For one, the experience led to her conversion to Evangelical Christianity and a fairly strong pro-life position; for the other, the experience solidified her views on the necessity of an abortion right.

- Sam Hawkins is a Presbyterian minister and part-time theologian who hails from the suburbs surrounding Cleveland, Ohio. He is sixty-two years old, married, and the father of two children. Sam believes that the church he serves has failed to provide an adequate theological understanding of prenatal life, the act of abortion, and women who have abortions. His views do not fit the usual categories of this debate. His final position is somewhat reluctantly pro-choice, yet he views the moral logic he employs as sympathetic to the concerns of those who are pro-life. As a minister and theologian, he plays a fairly visible role in the community and has never been shy about staking out his position, particularly his criticisms of the reigning political creeds on this issue. The problem as he sees it is that the debate over abortion has something of a life of its own which does not easily conform to the complications his view represents. In the church over the years, advocates of legal abortion have both embraced him as an innovator and denounced him (literally and to his face) as a traitor, while opponents to abortion have selectively used his arguments and authority when these suited their agenda and dismissed him as irrelevant when they did not. The nuance of his position, he complains, has been ignored.

All of these individuals and others we spoke to connect personally with the abortion controversy in various ways, as they do with other issues of the culture war. Yet in Part III we learn from these and many others that "middle America" is rather awkwardly equipped to meet the challenge of serious and substantive argument. A lack of knowledge about the issues is just one of the many obstacles ordinary citizens face. Strong and often conflicting emotions that are only weakly tied to any kind of tradition of moral understanding compound these difficulties. For some of the reasons why people seem ill equipped for public engagement, we turn to Part IV and a search into the workings of the range of institutions that encompass and support civil society.

The Institutions of Civil Society

It goes without saying that the institutions of civil society—a free press, public schools, churches and synagogues, and professional and philanthropic organizations—are essential to a vital democratic society.[74] In principle, these institutions mediate between the private individual and the imposing structures of government. They also represent a region of social life where people can engage each other over issues of common concern. In mediating between the individual and the state in this way, these institutions empower people, providing information and resources for them to participate more meaningfully in the organization of public life. Thus they represent the possibility of nurturing that common ground where the different interests and agendas of the culture war (all surrounding competing ideals of the public good) can be confronted head-on.

Part IV of this book explores the way in which these institutions function in the circumstances of the present culture war. To what extent do the mediating structures of civil society provide the foundations for civic competence among citizens? In Chapter Six I explore the ways in which many key civic institutions respond to the pressures of political partisanship. I give particular attention to the press, public opinion polling, professional associations (legal and academic, in this case), and religious institutions in terms of the character of their engagement with these issues of the culture war—the way in which the cultural conflict is mediated to citizens. To listen to activists on both sides, one would think that bias is the most significant failure of these institutions. But while bias is probably a legitimate complaint, a more serious problem is simply one of superficiality.

In Chapter Seven I examine the ways in which civil society educates citizens into the differences underlying the controversies of the culture war. If citizens and politicians do not have such an understanding, how can they engage in serious and substantive discourse? My special focus in this chapter is on programs of multiculturalism, which are embraced by nearly all institutions of civil society, yet promulgated particularly through the schools. Most of the contemporary reflection about multiculturalism is political in nature; everyone wants to know whose political interests are really being served. But my concern with multiculturalism is strictly educational: does multiculturalism do what it aspires to do? The short answer, as the reader shall see, is not encouraging, but the longer answer addresses multiculturalism's quite unintentional consequences. They are surprising and, in light of certain ideals of democratic practice, disappointing.

In Part V of this essay, I explore the meaning of all that we find in the search for substantive public reflection and argument for democracy itself. In Chapter Eight I examine the common links that make our democratic response to the culture war what it is. The problems, as we will discover, are formidable at the very least. Clearly if there is no meaningful response to the difficulties we face, the reality of democracy in America will become, and remain, a bitter and dangerous parody of the ideal we aspire to. But the various problems we encounter are addressable. Substantive democracy is possible. In Chapter Nine, I explore the practical ways in which democratic life might be invigorated to respond to the challenge; the practical ways in which conflict itself might be transformed.

Democracy and the Culture War: Looking Forward

This book, once again, is primarily a search for the common ground of substantive (as opposed to shallow) public engagement in all three of these regions of social life; a kind of engagement where ideals of the good can be forged and reforged, even in the trials posed by a culture war. The context is the controversy over abortion. This issue has many dimensions to it, and many aspects of it have no point of comparison with any other particular controversy in the culture war. All the same, because the conflict over abortion is of such consequence for American society, it may instruct us about the vitality (or lack of vitality) of democratic practice in response to a wide range of issues concerning race, the arts, education, family and family values, and sexuality—forums where the deeper matter of the common good is worked through. It may provide a glimpse into how American democracy at the end of the twentieth century mediates the historical challenges of our postmodern conflicts.

And so the search begins in earnest.

— PART II —

Searching Through the Special Interests

The Politics of Distortion

— 2 —

The Distortions of Rhetoric

What Activists Say,
But Do Not Quite Mean

It is a curious contrast. The moral, legal, and institutional factors that keep the controversies of the culture war in a deadlock are formidable, but as one meets the individuals who actually represent the various special agenda organizations, one cannot but hold out the hope that serious democratic argument is actually possible.[1] In our interviews with professional activists on both sides of the abortion controversy, my assistants and I found individuals who were passionate and dedicated but also sincere, personable, reasonable on their own terms, engaging, and both willing and capable of good discussion.[2] There is no denying that each of these individuals exudes a sense of urgency, and along with this is at least a small measure of paranoia—a look that inquired of us, "Who are you really?" and "What are you really after?" But any reticence they may have had before meeting us typically faded away in a few minutes of conversation.

Among these activists we also found individuals who held views that hinted of moderation: pro-choice activists who recoiled at the idea of late-term abortions; pro-life activists who recognized that in rare, difficult circumstances abortion would have to be allowable. Our experience corresponded in every way with Kristin Luker's in her study of women activists in the abortion controversy: these activists are people who care deeply about the meaning of abortion for themselves, for others, and for the communities they live in, and they are real people—not the two-dimensional caricatures they often seem through media presentations.

Sitting face-to-face with the activists, one cannot help but to empathize with the stories they tell, their concern, and the circumstances that have led them to carve out their particular niche in this public battle. Yet the abortion controversy cannot be adequately understood through an empathetic rendering of the activists' worldviews. It is essential to understand something about the rhetorical character of the public "debate" as well.

The Distortions of Rhetoric

If there is one common thread running through the rhetoric on both sides in the abortion controversy, and in the culture war as a whole, it is distortion. By "distortion" in public rhetoric I am *not* speaking of deliberate deceptions used to mislead the public. This is not to say that deception does not occur, but as a deliberate act of organizational policy it is fairly rare. Lying does not pay in the long run, because those who do it are almost invariably found out and exposed.

Rather, the distortions of rhetoric to which I refer have a more technical meaning.[3] They are a particular kind of speech act or public utterance, whether expressed verbally (as in a speech, proclamation, sound bite, or chant), in written form (as in a political advertisement, direct mail solicitation, bumper sticker, or magazine article), or in a symbolic gesture (as in a placard, photograph, or display). What distinguishes this kind of speech act is that it represents an overstatement of a point of view, creating much the same effect as a misshapen mirror at an arcade—elongating, shrinking, or fattening the reality that the speaker is attempting to address. Quite literally, it is rhetorical hyperbole whose main purpose is to appeal to the *emotional* predispositions of the listener. It is not as though these speech acts are technically untrue or unjustifiable by those who give voice to them, but they stretch, bloat, or conflate realities in order to evoke a visceral response from the listener. When public discourse is framed by these kinds of speech acts, public understanding becomes framed more by emotionally evocative images than by either the principles or traditions of moral logic or the factual foundations of rational understanding. We see these distortions, then, in pronouncements or symbols that exaggerate for effect. The idea of distortion becomes clear in the following contrasting illustrations.

On an early spring afternoon in 1989 in Los Angeles, Operation Rescue held a press conference in a typical meeting room filled with wires, microphones, bright lights, and television cameras, along with technicians and journalists. Operation Rescue leader Randall Terry walked up to the microphones and spoke solemnly to the crowd in attendance: "I appreciate you coming today. This story is not about Randall Terry, nor is it about Operation Rescue. It is about little children brutally murdered. I believe many of you want to report this story with integrity. All I ask is that you show the American public the truth and let them decide how they feel." At this point, an assistant walked forward, placed a small coffin on a table to Terry's left, and opened the lid. Inside was a dead fetus/pre-born baby, at roughly four and a half months of gestation. Terry continued: "This is Baby Choice. She was murdered by a salt solution at nineteen weeks. She will answer all your questions." With this, Terry and his staff walked out of the press conference, got into their cars, and drove away.

This may not have been the highest moment in the unfolding discussion of abortion in America, but it did succeed in projecting the image that what was being aborted was not just fetal tissue—a medical abstraction with no greater significance than an appendix—but a distinguishable human form. Such political theater is imitated in slightly less dramatic ways by photographs of aborted fetuses or fetuses alive and in the womb. Typical is the mailing from Human Life International that showed side-by-side photographs of an eight-week old fetus before and after an abortion. Along with this was the commentary, "The proof . . . about the merciless slaughter of innocent babies . . . is in the photo." This imagery is graphic and provocative, to say the least, and is probably unmatched by anything offered up by pro-choice activists. Coming close, however, is the image of a bloody metal coat hanger. Often seen on placards at rallies, in political advertisements in newspapers, or in mass mailings, the coat hanger is typically accompanied by statements along the lines of "Never again." Here the image is of women risking their lives and even dying in order to maintain reproductive autonomy.

The dead baby/fetus and the coat hanger are both graphic and emotionally evocative images of what legal abortion, or the lack of it, entails. The meaning of each symbol is projected to be self-evident, and each is elevated to imply a general principle, but symbols like these are never self-interpreting. Each image purports to announce, in effect, the bottom line of the abortion issue, but for most Americans it is not. More of the story must be filled in before they can make some kind of informed judgment about the real meaning behind these graphic displays.

If the one type of distorted speech act is defined by the use of potent symbols and images, a second type involves the manipulation of facts. Consider how the number of abortions in America is portrayed. All of the major pro-choice organizations emphasize in their literature and in public rhetoric that 91 percent of all abortions performed in America each year take place in the first trimester of pregnancy.[4] By contrast, pro-life activists frame the very same issue by noting the actual numbers of second and third trimester abortions. On average, we are told, nearly 160,000 second- and third-trimester abortions take place every year, which translates into more than four hundred such abortions every day. Of these, roughly 18,000 are of unborn children at the point of viability, a figure equal to 50 such abortions daily.

Both ways of describing the volume of abortions performed in America each year are correct, but each description has a notably different effect. The first makes the number of second- and third-trimester abortions seem small, if not insignificant; the second makes the number of such abortions seem shockingly large.

A third illustration of how speech acts distort public communication is found in the use of "narrative" or stories. One of the celebrated stories invoked by pro-choice activists is that of seventeen-year-old Becky Bell of Indianapolis, Indiana, who died in 1988 in the alleged aftermath of an illegal abortion. In 1984, the Indiana state legislature voted to require that girls under the age of eighteen secure either a parent's permission for an abortion or special judicial consent. For reasons that are not altogether clear, Becky Bell, who was four months pregnant, decided that she could do neither. According to pro-choice advocates and the girl's parents, Becky either had someone try to induce an illegal abortion or tried to end the pregnancy herself.[5] Whatever the case, infection quickly followed, generating a severe case of pneumonia. Within a week she was rushed to a local hospital, where she died.

In the wake of the tragedy, Bell's parents became spokespeople for the Fund for the Feminist Majority and Planned Parenthood, speaking around the country and appearing in political advertisements denouncing parental consent laws as something that severely restrict a teen's access to safe, legal abortion.[6] "She died," as her father put it, "because of a parental consent law that we didn't even know existed." Eleanor Smeal of the Fund for the Feminist Majority echoed the claim, saying, "These laws kill young women, and we want people to see that damage." "Becky Bell Brigades" were proposed that would canvass high schools and colleges across the nation to create pressure to repeal such laws.

On the other side are stories involving crippling regret after abortion. Not atypical is the experience of Nancyjo Mann. In 1974 (a year after the *Roe* decision was handed down), with two young children already and five and a half months pregnant with her third, Mann's husband abandoned her. Her mother and brother encouraged her to have an abortion, saying that no other man would likely want her with three children, let alone the two she already had, and that she would probably never amount to much if she did not take control of her life right then. What began as reluctance before the abortion grew into deep remorse and guilt after the procedure. Indeed she chose to be sterilized later, saying that she "couldn't cope with the idea that [she] could possibly kill again."[7] Many years later she founded Women Exploited by Abortion (WEBA) because she felt, in her own words, "ripped off by the abortionists who trivialized the nature of the deed and conned by a legal system that stretches 'freedom of choice' to include the painful destruction of children."[8]

In both of these stories, the larger issue of abortion is made gut-wrenchingly tangible for those who hear them. It is only natural to feel some sympathy for the people involved. Rhetorically speaking, however, these narratives become the prism through which the listener understands and interprets the *entire* matter of abortion. At a certain level, each story presents itself as characteristic of the experience of every woman who is either denied or gets a safe, legal abortion. Collectively these kinds of stories, symbols, facts, and pronouncements—speech acts all—dominate the framework for addressing the complex issue of abortion.

A Glossary of Rhetorical Distortions

The controversy over abortion is overrun with such distortions. They are all familiar, for they are made by the individual and institutional actors repeatedly and, often enough, officially. When brought together, these statements and the distortions they create form an exchange that runs the length and breadth of the abortion controversy. What follows here is an abbreviation of such an exchange, with each statement taken verbatim from the activists themselves.

Words of salutation:

Pro-choice:	Pro-life:
Keep your laws off our bodies![9]	
	Stop abortion on demand![10]
Keep your rosaries off our ovaries![11]	
	Abortion is murder![12]
Keep your cross out of our crotch![13]	

Terms of endearment:

Pro-choice:	Pro-life:
Anti-choice extremists![14]	
	Murderers![15]

(Cont'd)

Terms of endearment:

Pro-choice:	Pro-life:
Anti-choice zealots![16]	
	Pro-death activists![17]
Anti-choice absolutists![18]	
	Secular humanists![19]
Self-righteous anti-abortion forces![20]	
	Radical feminists of the pro-abortion lobby![21]
Anti-female bigots of the religious right![22]	
	[Your] programs are anti-child and anti-family![23]
Ultra-fundamentalist band of moralists [who] seek to impose its will on the rest of us.[24]	
	Ultra-liberals…who promote immoral sex, condoms, and abortions in public schools![25]

The accusations:

Pro-choice:	Pro-life:
The well-financed anti-abortion minority in this country is determined to destroy our individual liberty and to impose on us their specific religious belief. And	

(Cont'd)

The accusations:

Pro-choice:	Pro-life:

their efforts are vicious and re-lentless.[26]

When pro-choice organizations talk about "unwanted" children, they presume that they have a right to dispose of unwanted people any way they wish.[27]

[You] anti-choice extremists want to silence discussion and take away all of our choices, one by one.[28]

When [abortion-rights groups say a woman has a] "right to choose," what they don't say is "right to choose to kill another human being." You don't finish the sentence.[29]

[So-called 'pro-lifers' represent] a callous and vocal minority [that wants] to hurl the nation back into the frightening era of back-alley abortionists...terri-fied young women...and ruined lives.[30]

Abortion advocates are not of-fering choices; they are offering abortion—period. "Choice" ad-vocates have yet to provide the support necessary for women to make any choice other than abortion.[31]

(Cont'd)

The accusations:

Pro-choice:	Pro-life:

The "Right to Life" people call themselves "pro-life"...but whose "life" are they pro? Certainly not the life of the mother. Certainly not the life of a child born defective, fatally ill, destitute, or simply unwanted. You "pro-life" people are simply anti-abortion.[32]

Every day 4,300 unborn babies are killed by injections of chemical poison or dismembered by suction machines.[33] Abortion advocates foster public ignorance about this because it provides them with the perfect climate to win converts with their carefully-crafted populist "choice" and "keep-the-government-out-of-personal-lives" rhetoric.[34]

Women have a fundamental right to abortion.[35]

Planned Parenthood, in defiance of the law, coerces women to have abortions.[36]

Every person has a right to reproductive autonomy.[37] It's incorrect to call us pro-abortion. We represent the most neutral of all positions; we defend the RIGHT to choose whether or

(Cont'd)

The accusations:

Pro-choice:	Pro-life:

not we, as individuals, elect to exercise that right.[38]

Abortion is murder! It's infanticide. No better than legalized killing.[39]

Abortion is a vital and necessary aspect of reproductive health care.[40]

Abortion is an intolerable evil in this country.[41]

The radical right batters family planning efforts.[42]

Abortion is not family planning.[43]

Anti-choice extremists...will stop at nothing—not at distortion...not at verbal assaults during their "rescues"...not even at firebombing a clinic— if that is what it will take to destroy choice forever.[44]

Our opponents try to keep the truth sealed from the public, because to disclose it would be to unveil their true extremist stripes.[45]

We discuss alternatives in a responsible way. But extremists who lie are endangering people in crisis.[46]

Of those who perform abortions

Pro-choice:	Pro-life:
Health care professionals[47]	
	Blood-sucking hyenas![48]
Physicians[49]	
	Death merchants![50]

Characterizing the law

Pro-choice:	Pro-life:
The current law is actually a compromise between both sides. In *Roe v. Wade* the Court carefully mediated between (1) a woman's fundamental interest in personal privacy which included the decision to terminate a pregnancy; (2) every state's interest in promoting the health of its female citizens; and (3) a state's interest in the potential life of a fetus that is viable. To dismantle this compromise is to demonstrate no respect for women's fundamental rights and women's ability to make wise, judicious, and moral decisions.[51]	
	[The current law is] abortion on demand until the cord is cut.[52] Abortionists...kill human beings in the womb for any reason at any time during the 9 months of pregnancy.[53]

Characterizing parental notification

Pro-choice:	Pro-life:

Unable to stop abortions for all women, anti-choice extremists have decided to concentrate on those women least able to defend themselves from political assaults on their privacy and safety: the young and the poor.[54]

It is ironic that the people who cry "free choice" are unwilling to give any choice to parents about their children's sex lives.[55] A 13-year-old girl cannot get her ears pierced without parental consent. But she can have a legal abortion and her parents will never be told.[56]

The primary intent of those who promote parental consent and notice laws is to restrict abortion, not to encourage family communication.[57]

They are silent about the hundreds of teenagers who have been killed or crippled by so-called "safe, legal abortion."[58]

On the safety of abortion

Pro-choice:	Pro-life:

Women who have abortions are less likely to suffer psychiatric disability than women denied abortions.[59]

One psychological effect that we see is guilt. We see it all the time along with mourning, re-gret, and remorse.[60]

The American Psychological Association is on record as having said that severe negative reactions after abortion are rare and can best be understood in the framework of coping with normal life stress....Government restrictions on abortion are more likely to cause women lasting harm than the procedure itself.[61]

Long term complications from abortion occur in 20% to 50% of all aborted women. No less than 90% of women who have aborted experience moderate to severe emotional and psychiatric stress following abortion.[62] Post abortion stress even increases the probability that a woman will become involved in a pattern of child battery.[63]

Visions of the apocalypse

Pro-choice:	Pro-life:

We need to begin to highlight for the American public how grave a risk women face with the impending overturn of *Roe v. Wade*. It is very difficult for people to understand the grave consequences—the medical condition of women, family welfare, social unrest, and political upheaval. People need to begin to consider America without *Roe*.[64]

Americans do not approve of abortion on demand for nine months, abortion being used for purposes of birth control, abortion being advocated for young children behind the backs of parents. These are the common practices in this country today and are part of the reason why abortion is such an insidious social problem.[65]

The majority of Americans do not approve of this destruction of abortion rights.[66]

Abortions don't take place in bedrooms. Abortion is not a private matter. Killing is not a natural part of sex.[67]

(Cont'd)

Visions of the apocalypse

Pro-choice:	Pro-life:

I don't want to sound overly dramatic here, but I really do envision political and social upheaval. I envision a nation where women are faced with the choice between a forced unwanted pregnancy or an illegal abortion. Poor women at risk for their lives and health. Families losing mothers. I really believe that it's a devastation to our country.[68]

To allow one age group of humans to be killed because they are socially burdensome will lead inexorably to allowing the killing of other humans at other ages who have become socially burdensome.[69]

Women face the loss of their fundamental ability to make decisions about the most personal and the most important aspects of their lives. Women—particularly the poor, rural, and young women who find themselves faced with crisis pregnancies in states where abortion will be made illegal—will be subject to illegal abortion very quickly, and that puts women's lives at risk in addition to their health.[70] And

(Cont'd)

Visions of the apocalypse

Pro-choice:	*Pro-life:*

let's not forget that the anti-choice activists won't stop with the destruction of abortion rights. They're also determined to outlaw contraception and to turn back the clock on the fundamental right to privacy guaranteed under our Constitution.[71]

Abortion has already killed 25 million preborn babies. How many of our elderly will ultimately be sacrificed to balance the budget?[72]

Et cetera, et cetera, et cetera . . .

An observation made earlier is worth repeating: clearly more is involved in this exchange than simply the articulation of different perspectives on the same issue. At the same time, less is involved than the deliberate attempt to deceive listeners. The statements may be justifiable in every case, but there is nevertheless a clear and consistent overstatement, contorting the realities to which the speech act refers. Is it really true, as Concerned Women for America puts it, that "Planned Parenthood, in defiance of the law, *coerces* women to have abortions" (emphasis added here and in following quotes)? Is it true, as the Religious Coalition for Abortion Rights claims, that "so-called 'pro-lifers' confront patients and staff by day—and *plant lethal bombs by night* to frighten women from seeking vital and necessary reproductive health care?[73] Are we to believe that the "ACLU *Demands* Infanticide"?[74] Is Patricia Ireland correct in saying that a *"holy war is being waged on women* with the end of creating a theocracy in the 21st century"?[75]

I have argued elsewhere that the technology and marketing of contemporary public discourse (for example, through sound bites, political advertisements, billboards, and direct mail) are factors contributing to the distortion of public speech.[76] They define an environment that predisposes a dialogue of exaggeration, sensationalism, and superficiality. But to affix blame on impersonal technologies or uncontrollable market imperatives does not exactly exonerate the activists from responsibility. Individuals and organizations that choose to engage each other with these technologies and in this environment are, at some level, accountable for the consequences.

Of Dead Babies and Coat Hangers: The Activists Reflect on the "Debate"

As one might expect, though, the activists themselves do not quite see it this way. Certainly their opponents are guilty of sensationalizing and distorting public debate, but not they. Consider first how activists on each side regard their opponents' contributions to public discourse.

"Lies!" This was how Bob, at the Christian Action Council, described the way pro-choice groups describe abortion. "When a woman comes into a crisis pregnancy center [CPC] and sees photographs of prenatal development, she's shocked because she inevitably will say, 'Planned Parenthood just told me [the fetus] was pregnancy tissue; it was just an unconscious blob of cells; That [abortion] was just a menstrual extraction . . . they never told me this' [referring to the photographs]. [Our opposition] lies to these women. . . . They are not told the truth about the baby." He had the same opinion of Planned Parenthood's ad campaign against pro-life crisis pregnancy centers: "[Their accusations] are lies. They say that we pretend to be abortion clinics so that we can trick women to coming to us. When women do come in, they say we give them false information about abortion and that we harass them—terrorize them emotionally so that these women do not get abortions. The fact of the matter is that CPCs associated with the Christian Action Council are scrupulously honest in their dealings with women."

John, representing the National Right to Life Committee, had the same view of the opposition's rhetoric: "Have you noticed the logo for NARAL? It is half of the face of the Statue of Liberty. The whole face is not shown. This is typical for them. They only speak half-truths." A spokesperson for the American Life League made the same point: "They have a habit of lying, and they just keep doing it. Some of them don't even recognize they're lying, because they do it so often they cannot discriminate between truth and error."

Echoes of these claims can be heard on the other side of the grand canyon of abortion politics. "Total bullshit!" said one attorney in the upper reaches of NOW in response to pro-life attempts to prohibit gender-selection abortions, require informed consent, and block the introduction of RU486. "Excuse my language, but [their claims] represent an attack on women. . . . They imply that women are irresponsible, that they don't take decisions like this seriously, and that women need the state to come in and guide them, propagandize them, and if they don't comply, then penalize them. . . . Everything they say misrepresents the facts. The reason is that their goal is to stop abortions, not to help women." Susan at the Religious Coalition for Abortion Rights held the same view: "The major terms of the anti-choice movement manipulate the truth. For example, the term *unborn child* or *unborn baby* gives the impression that a fetus is actually a baby, which it is not. A fetus is no more an 'unborn child' than we are 'undead corpses.' The anti-choice movement does this so that people feel that a fetus is life and therefore, abortion is murder. . . . Their claim that abortion is used as a form of birth control falls into the same category. . . . It is very manipulative."

It is not surprising that activists are considerably more generous when reflecting on their *own* use of rhetoric. Dorothy, of Concerned Women for America (CWA), justified her organization's rhetoric by saying that it is used by both sides. Such language "has always been a way of fighting the battle." For CWA's part, "we use a language that people can understand what we are saying. We don't want anybody to misunderstand where we're coming from." (Few could possibly have any doubts about that.) Bob of the Christian Action Council, admitted that his organization too sometimes uses what he called "colorful language" but does so, he said, only if it is accurate. "For instance," he explained, "I think an abortionist is a butcher, pure and simple. He's butchering a child. He's carving that child up like a Thanksgiving turkey. That's what an abortion does. [For this reason] I will call an abortionist a butcher." Like a Thanksgiving turkey? Colorful? Indeed! Accurate? Well, not exactly.

The defense of "colorful" rhetoric is fully made by pro-choice activists as well. For example, an executive with Planned Parenthood justified the slogans used by her organization by saying that "messages like this are designed to get the attention of the American public who don't focus on this issue." We asked specifically about an advertisement placed in *Time* magazine that featured the headline, "How would you like the police to investigate your miscarriage?" She explained, in response, that "the impact of restrictive laws can, in fact, lead to that kind of government intrusion, and while I think *it may be an extreme example*, its purpose was to demonstrate to people, who don't normally focus on this issue, what's at risk" (emphasis added).

The irony of failing to see in their own rhetoric the same kinds of distortions they decry in that of their opposition was crystallized when the activists from each side reflected on their opposition's use of either coat hangers or photographs of dead fetuses for symbolic purposes. Consider the following exchange with Susan of the Religious Coalition for Abortion Rights:

INTERVIEWER: Is a coat hanger an appropriate symbol for the pro-choice movement?

SUSAN: The coat hanger is a very powerful reminder and symbol for those women who lived through and experienced the days when abortion was illegal. . . . It gets them back to that emotional place in themselves. It reminds them of what it was like. . . . For younger women who did not experience that time, it's just kind of a chilling visual that makes us feel uncomfortable because we didn't experience that. . . . It doesn't feel so good to see that. I mean it does make me feel kind of sick, but then it's accomplishing its goal.

INTERVIEWER: But what about the use of dead fetuses used by the pro-life? Doesn't that do the same thing?

SUSAN: Right, but it's manipulative. When they show you a fetus or pictures of fetuses, they are always practically full term, and they say this is what abortion does. No, it doesn't. They don't show you fifteen-week old fetuses, which is the outside limit for 80 percent of all abortions. . . . Sure, these pictures make you sick. It's just like the sick idea that a woman who's eight months pregnant is going to run to get an abortion. It's just not true. It's manipulative. By the way, the fetuses they show are late term, [but] the coat hanger was used any time during pregnancy.

The conversation went much the same way with Joanne of the National Organization for Women.

INTERVIEWER: What do you think when pro-lifers use dead fetuses or pictures of dead fetuses to communicate their message?

JOANNE: I think it's obscene. If you have respect for life, why would you take what you consider life and tote it around the country? It's just obscene! It's an obscene form of bullying. Moreover, I think it's probably disrespectful to everybody concerned—including themselves! It is demeaning, and I don't think it's effective.

INTERVIEWER: What about when pro-choice advocates use coat hangers to communicate their message?

JOANNE: Well, I think coat hangers are a symbol of one of the major ways women self-aborted in this country.

INTERVIEWER: Is that really true?

JOANNE: Oh, yeah. This is an instrument that was used, that *will* be used.

For pro-lifers, the rhetorical purpose of these opposing images reads quite differently. Listen to John at the National Right to Life Committee:

INTERVIEWER: Why does the pro-life movement show dead fetuses or pictures of fetuses in gestation, as in the film "The Silent Scream"?

JOHN: These pictures show the humanity of the unborn. Pro-abortionists always want to dehumanize the child by calling it a fetus, or a blob of "pregnancy tissue." Pro-abortionists think these pictures are inflammatory, but only because it's the truth.

INTERVIEWER: They can be fairly gruesome, can't they?

JOHN: Well, it's true. We see pictures of the results of abortion—pre-born children who were pulled out of a dumpster in Houston,

Texas, and in California—but they are very, very powerful tools for motivating people who may be pro-life, but are ambivalent or not activated. . . . When people see what happens in abortion [in these] gory pictures, people identify with that unborn child and conclude that what you are doing is fundamentally wrong.

INTERVIEWER: What do you think of your opposition's use of coat hangers as a symbol?

JOHN: There's no question that there were some illegal abortions before *Roe,* but to suggest that hundreds of thousands of women died from illegal or self-induced abortions is a deliberate fabrication of the data. Nobody knows. It's just a made-up number. There certainly was not an epidemic of deaths from illegal abortion as they would have you believe.

And then there was Pete, with Missionaries to the Preborn, who himself has shown dead fetuses:

INTERVIEWER: How do you feel about protesters carrying around aborted fetuses?

PETE: I am a tremendous advocate of it. When people look at a dead child and they realize that this happens about fifteen to twenty times a day within 20 or 30 minutes of where they live, work and worship, the reality begins to sink in.

INTERVIEWER: Does it sink in or are people just grossed out?

PETE: They might be grossed out, but they can't deny what they're seeing. . . . You see, I want to make it so that people see and listen to the testimony of the child himself. It is the same as in the story of Levite's concubine, told in Judges 19 of the Old Testament. After the Benjamites gang-raped the woman and left her dead, he cut her body into twelve pieces and sent them all over Israel, saying that never before has something this horrendous happened. He let the dead woman testify to their [the Benjamites'] sin. It was direct testimony. It is the same with an aborted baby: "Innocent blood cries out from the ground." It just cries out to anybody who has a shred of justice in them.

INTERVIEWER: Is it the same when feminists show coat hangers?

PETE: Well, that's bogus. They have consistently lied on that score. They focus on something that is statistically marginal. The aborted baby is real every time.

Intention, Technology, and Reality

Debates over public policy, as Peter Berger has observed, are very often debates over language.[77] Is the object being aborted a fetus, or an unborn baby? Is abortion murder, or a safe surgical practice? Is one side's rhetoric obscene, demeaning, and manipulative, while the other's is realistic or just slightly colorful? Are people who blockade abortion clinics engaging in civil disobedience in the name of protecting life, or are they practicing terrorism against women?

The tug of war over language obviously goes far beyond the abortion dispute. Is affirmative action a policy of racial justice or reverse discrimination? Are the opponents of homosexuality and gay rights homophobic or defenders of the family? Is the work of avant-garde painters serious art, or trash? Are opponents of some textbooks violating the First Amendment or are they maintaining community standards? And so on. We have seen in some detail how important and distorting speech acts are in the abortion controversy. They have a similar significance and distorting effect when examining the way other controversies are discussed.

The reason language is so important to public policy is not difficult to discern. Language both reflects and shapes social reality, for words themselves frame how we think about experience. Thus those who have the power to establish the language of public debate will have a tremendous advantage in determining the debate's outcome. Linguistic victories therefore translate into political victories. Activists on both sides themselves acknowledge this: "Language is everything," as one Planned Parenthood executive put it.[78]

But the language of public debate over this issue is symbolic in a more visceral way. Susan of the Religious Coalition for Abortion Rights put it well, saying, "This is a visual war we're fighting here" that is perfectly suited "for the thirty-second sound-bite society we live in." Not only does the rhetoric compete according to a zero-sum calculus whereby one side's gains are the other side's losses, but the conflicting sympathies and sentiments play by the same rules as well.

There are no laws against this, but the outcome is clear: distortion in the way we come to understand important and controversial issues.

Many of the activists we interviewed admitted that when speaking to a live audience, they will tone down their rhetoric. They all agreed that in face-to-face conversations, the rhetoric they use in political advertising, at rallies, and in direct mail would put people off. But it is the rhetoric used in political advertising, in direct mail, in television sound bites, and at rallies that is accessible to the largest number of people. As such it forms a backdrop—the lowest common denominator—for all other discussion. It cannot be discounted or ignored, for it constantly (if only implicitly) defines the rhetorical framework of all other moral, political, and legal exchanges on the issue.

In the context of such communications technology, the intentions of the actors involved would seem quite irrelevant. Even if the activists could generate enough ironic detachment to see the exaggerations in their own rhetoric (and not just the manipulations in that of their opponents), as long as they and the institutions they represent continue to engage in the current style of public speech, the "debate," such as it is, will not change in any remarkable way. The outcome, of course, is a thinning out, a shallowing, of the democratic imperative.

— 3 —

The Distortions of Interest

What Activists Would Rather Not Talk About

Sincerity is one of the hallmarks of those passionately engaged in the controversies of the culture war. Such sincerity is real, not feigned. If it were the only factor animating people on both sides of the controversies, perhaps one could go beneath the various distortions of rhetoric each side is prone to perpetuate. But for better or for worse, it is not the only factor.

A second kind of distortion to public discourse prevalent within the special agenda organizations comes from the play of unacknowledged and unexamined interests that invariably animate groups in their actions and arguments. The legitimacy of those interests is not really the first issue; someone could judge the material interests or social advantages afforded to a group to be either justifiable or unjustifiable. The problem is that when practical advantages go unacknowledged in public, the serious deliberation of public disputes is made all the more difficult. For one, public debate can only be incomplete when information is held back. How can political leaders (as well as the general public) assess an issue or formulate policy without knowing all the relevant facts?

In this chapter I explore some of the interests at play in the abortion controversy. My purpose is not so much to expose these interests to public scrutiny as to show how they further polarize public exchange.

Institutional Interests

The first and most obvious interests are institutional in nature. Though special agenda organizations range considerably in size and capacity, the ones that are most prominent (in part because of the quantity of mischief they create) have a propensity to develop into fairly large, independent bureaucracies with interests of their own—interests that are often independent from the issues for which they stand. This is why special agenda organizations rarely go out of business but instead evolve as they shift their focus from older, "resolved" issues to new ones. For example, Clergy and Laity Concerned About the War in Vietnam shortened its name at the end of the war to Clergy and Laity Concerned—that is, concerned about promoting a general progressive agenda in public policy. Likewise, after its 1984 boycott campaign against Nestlé (because of the latter's marketing of infant formula in Third World countries) succeeded, the group INFACT became an organization committed to a reduction in nuclear weapons production.

This inclination for organizations to outlive their founding purposes is no less evident in the realm of abortion politics. Before 1973, for example, NARAL was the acronym for the National Association to Repeal Abortion Laws. After *Roe* legalized abortion in that year, however, the acronym was preserved to represent the newly rechristened National Abortion Rights Action League. One sees the shuffling of priorities among pro-life organizations as well in their effort to diversify (through both legal initiatives and social action) their focus from abortion to concern for the terminally ill and the elderly. One reason for this sort of flexibility is that the professionals who staff the groups have an interest in preserving their own jobs. For these institutional reasons alone, then, conflict is not easily resolved.

What Men Have at Stake

One of the triumphs of the women's movement has been to bring about a broad recognition that there are often significant differences between the experiences of women and those of men. We now recognize that to study men with the presumption that one's findings are valid for women is methodologically flawed. Thus it is virtually unimaginable (and quite rightly so) in social scientific circles to study white men and imagine that the results can be generalized to anyone besides white men. Presumably this also cuts the other way. In her work, Kristin Luker focuses exclusively on the worldviews and life circumstances of *female* activists. Clearly a serious study of male activists is called for, but even without such a study, one can speculate as to what men may have at stake in the controversy over abortion.

The question of what motivates men to take sides or to participate in the abortion debate is relevant for empirical reasons. For one, while the greatest support for the pro-life movement comes from women,[1] it has been men—Randall Terry, Joseph Scheidler, Robert Marshall, Tom Glessner, Richard Glasow, and so on—who are often the leaders and spokes*men* for pro-life organizations. Second, though women's organizations are most visible in the defense of abortion rights, public opinion polls regularly show that males in their early twenties are among the strongest supporters of liberal abortion laws. Thus we see that men are quite relevant to the discussion—but what do they have at stake in this issue?

First let us consider the pro-life side of the controversy. Suppose a male pro-life activist is genuinely concerned about protecting the life of the unborn. He believes the unborn to be human, deserving our protection as part of the human community. Abortion, therefore, is akin to murder: legal abortion is a grave social and moral injustice and, on a societal scale, it is tantamount to genocide.

Even if this is the case, a male pro-lifer's objections to abortion implicitly endorse a division of labor in which women, by virtue of their anatomy, are largely relegated to the role of caregiver and therefore made dependent upon an economically independent male. A pro-life male, especially one who relies upon Scripture or a socially conservative religious and moral tradition (as many pro-life advocates are inclined to do), may respond, "This is the way it *should* be, particularly through the child-rearing years." The problem is that childbearing and child rearing need not necessarily be linked. Pro-life men could just as easily stay at home and allow their wives to work; moreover, day care could be encouraged as another alternative for families where both parents prefer or need to work. If the protection of the life of the unborn child is nonnegotiable, certainly the matter of who cares for the children *is* negotiable—especially considering that a woman's economic independence is one of the central priorities of pro-choice activism.

Clearly the suggestion that pro-life men should be willing to care for their children in order that their wives may work is not, in itself, going to satisfy pro-choice advocates. Work aside, pro-choice activists do not think that a woman should have to endure the trauma of a pregnancy against her will. Even so, the issues of child rearing and a woman's economic independence are paramount to the debate. Thus it is noteworthy that pro-life men are generally unwilling to recognize these concerns and to search for points of negotiation (say, through a reworking of the traditional division of labor in order to allow women the freedom to pursue economic independence if they so desire). But the general willingness to rework the so-called traditional family is not forthcoming. Not only are such alternatives rarely heard, organizations pushing the pro-life agenda tend to oppose day care options that would allow women the flexibility and opportunity to work outside of the home. They also tend to oppose family-leave legislation that would enable both men and women to take leave from work at the birth of a new baby. Naturally, these actions only bolster the arguments of pro-choice advocates who demonize the pro-life movement for its unspoken agenda to recreate a patriarchal social order. To be blunt, when accused of relegating women to the kitchen, pro-life men have reason to duck for cover; their broader interests are being challenged.

This situation is coupled with a general tendency in the pro-life movement (with its prominent male leadership) to depict women who choose abortions as models of moral callousness, selfishness, and irresponsibility. (Take, for example, a statement made by Judy and Paul Brown of the American Life League: "When NOW says . . . 'every child a wanted child' this means 'we kill children we are too selfish to care for.'")[2] Besides being fundamentally condescending, this portrait fails to describe the empirical realities or intentions of most women seeking abortion. It does not recognize that the decision to have an abortion can be made by a responsible moral agent in the context of a life that strives to be moral and responsible. Thus, when pro-life men refer to women seeking abortions as self-indulgent, they betray a broader discomfort with nontraditional views of sexuality, especially female sexuality. Here again, if abortion were the exclusive concern, issues of sexuality could be separated out from it. Invariably, though, issues of sexuality are not separated out, thus reinforcing pro-choice suspicions that pro-life men want *more* than to stop abortions.

But now consider men on the pro-choice side of the controversy. Suppose a pro-choice fellow is genuinely concerned to see the economic and social liberation of women, as feminist arguments articulate it. He believes that men have oppressed women for too long, and he is therefore committed to structural changes in society that would allow women to achieve their full potential in the public sphere. One such structural change is the legal guarantee of a woman's reproductive autonomy. To the pro-choice male, abortion is not a philosophical problem. He does not believe that fetal life is worthy of protection; legal abortion is essential to a woman's equality with men. The guarantee of a woman's equality with men outweighs any claims the fetus might have on the right to life.

But by vesting all reproductive responsibility in the woman, a pro-choice male creates a situation in which men can easily rationalize their irresponsibility toward women who choose not to abort.[3] As Daniel Callahan has put it, "If legal abortion has given women more choice, it has also given men more choice as well. They now have a potent new weapon in the old business of manipulating and abandoning women."[4] Given that 80 percent of all abortions are sought by single women (according to Alan Guttmacher Institute statistics), the advent of reproductive rights has created a situation in which a man can coerce a woman to have an abortion by denying his responsibility toward her, or even abandoning her when she gets pregnant and "chooses" to carry the child to term. According to feminist legal scholar Catharine MacKinnon, "Sexual liberation in this sense does not free women, it frees male sexual aggression. The availability of abortion thus removes the one remaining legitimized reason that women had for refusing sex beside the headache."[5]

The anecdotal evidence for this interpretation is compelling.[6] Consider an encounter captured in the CBS documentary "The

Vanishing Family: Crisis in Black America," shown on January 26, 1986. The scene is a ghetto in Newark, New Jersey, and journalist Bill Moyers is speaking to Timothy, a man in his early thirties who has fathered six children with four different women.

MOYERS: People out there watching are going to say, "Why didn't he think about [his responsibility] before he brought six kids into the world?"

TIMOTHY: Well, the mother had a choice. She could have an abortion or she could have the child. She decided she wanted to have the child, so therefore, I guess it's not sweating her.

MOYERS: So do you think it's her fault that she got pregnant?

TIMOTHY: Well, maybe, maybe not. I say, "Mama's baby, Papa's maybe." Ya know what I mean?

MOYERS: (later in the interview) Would you have had all these kids if you had thought about it?

TIMOTHY: No.

MOYERS: All were an accident?

TIMOTHY: Yeah, you could say that.

MOYERS: Were you just having a good time?

TIMOTHY: (Smiling, a little embarrassed and a little proud) Yes, I had a lovely time. I enjoyed myself.

Empirical studies have also demonstrated that male coercion and pressure play a sizable role in many women's abortion decisions. A survey from the Medical College of Ohio, for example, examined 150 women who "identified themselves as having poorly assimilated the abortion experience."[7] Of the 81 women who responded, more than one-third felt they had been coerced into their decision. Fewer than one-third of the women initially considered the abortion themselves. In Mary Zimmerman's study of women who had undergone abortions, she found that men who were informed of the pregnancy supported their partner's initial decision to abort by a margin of two to one. In cases where women initially chose to bear the child, their male partners were opposed to the decision by a margin of eight to

one. In all of these cases the man withdrew his support for his partner, "thereby eliminating that alternative."[8]

Even in Carol Gilligan's famous study *In a Different Voice*, not all
of the women's abortion decisions she recounts were independent,
moral choices. Male coercion played an important role in about one-
third of the cases cited. The men in these women's lives were unwilling to provide their partners with the moral and material support for
pregnancy, childbirth, and child rearing.[9] As one of Gilligan's respondents noted, "He made me feel that I had to make a choice and there
was only one choice to make and that was to have an abortion and I
could always have children another time, and he made me feel if I
didn't have it that it would drive us apart."[10] In all these cases, the
logic goes something like this: since the man was willing to pay for an
abortion, and since the woman had a constitutional right to get one
even if he wished to prevent it, by her failure to obtain an abortion
she took sole responsibility for the child. Therefore, the man should
not be liable for any child support.[11]

Liberal abortion policy has created a climate where men can enjoy
sexual relations with little or no concern for consequences. It does
not require great imagination to see that this may explain the thousands of dollars the Playboy Foundation (as in *Playboy* magazine—
hardly known for its feminist sensibilities) provided during the 1980s
to the ACLU Reproductive Freedom Project, Catholics for a Free
Choice, the National Abortion Federation, NARAL, the NOW Legal
Defense and Education Fund, Planned Parenthood, and the Religious Coalition for Abortion Rights.[12] *Hustler* magazine is also reported to have given money to women's groups concerned with
abortion.[13] Abortion is often misrepresented as solely a women's issue; clearly, however, it is a men's issue as well as long as men are interested in protecting their sexual liberty.

Thus men have a keen, if indirect, interest in the outcome of the
abortion controversy. Though they can argue effectively on both sides
of the issue, the implicit stake that both pro-life and pro-choice men
have in this is ironically much the same. In both cases it is the power
to shape women's life circumstances for them: on the one hand, to
compel them to stay at home and raise a family, and on the other, to
compel them to choose abortion so that men may resist responsibility

for their sexual behavior. Either way, men are in positions to press their advantage, making matters more, not less, difficult for women.

Pro-Choice Tactical Interests

A key tactical advantage of the pro-choice position is economic in nature. Abortion, in a word, is profitable.

It is true that abortion is far from being the most prestigious or the most lucrative of medical specialties. Moreover, doctors specializing in abortions are regularly under siege from protesters and largely isolated from their colleagues. These doctors themselves complain of being heavily stigmatized. As a consequence, fewer and fewer doctors are willing to enter the field.[14] In hospitals, special bonuses are sometimes offered to interns and residents who will perform the procedure. Nevertheless, for those who do perform abortions as a part or all of their practice, it can be a lucrative business.

Consider first that most abortions are performed in specialty clinics. According to one study, 25 percent of all abortion providers perform roughly 80 percent of all abortions. At the Northern Illinois Women's Center outside of Chicago, for example, doctors perform approximately 3,500 abortions every year. In 1985, when the director of this center, Dr. Richard Ragsdale, went to court to protest Illinois statutes regulating his practice, he testified that the average abortion costs $250, though he did perform abortions on indigent women for lesser fees or for free. At this rate his clinic's income would have been more than $750,000. In the Routh Street Women's Clinic in Dallas, Texas, doctors perform about 4,000 abortions a year, suggesting (by the same calculations) an income of up to approximately $1 million per year.[15] In actual number, approximately 1.2 million abortions take place in about 800 nonhospital facilities across the United States annually.[16] This averages out to about 1,500 abortions per clinic; at about $250 per abortion, the income generated from these abortions is approximately $375,000 per clinic.

The largest provider of abortion services is Planned Parenthood. During the late 1980s and early 1990s, roughly 100,000 abortions were performed at their clinics annually. At an average cost of $215 for a first-trimester abortion, total income from abortions is about

$20 million or more. This revenue, along with government grants and private donations, funds staffing and operation for the organization and its 171 affiliates. Although the medical practice of abortion is a small part of the medical/pharmaceutical sector of the economy, in the decade following *Roe,* it was something of a growth industry, with an increase in abortions of about 150 percent.[17] The annual number of abortions has held steady at approximately 1.6 million for the last several years, after first reaching 1.5 million in 1979.

Abortion is also a largely unregulated business. As noted in Chapter One, most of the efforts to regulate the practice of abortion between 1973 and 1989 were judged unconstitutional. Some states have been able to enact parental notification restrictions, clinic operation restrictions, and the like, but the number of government regulations enforced on specialty clinic operations has been fairly small. Pro-life advocates are not too far off the mark when they argue that abortion is "the largest unregulated business in America."[18] Yet this is only true insofar as government intervention is concerned. Many clinics are self-regulated through their association with larger associations of abortion providers (of which the National Abortion Federation, with a 1992 membership of about three hundred clinics, is the largest).[19] As a consequence, abortion in general is a fairly safe procedure. According to national statistics, abortions in the first trimester (seven to thirteen weeks) and early second trimester (thirteen to sixteen weeks) are among the safest outpatient procedures available in the United States. Estimates suggest that major complications occur less than 1 percent of the time.[20]

Complications do occur, though, and often enough they occur in *legal* clinics where the staff are either incompetent or poorly equipped. The cases can be quite notorious. There is, for example, the Dadeland Family Planning Center in Dade County, Florida, where physicians sometimes would perform fifty to sixty first- and second-trimester abortions per day. Fifteen lawsuits were filed against the clinic in just ten years: the clinic advertised falsely, one of its doctors was reprimanded by his state licensing board for gross malpractice, and another was responsible for more than a half million dollars in out-of-court settlements for abortions gone awry. Over the years uteruses were ruptured, colons were perforated, hysterectomies were performed in emergency, many women were told they were pregnant when they were not, and one unfortunate woman died.[21]

Another notorious clinic is the Hillview Women's Medical Surgical Center in Maryland, outside of Washington, D.C. In this clinic, where approximately five thousand abortions were performed annually, one thirty-four-year-old woman died under general anesthesia, and another thirty-two-year-old woman suffered severe brain damage and near-total paralysis when the anesthesia she received constricted her throat, stopping the flow of oxygen to her brain. In both cases, anesthesia was administered by unqualified and unlicensed personnel. And then there was the Water Tower Reproductive Center in Chicago, where the clinic owner and chief abortion provider, Dr. Arnold Brickman, performed hundreds of abortions on women who were not pregnant, performed incomplete abortions, refused to admit public health inspectors on the premises, performed abortions without a clinic license, and had his license revoked for gross malpractice in the treatment of an eighteen-year-old woman who bled to death after an abortion[22].

These are atrocity stories, and pro-life advocates naturally have an interest in giving them as much play as possible. But they are not fabricated, and indeed, they are more numerous than one might imagine.[23] Invariably they are a source of deep embarrassment to abortion-rights advocates, who repeatedly emphasize the importance of protecting women's access to "safe, legal abortion." In the CBS "60 Minutes" exposé of the Hillview Women's Medical Surgical Center, for example, journalists found that several abortion-rights activists knew about the unsafe practices of the clinic but did not want them publicized. One pro-choice leader associated with the National Abortion Federation conceded: "This is the last thing we need. We had hoped that [this incident] wouldn't get national publicity because of the political nature of all of this."[24] Likewise, pro-choice leaders in Florida did not want the facts about the Dadeland Family Planning Center to get out. "This will hurt us," said one activist there. Patricia Windle, another advocate of abortion rights and a clinic owner in Florida, agreed: "The hysteria is already bad enough and we don't want to give the hysterics weapons."[25]

But the ethical questions raised by the existence of such negligent but legal abortion facilities are unavoidable. Law and public policy could make such clinics safer. Invariably, however, legal regulations are fought by the ardently pro-choice. "In my gut," said one full-time pro-choice activist, "I am completely aghast at what goes on at that place [the Dadeland Family Planning Center]. But I staunchly oppose anything that would correct this situation in law."[26] But why?

For years the pro-choice establishment has feared the slippery slope of abortion regulation, believing that if it gave an inch toward regulation, pro-life activists would move a mile toward the ultimate elimination of abortion rights. This argument extends not only to the imposition of safety standards on clinics offering abortion but to laws mandating parental notification, informed consent, waiting periods, prohibitions against gender-selection abortions, and so on.

From a purely monetary perspective, regulations on abortion would also cut into the profit margin of running a clinic. To impose hospital standards on specialty clinics, providers complain, would increase the cost of abortion to such an extent that many clinics would be put out of business and the price of abortion would rise out of reach for many women. Other regulations, like parental notification, would potentially decrease the available clientele: according to data collected in the 1980s, about two hundred thousand abortions were performed on minors seventeen or younger, including about fifteen thousand abortions on girls under the age of fifteen.[27]

One need not gainsay the sincerity of pro-choice advocates worried about the reversal of *Roe v. Wade*. Their fears about a slippery slope are well-founded—if given an inch, pro-life organizations *would* want to take a mile. But this does not negate the fact that powerful economic incentives nurture the initiative to maintain unrestricted access to abortion. It is not in the interest of the abortion industry to be regulated further. In this light, it is also disingenuous for a group like Planned Parenthood to say that it is a nonprofit organization. Planned Parenthood's nonprofit status only means that its income is not taxable; salaries are paid, clinics and family planning centers advertise, and the national headquarters is funded in part on the revenue generated by abortion. In the end, the championing of abortion rights of some organizations on the pro-choice side of this controversy is inseparable from their economic interests.

Pro-Life Tactical Interests

Pro-life advocates also have a tactical interest that goes largely unacknowledged in public discussion. In brief, it is impossible for the overwhelming majority of pro-life advocates to separate their commitment to the unborn from their deeper commitment to the reassertion of traditional moral and religious authority in society. It is this embrace of traditional authority that animates their passion for unborn children, their commitment to traditional authority that orders their conception of family life (including the division of labor between men and women, as mentioned earlier), and their submission to traditional authority that gives meaning to the lives of individuals and the communities active in the pro-life movement.

For example, on "Sanctity of Human Life Sunday" in the spring of 1992, a young minister made the curious claim that abortion-rights activists were not bad people—they just did not understand that what was being aborted was a human child made in the image of God. "If we can only teach them this," he said, "they will come around and support the right to life for the unborn child." His views are, needless to say, naïve. No amount of education or coaxing is likely to convince the ardently pro-choice, whose worldview is completely alien to the religious self-understanding of the pro-life side. Traditional authority holds no binding meaning for the progressive abortion-rights advocate. To reassert it in the social order, then, would be literally oppressive to the pro-choice community. Without the premise that fetal life is sacred (a premise that traditional authority provides), the fetus will remain an abstraction—"potential life" at best.

This leads to a tremendous irony. Even though most American women are largely sympathetic to the pro-life side of the controversy (as will be seen in Chapter Four), and despite the fact that grass-roots supporters of the pro-life movement have a genuine concern for the lives of real women (expressed in private charity), the pro-life movement finds it nearly impossible to shake the image that it is hostile to women. From the pro-life perspective, life in any form is more important than liberty or choice. Without the ontological presuppositions that traditional authority provides, this makes it look as though the pro-life are saying that the life of the fetus is more important than the life of its mother, a woman already integrated into the social world. That explains why, from the moment of conception, the child's right to life takes precedence over the desires of its mother.

Pro-life public policy appears to reinforce the premise that women take a secondary place to fetal life. For example, while pushing for tough pro-life legislation, conservative U.S. administrations in the 1980s and early 1990s undermined the study of teen sexual behavior designed to help understand and address the concerns of adolescents and young adults,[28] blocked legislation containing initiatives specifically oriented toward women's health concerns,[29] expressed little concern in public policy—despite their support for parental notification—with how communication between daughters and parents might be improved, and took no initiatives toward expanding social welfare for women who chose life for a child. Pro-life leaders themselves, in their single-minded pursuit of overturning *Roe v. Wade*, endorsed these policies without complaint or criticism. And why should they make a fuss? It was in their broader interests to do so because these policies reflected their basic attitudes toward teen sex, traditional families, and contraception. It is not surprising, then, that pro-choice advocates claim that pro-lifers care about the child from conception until birth, but not after that.

In sum, just as one cannot separate business interests from the practice of abortion, so it is impossible to separate pro-life opposition to abortion from the traditional moral authority and social order it implies.

The Distortions of Interest

The interests at play in the abortion controversy are just an illustration of unacknowledged and unexamined interests involved in all disputes of the contemporary culture war. In the church/state dispute, for example, the different interpretations of the Constitution reflect the opposing interests of theists and secularists.[30] In the dispute over homosexuality, the interests reflect privileges afforded to competing ideals of social and sexual intimacy. The conflicts over multiculturalism, race, freedom of free speech, sexual harassment, values in schools, and so on are similarly animated by competing social advantages.

Why are these interests (and others I have not covered here) unacknowledged by actors in public dispute? One reason is that for advocates on each side of every controversy, it is imperative to gain the

moral high ground—to exalt itself as the champion of truth and justice, while denigrating the opposition as the enemy of these ideals.
The legitimacy of claims made depend upon this; yet the vested interests inherent in each position strain the credibility of such claims.
The realities of social or material gain dilute if not discredit the public image each side is so eager to present. So it is in cases where pro-
life "crisis pregnancy centers" are shown to advertise themselves
falsely as providing abortion services as a pretext for luring unsus-
pecting pregnant women in to change their minds. So it is when it
becomes clear how much money some physicians make off of an
abortion practice.

A second reason why interests remain unacknowledged is that it
is very difficult to extricate oneself or one's cause from them. They
are just there, complicating matters. It thus remains an added interest of opposing factions to keep such matters subdued. Yet it is because these interests are there, out of sight, that public discourse
stays entrenched in polarized camps. The legitimacy of social advantages is never itself discussed openly. When the issue of their existence is raised by one side or another, the process is inevitably
enveloped by an endless volley of accusations and counteraccusa-
tions: "It is an interest!" "It is not!" "Is so!" "Is not!". . . The effect is
to shut down substantive exchange.

The interests, though, are part of the substance of the dispute.
Not to acknowledge them and allow public discussion of them is to
misconstrue central issues at stake.

The Politics of Distortion

With all of this in mind, let us return to the original question: what is
the possibility of a serious and substantive moral and political debate occurring among the individuals and organizations that are
most prominent in the controversy—the activists and the special
agenda organizations? The reason why the sincerity and seeming
reasonableness of the activists (observed at the beginning of Chapter Two) do not get translated into the public debate itself is because
inflammatory rhetoric and vested interests are mostly a function of
larger social processes, not individual intent. However well-mean-
ing any individual actors may be, they have little control over these

social dynamics. Movements, and the historical factors that put them in motion, are truly greater than the sum of their individual members. Thus it is largely in the nature and identity of contemporary social movements (and the specific organizations that they comprise) that discourse about public policy is distorted.

There is, of course, place and opportunity within these organizations for a kind of high-minded and courageous leadership capable of speaking to the concerns of all rather than the special interests of the few; a leadership that insists on the complete integrity of its own public speech. In this sense, public discourse need not be quite so superficial and antagonistic. But what incentives are there for such leadership if the "other side" is taking the low road, getting away with it, and gaining ground because of it? In this kind of cost-benefit analysis, the bottom line is clear: persuasion is a waste of time and money. So long as the movements remain as they are and remain the principal voices of what passes for debate, the symbolic realities to which the various issues of the culture war point are not likely to be reflected upon and discussed on their own terms.

But to hold the special agenda organizations exclusively responsible for denigrating democratic discussion and debate in this way— for fashioning and fostering shallow democracy—goes too far. In democracy, ordinary citizens theoretically have a voice in the shaping and the conduct of public life and are thus capable of exerting pressure upward, holding such organizations accountable to a higher level of engagement. The next two chapters consider the story of middle America in the midst of the culture war's challenge to democratic life and practice.

— PART III —

Searching Among Middle America

The Politics of Ambivalence

— 4 —

The Anatomy of Ambivalence

What Americans Really Believe About Abortion

Carl Bowman, coauthor

If the possibility of serious and substantive argument is slim among those who give voice to the controversy, what about the possibility of such reflection and debate among typical Americans?

For most Americans, the clashes of the special agenda organizations are far removed from their experience. Muffled sounds of distant battles can still be heard, but most of the time they are not of immediate concern. And so it should be; survival away from the front lines is hard enough as it is. But perhaps in the relative quietude of what is called middle America, in the commonsensical ways in which ordinary citizens view the world and live their lives, one can find the grounds for the kind of serious and substantive discussion that will permit a constructive response to the strife of the culture war. This is the task of the next two chapters. The case through which we examine the broader matter is, again, abortion.

We begin by probing the public mind, considering in some depth how typical Americans view abortion and the related controversy. We do so through the tool of public opinion surveys.[1] There are many of these surveys that we will refer to, but we key on an unusual

85

one conducted by the Gallup Organization in the summer of 1990.[2] What makes this survey unique is that it was designed to probe in greater depth than ever before the complexities of American public opinion on the subject. What we learn is really quite different from the familiar nostrums recited by the talking heads of public opinion research. We learn that the activists have it mostly wrong. First they misunderstand their own constituencies—the rank-and-file support for both the pro-life and pro-choice movements is not nearly so "pure" ideologically as they say it is. Second, they misunderstand those Americans who are more or less in the middle of the controversy. These Americans are not at all dim-witted or muddled as they are often described by the activists. They are ambivalent, to be sure, but ambivalent in the most fascinating ways.[3]

We begin, though, with a look at how Americans understand the disposition of law toward abortion. Can we find the grounds for serious and substantive debate in middle America? Here we find our first clue.

How Americans Understand the Law

Given the years abortion has been an issue and the emotional investment some people have made in arguing about it, one would imagine that most people form their opinions on the basis of a solid understanding of the facts at hand. What we learn, however, is that in middle America, the debate about abortion is carried on in a context of colossal ignorance.

Consider this. The very day Supreme Court Justice Thurgood Marshall retired from the bench in 1991, speculation about the fate of *Roe v. Wade* began to pick up. A new justice, everyone was thinking, could be the decisive vote in any effort to overturn the 1973 *Roe* decision. Peter Jennings of ABC News announced that evening the results of a new ABC/*Washington Post* survey showing that about six of every ten Americans favored keeping *Roe v. Wade* intact. On the surface his announcement seemed to provide compelling evidence to his audience for maintaining the legal status quo. But what Mr. Jennings did not say was that only about one out of every ten Americans has any real understanding of what *Roe v. Wade* actually mandated.[4]

According to the Gallup survey, one out of four Americans thought *Roe* made abortions legal only during the first three months of pregnancy and regardless of a woman's reason for wanting one. Another one out of six believed the decision permitted abortions only during the first three months and only when the mother's life or health was threatened. Four percent actually believed that the decision outlawed all abortions in the United States. Finally, almost half (43 percent) collectively shrugged their shoulders, openly confessing their ignorance of the outcome of this landmark case. Another survey conducted by a Gallup affiliate at about the same time framed the question negatively, and the results were the same: 80 percent of those polled disagreed that abortion was available through all nine months of pregnancy, and indeed, 65 percent disagreed strongly![5]

The American public showed a similar lack of knowledge about the more recent *Webster* decision, though in this case they were a bit more aware of just how uninformed they really were. Roughly 80 percent of the respondents admitted they were not at all familiar with the decision, and only one in ten got it right that after *Webster,* abortions legal in one state could be illegal in another. Add to this the fact that eight out of ten Americans in another survey either underestimated the number of abortions performed every year or else knew so little that they could not even hazard a guess, and you have the makings of profound legal illiteracy.[6] After twenty years of ceaseless commentary in the media and heated debate by political pundits, almost half of all Americans still admit to having no knowledge of what *Roe* accomplished, and most of the rest get it wrong.[7]

The depth of this mass legal illiteracy has tremendous social and political implications. Consider first how it relates to the public's views of specific abortion policy proposals. The majority of Americans say they want to keep *Roe* intact, but they also favor proposals that would restrict (some severely) what it currently allows, if not undermine it altogether (see Figure 1). For example, 86 percent of all those surveyed favor informed consent; 84 percent favor health

Figure 1

Popular Support for Abortion Legislation

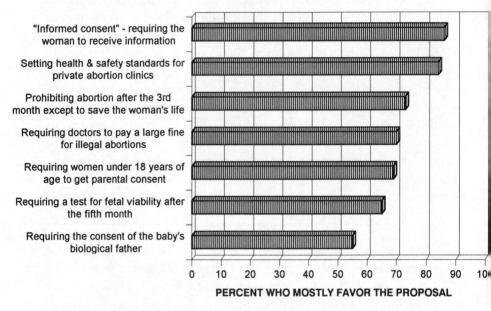

Question: "Here is some legislation on abortion that is being considered in some states. Please indicate whether you mostly favor or mostly oppose the following proposals."

and safety standards for private abortion clinics; 73 percent would prohibit abortion after the third month except to save the mother's life; 70 percent would require doctors to pay fines for performing illegal abortions; 69 percent favor restrictions on the use of abortion for the purposes of birth control; 69 percent favor parental consent for teenagers seeking an abortion; and 65 percent favor laws requiring a test for viability after the fifth month. Also receiving broad support are proposals requiring the consent of the baby's biological father (55 percent) and prohibiting the use of fetal tissue for medical research (41 percent). The wide public support for these proposals, in conjunction with public support for *Roe,* is understandable *only* if people imagine *Roe* to be something it is not.

Consider, too, how this legal illiteracy relates to the ebb and flow of passions on both sides. The Gallup study suggests that public opinion on abortion is becoming more polarized. When asked if their views had drifted in the preceding two years, more than one-third of those surveyed said yes: the pro-life tended to say they had become even more pro-life in their views, while the pro-choice had become even more pro-choice. Moreover, two out of every five respondents said they would not vote for a political candidate whose abortion stand they disagreed with, even if they were in agreement on most other issues. Similarly, a 1990 Wirthlin study reveals that nearly one-fifth of all Americans feel so strongly about this issue that they say they would base their vote solely on a candidate's position on abortion;[8] among these Americans it is the pro-lifers who are more single-issue driven.[9] The Gallup study suggests that, other things being equal, a clearly pro-choice candidate stands to alienate 20 percent of potential voters, while a clearly pro-life candidate stands to lose only 12 percent as a consequence of his or her abortion stand.[10]

Despite pro-life political passions, however, there is evidence that the abortion-rights position is gaining support at the expense of the pro-life movement. Roughly one out of every eight Americans who positions himself or herself in the middle or as moderately pro-life says that he or she drifted closer to a pro-choice position, while almost no one in the middle or on the moderately pro-choice side says he or she has moved closer to the pro-life side of the debate.[11] The difference is subtle but significant. These tendencies in public sentiment become even more interesting when we realize that they take shape without a clear understanding of the law that is so passionately contested.

In the end, public ignorance about abortion law suggests that people are arguing with phantoms, not with each other and certainly not over the facts of the legal dispute. If people agreed on what they were disagreeing about, not only might the quality of public debate

be enhanced but the entire map of the controversy could well be re-
drawn.

Where Americans Really Position
Themselves in the Controversy

To listen to the activists, there is no point to a debate among the
larger population of Americans because the vast majority—so they
tell us—have already made up their minds. Indeed, one of the curious features of the abortion war is that each side claims that the majority of Americans support its platform. Thus NARAL, for example,
claims that "opinion polls clearly show that four out of five Americans reject our opponents' goal of outlawing all abortions." At the
same time, the National Right to Life argues that the "vast majority
of Americans reject abortion on demand."[12] Back and forth it goes,
both sides correct in their own way but leaving an impression that is
not exactly correct, namely, that those who disagree with them are
out of the mainstream of American life. The activists themselves
know the survey data well enough to know that they can only make
their majoritarian claim with certain qualifications. Ah, details, details—not surprisingly, the qualifications are never provided. Ma-
joritarianism, after all, has its ideological uses.

The reality, no matter what public opinion poll you consult, is that
most Americans land somewhere in the middle of this debate. The
figures will vary from poll to poll, but the general distribution of
opinion is about the same: hardened opinion at each end of the debate and a larger, softer middle (of roughly 60 percent). In the
Gallup survey mentioned above, about one-fourth (26 percent) of
the respondents positioned themselves as strongly pro-life; just under one-fifth (17 percent) identified themselves as strongly pro-
choice; and the remainder (55 percent) put themselves somewhere
in the middle as either moderately pro-life (16 percent), moderately
pro-choice (16 percent), or neutral on the issue (23 percent; see
Figure 2). The only way to find a majority on this issue is to fabricate
one—which, of course, each side is quite happy to do.

On this general point, it is worth noting that there is no "gender
gap" in this overall distribution of opinion. This is not, in other
words, an issue dividing pro-choice women against pro-life men; in

Figure 2

How Americans Identify Themselves on Abortion

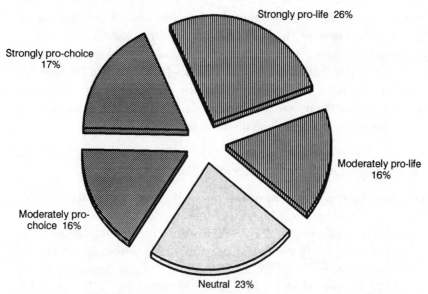

Strongly pro-life 26%

Strongly pro-choice 17%

Moderately pro-life 16%

Moderately pro-choice 16%

Neutral 23%

Question: "Which would you say best describes your general outlook on the abortion issue—strongly pro-life, moderately pro-life, neutral, moderately pro-choice, or strongly pro-choice?"

fact, women were more likely to be pro-life (43 percent) than pro-choice (33 percent).[13] There is also no substantial racial gap. If anything, blacks were also more likely to say they were pro-life than pro-choice.[14] But the clearest gender and racial differences pertain to the *intensity* of opinion. Women were more likely than men to be either strongly pro-choice or strongly pro-life, and black Americans (like males in general) were more likely to identify themselves as neutral or indifferent.

Another factor that contributes to the varying intensity of opinion is whether abortion is an abstract issue or one made concrete through some level of personal experience. In brief, when abortion becomes a personal reality, people are much less likely to be ambivalent about it. For example, personal acquaintance with someone who has had an abortion (and about half of all respondents said they knew someone who had) seems to crystallize one's opinion at either end.[15] Also, women who have considered abortion for themselves at one time or another (16 percent of all the women surveyed had) are highly likely to take a strongly pro-choice position, where those women who have not considered it for themselves but know someone who has actually had one are much more likely to be strongly pro-life.[16]

What is the substance behind the labels people use to describe themselves? After a brief overview of the moral meaning Americans impute to abortion, we will look more carefully at the movement constituencies and the allegedly muddled middle.

Moral Opinion About Abortion: A Brief Overview

It takes the special talent of the modern survey researcher to collapse a complex, multilayered dilemma, like a used cardboard box, into a single plane. A CBS/*New York Times* poll conducted in the spring of 1989, for instance, posed the yes/no question "Is abortion murder?" and found that slightly more Americans said yes (48 percent) than no (40 percent). Similarly, a *Los Angeles Times* poll of women conducted a month earlier found a similar pattern but slightly more uneven (58 percent saying it was murder, compared to 34 percent who said it was not). In both cases, a simplistic question yielded a simple and not terribly illuminating response. The ethical dilemma of abortion is considerably more complex: what is the meaning of *murder?* Who or what is or is not being murdered? All of these issues need addressing, and while it is impossible for every public opinion survey to go into great depth on this issue, it is possible to go further than a simple yes/no question.

The Ethical Meaning of Abortion

When asked to choose from an expanded series of statements the one that best conveys the ethical meaning of abortion, almost four out of every ten Americans (37 percent) say that "abortion is just as bad as killing a person who has already been born; it is murder." Together with another tenth (12 percent) who said that it is "murder, but not as bad as killing someone who has already been born," that makes about half of the adult population who, at least in the abstract, view abortion as a very serious moral offense. Yet almost three out of every ten Americans (28 percent) say that "abortion is not murder," even though they concede that it "involves the taking of human life." And another 16 percent say that abortion is nothing more than "a surgical procedure for removing human tissue" (see Figure 3). Thus we see an entire spectrum of opinion on the ethical meaning of abortion, with most Americans at least agreeing that the act has serious ethical significance.

Figure 3

Is Abortion Murder?

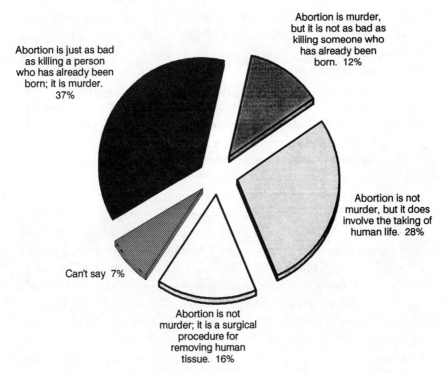

Abortion is murder, but it is not as bad as killing someone who has already been born. 12%

Abortion is just as bad as killing a person who has already been born; it is murder. 37%

Abortion is not murder, but it does involve the taking of human life. 28%

Can't say 7%

Abortion is not murder; it is a surgical procedure for removing human tissue. 16%

Question: "Which of these statements best describes your feelings about abortion?"

The Matter of Personhood

But what explains this range of moral assessments? The most generous assumption one can make is that people come to different conclusions about the meaning of abortion because they have
fundamentally different ideas about who or what is being aborted.
This, not surprisingly, appears to be the case. It makes no more
sense to talk about "murdering" a fetus that is nothing more than a
part of a woman's body than it does to speak of a "harmless surgical
procedure" that terminates the life of a human being. The ontological status attributed to embryonic life is directly linked to the level
of moral outrage or indifference that is evoked.

What status, then, do Americans attribute to the developing human embryo? And when, in their minds, does it first become a person? Given a range of choices, most Americans (nearly six in ten) say
that the fertilized egg inside a mother's womb first becomes a person at the moment of conception. About half that number believe it
becomes a person either at quickening (when the mother first feels
movement) or at the point of viability (when the developing baby
can survive on its own). Not surprisingly, the vast majority of those
who call themselves strongly pro-life (86 percent) fix personhood at
conception, while viability is the point of distinction for the strongly
pro-choice. While Americans differ in the precise moment that they
view as morally pivotal, they are almost universally agreed that this
moment occurs sometime *before* birth. Less than one in ten believe
that an embryo is not a person until the moment of birth.

Naturally these views are interwoven with people's ideas of the
qualities that make up "personhood." Only a very small number of
Americans believe that the main attribute distinguishing humans
from other forms of life is their membership in a community (1 percent), their capacity to experience a range of emotions (5 percent),
or their ability to work and be productive (3 percent).[17] When all is
said and done, opinions on the meaning of personhood tend to settle
on one side or the other of the Enlightenment divide: a large group
of Americans (36 percent) believe the most important feature of human life is its creation in God's own image, while an even larger
group (49 percent) believe it is the human ability to think and reason. Those who view personhood as a function of an ability to think
and reason are varied in their ethical evaluation of abortion—a plu-

rality (37 percent) see it as "the taking of human life" but stop short of calling it murder; a quarter see it as full-fledged murder; and another quarter see it as nothing more serious than a surgical procedure. A stronger consensus emerges among those with a sacred view of personhood, more than half of whom see abortion as full-fledged murder, and only a few of whom (7 percent) would cast it as a surgical procedure (see Figure 4).

Balancing "Rights"

The other considerations that weigh heaviest in the ethical equation are the civil liberties of women and the sweep of government regulation. Yet when a fetus's right to life is weighed against a woman's right to choose, the Gallup study shows the public to be fairly conservative toward the preborn child. When asked "At what point in a pregnancy do you feel that the unborn child's right to be born outweighs the woman's right to choose whether she wants to have a child?" one-half of all surveyed say the right to be born outweighs the right to choose at the instant of conception. Another third believes this occurs sometime during the pregnancy, and less than one in ten (8 percent) believes the right to choose takes moral priority right up until the moment of birth.[18] At least at this philosophical level, two-thirds of the public are quite nervous about the practice of abortion after the first trimester, and most of the rest are opposed after the point of fetal viability.

Abortion in Its Context: The Hard Cases

But certainly the circumstances in which a woman contemplating abortion may find herself make a difference in the moral evaluation. Indeed, the moral ambivalence we have already begun to see in the general public is confirmed when considering the effect of these circumstances. Here the patterns of public opinion could be described as a series of shifting balance points.

Imagine trying to balance a long stick horizontally on your finger. To balance the stick alone, you would have to position your finger right in the middle. If a heavy weight were attached to the left and a lighter weight attached to the right, the balance point would shift

Figure 4

The Moral Meaning of Abortion

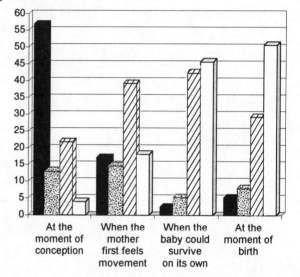

Percent who say abortion is. . .

■ Murder - it is just as bad as killing someone who has already been born

▨ Murder - but not as bad as killing somone who has already been born

▱ Not murder - but it does involve the taking of human life

☐ A surgical procedure for removing human tissue

PERSONHOOD BEGINS. . .

Responses to the question "Which of these statements best describes your feelings about abortion?" for groups with different conceptions of when personhood begins

from the middle over to the left. This is what happens to public opinion when it is faced with the morality of abortion in the complex range of real-life situations and circumstances: the greater the weight of seeing the pregnancy through to term, the more the balance point shifts toward the abortion option (see Figure 5).

In the fairly rare situations of rape, incest, or danger to the life of the mother, for example, the balance point of public opinion is located toward a moral approval of abortion. At least seven out of every ten Americans believes that abortion during the first three months is acceptable under these circumstances. But in situations where a child would create an economic burden for the family, where the quality of life for the child or for the mother is deemed deficient, where a teenager would be required to drop out of school, or where abortion is being used as birth control or as a means of selecting the gender of a child, the balance point shifts toward moral censure.

In all of these situations, the level of acceptability in the public (however high or low) drops dramatically if the abortion is to take place after the third month of the pregnancy (see Figure 6). Americans thus make subtle moral distinctions between situations in which

Figure 5

Shifting Balance Points

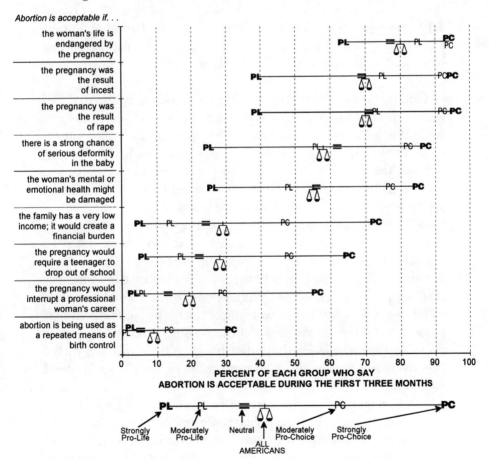

The complexity of moral approval and censure on abortion

abortion is justifiable and those in which it cannot be morally sanctioned. It is very clear that since most abortions are not performed for medical reasons or reasons pertaining to rape or incest, the majority of Americans would morally disapprove of the majority of abortions currently performed.

But here we reach an important qualification. While the majority of Americans morally disapprove of abortion in the situations in which it is most commonly performed, many of these Americans nevertheless also seem willing to live with a law that makes it possible for a woman to get an abortion during the first three months of pregnancy almost regardless of the reason. The classic illustration of this fact is that while half of all Americans (48 percent) agree in the abstract that abortion is murder, and another 28 percent believe it is the taking of human life, most also agree that women should have the right to choose whether or not to have one.

The disjunction between what most Americans approve of and what they are willing to allow is not easy to square. Clearly one factor in this is a pervasive distrust of the power of the state to intervene in a person's decision, however unpleasant or morally dubious that decision may be. Fewer than one out of every five Americans believe that the government should have even a moderate amount of say in the abortion decision. A full 80 percent of those in the Gallup sample believe that a woman should have a greater say than the law, the courts, the state government, or the federal government. But curiously, however ubiquitous people's distrust of the state is on this matter, such distrust is also fairly shallow; people's responses in surveys as to the role of the state will differ depending on the wording of the question. If the issue is posed in terms of the government intervening "to restrict people's choices," they respond with predictable hostility; if it is in terms of the government intervening "to protect the unborn," they respond much more positively.

Given all of this, it is clear that neither outlawing all abortions nor maintaining liberal abortion policy is a proposal that sits well with the majority of Americans or even, as we shall see, with many of those at opposing ends of the controversy. So what of the movement constituencies—the rank and file of the movements?

Figure 6

When Is Abortion Viewed as Acceptable?

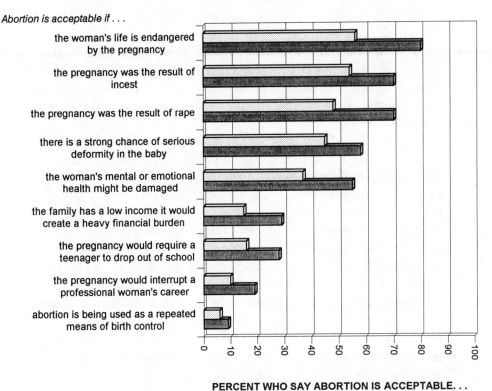

Abortion is acceptable if . . .

the woman's life is endangered by the pregnancy

the pregnancy was the result of incest

the pregnancy was the result of rape

there is a strong chance of serious deformity in the baby

the woman's mental or emotional health might be damaged

the family has a low income it would create a heavy financial burden

the pregnancy would require a teenager to drop out of school

the pregnancy would interrupt a professional woman's career

abortion is being used as a repeated means of birth control

PERCENT WHO SAY ABORTION IS ACCEPTABLE. . .

▦ *During the first 3 months* ☐ *After the third month*

Question: "I am going to read you some situations where a woman might consider having an abortion. For each situation, I want you to tell me whether you, personally, feel an abortion would be acceptable or unacceptable."

Learning More About the Rank and File

Combined with differences in ideas about when a fetus becomes a person, the divergence in ethical evaluations of abortion are remarkably sharp for Americans at polar ends of the controversy. Nearly nine out of ten of the strongly pro-life believe that a fertilized egg inside a mother's womb first becomes a person at the moment of conception, compared to about two out of ten of the strongly pro-choice who hold this opinion.[19] Not surprisingly, nearly eight out of ten strong pro-lifers believe abortion is just as bad as killing a person who has already been born; that it is literally murder. By contrast, less than one in ten of the strongly pro-choice make this same moral judgment.[20] Rather, among the latter, the plurality believe it is just a surgical procedure for removing human tissue.[21] (One-third of the strongly pro-choice, however, are willing to view abortion as the taking of human life, but not murder).[22]

It only follows from this that the strongly pro-life would disproportionately oppose abortion even in the so-called hard cases, while the strongly pro-choice would offer broad moral approval of abortion in many other, perhaps less urgent circumstances. And so each side does. A majority of the strongly pro-life do oppose abortion in the first three months in the circumstances involving rape, incest, and a "strong chance of serious deformity" in the baby.[23] Likewise, a majority of the strongly pro-choice individuals approve of abortion in the first trimester when the purpose is to relieve a family with a very low income of a heavy financial burden, in a situation involving a teenager whose pregnancy would require her to drop out of school, in circumstances that would interrupt a professional woman's career, and in a situation where the father of the unborn child abandons the pregnant woman.[24] Each in their respective ways places the movement constituencies dramatically outside the mainstream of American public opinion.

That opinion among the strongly committed on each side of the controversy divides in this way is unremarkable. What is much more interesting is the way in which the hard-core support for these movements deviates from the party line. Sizable minorities of the strongly pro-life *approve* of abortion in the first three months in the circumstances involving rape (39 percent), incest (39 percent), a threat to the life of the mother (64 percent), and a strong chance of a serious deformity in the developing baby (25 percent). A smaller, but still notable minority of these pro-life supporters even approve of abortion in these circumstances during the second trimester.[25]

Likewise, a significant minority of the strongly pro-choice say abortion is unacceptable in circumstances where a family with a very low income has a heavy financial burden (30 percent), a teenager's pregnancy would require her to drop out of school (26 percent), a professional woman's career would be interrupted (39 percent), the father of the unborn child abandons the pregnant woman (27 percent), abortion is being used as a method of birth control (67 percent), or abortion is used to select the gender of the child (77 percent). This departure from the pro-choice party line is reflected in views of the law as well. Thirty-seven percent of the strongly pro-choice favor parental consent laws; 53 percent favor a test for fetal viability; 25 percent favor laws requiring women to get the consent of the baby's biological father before having an abortion; 78 percent favor requiring women to receive information about fetal development and alternatives to abortion before going ahead with the procedure; 89 percent favor the passage of a law requiring health and safety standards for private abortion clinics; and 47 percent favor a restriction of abortions after the third month of pregnancy unless it is required to save a woman's life.

Even with these important qualifications, though, there is a relative moral and legal consistency at each end of public opinion on this issue. This consistency suggests, among other things, that like the movement activists who claim to represent them, most Americans have a position on abortion that is rooted in a larger cultural system. As with the activists, the strong pro-life and strong pro-choice supporters hold opposing views not only of abortion but, as mentioned earlier, of motherhood, human sexuality, and the family. Beyond these more obvious associations, though, their perspectives are directly related to even more fundamental assumptions about the sources of truth and of goodness, about the ultimate meaning of life, and so on—they are born out of a participation in distinct moral and religious communities. What this means is not only that their attitudes toward abortion are rooted in larger worldviews but that these worldviews are institutionally rooted within and sustained by *communities of moral conversation*. In fact, when all factors are weighted together, the commu-

Figure 7

How Moral Communities Identify Themselves on Abortion

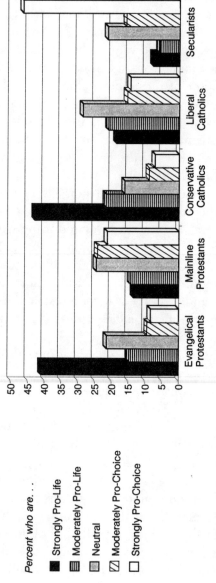

Question: "Which would you say best describes your general outlook on the abortion issue—strongly pro-life, moderately pro-life, neutral, moderately pro-choice, or strongly pro-choice?"

nity of moral conversation to which a person belongs is a much better predictor of position on the abortion issue than that person's education, regional identity, race, gender, or any other background factor (see Figure 7).[26]

The pro-life movement indeed draws disproportionately from the Evangelical Protestant and conservative Catholic communities.[27] More than half of all evangelicals and conservative Catholics could be identified as consistently pro-life in their commitments;[28] only about one-fifth of all mainline Protestants and about one-fourth of all progressive Catholics could be identified this way. Finally, fewer than one out of every ten secularists (those who claim no religious faith) finds himself among the consistently pro-life.

By contrast, most secularists (about seven out of every ten) position themselves decisively on the pro-choice side of the controversy, and more often than not, they are philosophically consistent and politically active in their commitments.[29] The pro-choice movement also draws from other communities of moral conversation: about one out of every six consistent pro-choice supporters is a progressive Catholic, and about one out of five is from the mainline Protestant community. Only a handful of evangelicals and orthodox Catholics (4 percent in each case) identify themselves as consistently pro-choice.

We will say more about how these religious and moral communities relate to attitudes about abortion shortly. For now it is worth observing that it is precisely because abortion opinion is rooted in different communities of moral discourse that the controversy remains so intractable. But this does not mean that substantive debate is impossible. To the contrary: now we have some idea about the terms by which serious and substantive argument can take place. More on this in later chapters.

How the Movements Are Outside of the Mainstream

As noted above, the strongly pro-life and the strongly pro-choice show themselves to be distinct from the mainstream of public opinion in their acceptance or unacceptance of abortion in hypothetical circumstances. But it is in the moral communities to which they belong that we see what really marks each side as being out of the mainstream.

While the various pro-life groups seem to share much in common on *this* particular issue, on other matters, the worldview of the committed pro-life supporter is markedly different from that of the majority of Americans, even that of its closest allies. Compared to the average American, the strongly committed pro-life supporter is significantly more conservative in his or her attitudes about all aspects of sexual morality and family life (especially the roles of men and women). They are also more conservative in their positions vis-à-vis electoral politics, and they are far more observant in such religious obligations as prayer and church attendance.[30] Needless to say, this only reinforces the nightmare of the pro-choice that the agenda of the pro-life movement is not just to end the practice of abortion but to reestablish a more traditional social order in American society.

Importantly, those who are strongly pro-choice (the rank-and-file support for the pro-choice movement) depart significantly from the national norms in just the opposite ways—that is, in their sexual libertarianism, their political liberalism, and their secularism. The most interesting way in which they are separated from the cultural mainstream, however, is in their moral approval of the notion that only life "worthy of living" should be protected (see Figure 8).

In terms of abortion, for example, the strongly committed pro-choice are two to three times more likely than the average American to say they would have an abortion if a baby has a genetically related mental or physical problem (such as mental retardation, blindness, a missing limb, a defective heart, or a terminal illness). Three-fourths of the strongly pro-choice believe that if a child will create a heavy financial burden on a family, abortion is acceptable, compared to just over one-fourth of the larger population (and compared to 93 percent of the strongly pro-life who *disagreed*). Three-fourths of the strongly pro-choice also agreed that "abortion is usually a better option than bringing a child home where it is not wanted," compared to one-third of the general population (and only 8 percent of the strongly pro-life); and 21 percent of the strongly pro-choice (three times as many as among all Americans) say that gender-selection abortions are acceptable during the first trimester, whereas 15 percent say they are acceptable in latter stages.

Figure 8

Matters of Life and Death

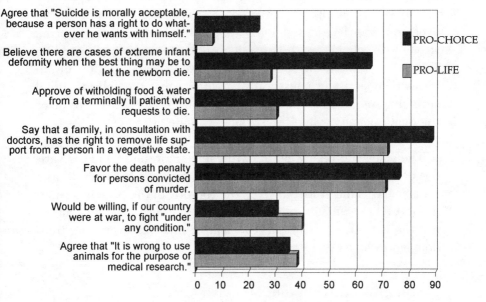

Percent of "Pro-life" and "Pro-choice" Americans Who
Give Each Response

*Responses of persons who identify themselves as "pro-life" and "pro-choice" to
a series of questions on life and death.*

If the pro-choice seem unconcerned for fetal life, they would
seem coldhearted toward the despairing and the vulnerable: while
the proportion is still just a minority (roughly one-third of their total
number), the strongly pro-choice are twice as likely as the average
American (and five times as likely as the strongly pro-life) to agree
that suicide is "morally acceptable because a person has a right to do
whatever he wants with himself." The pro-choice are also the least
likely of all Americans to say that someone who is depressed and
lacks the will to live is wrong to commit suicide. So, too, 67 percent
of the strongly pro-choice agree that "it would be best for all concerned to let a newborn infant with an 'extreme deformity' just die,"
compared to 37 percent of those neutral on abortion and 21 percent

of the strongly pro-life. The same general pattern of opinion plays out in moral judgments concerning the terminally ill patient who is in great pain and requests to die, and about the rights of family members (in consultation with doctors) to remove life support from a person who has lapsed into a vegetative state. Here, too, the strongly pro-choice are the least likely to favor the protection of life. Interestingly, the Gallup survey also showed—counterintuitively, in terms of liberal and conservative politics—that the self-identified strongly pro-choice are, by a small margin, the most likely to favor the death penalty, while the strongly pro-life are the least likely to favor it![31]

The association between the pro-choice movement and the various policies of medicalized death is too consistent to brush off as a statistical triviality. Indeed, given the rhetoric of the pro-choice and its kindred movements, one wonders whether death is the means or just the net effect of the quest for autonomy, empowerment, freedom, and a high quality of life.

Learning More About the "Muddled Middle"

But what of the majority of Americans who are in the middle of this controversy? At an ethical and philosophical level, most of these are willing to concede to the pro-life movement the notion that personhood begins at or near conception. Like those who are pro-choice, however, they hesitate to classify abortion as outright murder, even though they admit that it takes a human life. In general, most Americans live with a certain moral dissonance. For example, seven out of every ten persons who call themselves moderately pro-life believe that personhood begins at conception, yet less than half of those who take this position say that abortion is as bad as killing a person who has already been born. The pattern is virtually identical among those who call themselves neutral.[32] Even in the case of individuals who identify themselves as moderately pro-choice, a plurality (35 percent) believes that personhood begins at conception, yet less than a third of those who believe this are willing to call abortion full-fledged murder. For each of these middling groups, a large percentage of those who say personhood begins at conception also maintain that the abortion of such "persons" cannot be called murder, even though they say it ends a human life.[33] The discrepancy suggests that while they say the human embryo is a person, they view it as a lower level of person whose rights must be weighed against other considerations.

The Four Faces of Ambivalence

This only scratches the surface of the nature of ambivalence that characterizes the opinion of the majority of Americans. The character of moral reflection in the American public becomes more interesting, complex, and even three-dimensional when examined from a slightly different angle. We gathered a dozen or so questions in the Gallup survey dealing with the public's attitudes toward the status of the fetus, the moral status of abortion, the circumstances under which they think abortion is acceptable, whether they would have an abortion themselves (or encourage one for their spouse, girl-friend, or daughter) and how they position themselves on the social issue itself. These were combined in what specialists call a cluster analysis, and what we found is that there are disparate patterns of thinking on this issue. In between the consistently pro-life and consistently pro-choice positions are four relatively distinct positions of moral opinion (see Figure 9).[34]

Those who fall into the first cluster of ambivalent moral opinion could be called the *secretly pro-life*. These individuals are very much allies of the pro-life movement, for they believe that the fetus becomes a person from the moment of conception (or a little after) and, in principle, that the right to life outweighs the right to choose at conception. Even so they are reluctant to call abortion murder, and they are willing to say it is acceptable under the most difficult of circumstances. As it turns out, they might even consider an abortion themselves (or, if male, for a girlfriend, wife, or daughter) if they found themselves in these straits—such as a pregnancy resulting from rape or a fetus with serious genetic problems. What is so curious about this group, however, is that despite their distinctly pro-life moral leanings, they tend to think of themselves as neutral or even moderately pro-choice in the controversy itself.

Those who fit into the second pattern of moral ambivalence toward abortion could be called the *conveniently pro-life*. Like the secretly pro-life, the majority believe that the fetus becomes a person

Figure 9

Clusters of Moral Opinion

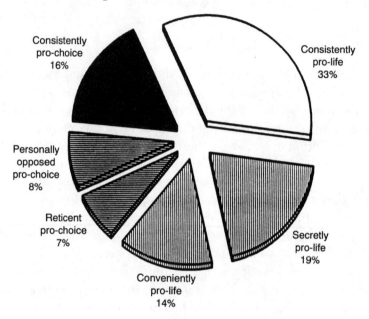

The structure of American ambivalence toward abortion

from the moment of conception, and that the fetus's right to life outweighs the woman's right to choose at conception or shortly thereafter. Unlike the secretly pro-life, however, they tend to believe that
abortion is murder. It is not surprising, then, that they tend to think
of themselves in the controversy as moderately or even strongly pro-
life. Yet when asked to consider specific situations under which
abortion might be acceptable, they are even more accepting of the
practice than are other pro-life Americans. Even more telling is the
fact that when faced with a personal decision about abortion, they
would not hesitate to have or at least strongly consider having an
abortion, especially under the more trying situations described
above. In general, these people are strongly pro-life in their philosophy, but pro-choice in personal practice.

Those in the third cluster of moral opinion could be called the *reticent pro-choice*. On balance these individuals think of themselves as moderately pro-choice and, to a certain degree, even morally neutral on the issue. Nevertheless, their assumptions about the nature of the fetus and whose rights should be protected are very much on the abortion-rights side of the debate. Specifically, they focus upon viability as a key point in the pregnancy, believing that personhood begins at this point or even later, and that the right to life does not outweigh the woman's right to choose until this point in the pregnancy. If they personally had to make the decision, faced with the likelihood that their child would have a genetic abnormality, they would either have the abortion or at least seriously consider it. What makes them uniquely ambivalent in their understanding of abortion is that they tend to be *reticent in conceding the moral acceptability of abortion to other people*. This ambivalence is also reflected in the way they identify themselves on the issue (namely, as neutral to moderately pro-choice). Perhaps one reason for this ambivalence has to do with their view of the ethical status of abortion itself. While they generally do not believe the act is murder, they do believe that it is the taking of human life. Thus they vacillate, and since they are not really positive one way or the other about abortion, they are pro-choice. In short, they are pro-choice by default, rather than by conviction.

The final pattern of ambivalence could be called the *personally-opposed pro-choice*. They are the mirror opposite of the conveniently pro-life, for they are pro-choice in philosophy but pro-life in personal practice. They believe that the fetus only becomes a person at the point of viability, or even later in the pregnancy. In line with this, the majority of these individuals state in principle that the unborn's right to life outweighs the woman's right to choose at about the fifth month. Is abortion murder within this group? Not really; while a good many will say that abortion is the taking of human life, they emphatically state that it is not murder. The predominant opinion is that abortion is only a surgical procedure for removing human tissue. Ethically, they show a fair degree of consistency with the pro-choice stance. Pro-choice by commitment, they view abortion as morally acceptable in many if not most situations. Yet what really sets the members of this coalition apart is their emphatic *un*willing-ness to consider an abortion for themselves—even, for example, if their baby were shown to have serious genetic problems. Only in the most extreme and trying situations would abortion ever be a per-sonal consideration.

Moral Communities and Community Integration

If the communities of moral conversation people belong to figure so prominently in how they place themselves in the controversy and in their thinking about the issue, how do these communities relate to the patterns of ambivalence among those in the middle? Figure 10 displays the distribution of abortion attitudes within these commu-nities. Though evangelical Protestants and orthodox Catholics are disproportionately pro-life and consistently so, about one out of five from their ranks would be considered secretly pro-life. Another one out of eight would fall into the conveniently pro-life category, pub-licly approving of the pro-life agenda yet personally given to the abortion option.

Mainline Protestants are the least homogeneous in their views of abortion, perhaps reflecting the theological diversity of this commu-nity. One-fifth of mainline Protestants are pro-life in their moral commitments but think of themselves as neutral or pro-choice and tend toward a pro-choice political philosophy. About one of every ten is strongly pro-choice in both political and moral philosophy, but would not personally consider abortion. In short, there is no main-line of moral thinking among Protestant mainliners—in this diverse community, both concern and deep ambivalence abound.

As we intimated before, liberal Catholics, like their theologically conservative counterparts, tend toward the pro-life side of the con-troversy, but they are much less resolute—less than one out of four are consistently pro-life in their commitments. About a fifth of all liberal Catholics are privately pro-life but would balk at strong pro-life legislation, and another fifth are conveniently pro-life, opposed to abortion in principle but pragmatists when push comes to shove. About one out of every six progressive Catholics takes a halfhearted pro-choice stand, being either reluctantly or personally opposed.

Figure 10

How Moral Communities View Abortion

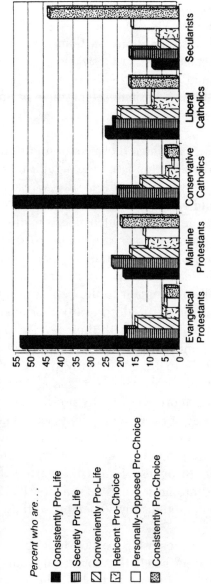

The Impact of Faith on the Clustering of Abortion Attitudes

Finally, while most secularists are ideologically and publicly committed to progressive abortion policy, a significant minority of these would not consider abortion for themselves, even in the most difficult circumstances. So, too, a sizable group of secularists (about 16 percent) would come out as secretly pro-life, the main qualification being that they hesitate seeing their perspective legally imposed on others.

The distinct ways in which these communities of moral conversation relate to the abortion issue are significant in light of the ancient wisdom, drawn from earlier survey research, that the only factor that could accurately predict polar attitudes toward abortion was the frequency with which a person attended religious services. The indicators used in this earlier research were crude in that they never probed the content of a person's deepest moral beliefs and commitments, but they did point out an important fact: it is not just intellectual assent to the beliefs of a moral community that shape a person's attitudes toward abortion, but rather a person's belief in combination with their level of participation in the rituals of community life. Thus while evangelicals as a group are much more likely to be consistently pro-life than are mainline Protestants, evangelicals who *participate actively* in their moral communities are more consistently pro-life than evangelicals who do not. Three out of every four evangelicals who attend religious services more than once a week are completely and consistently pro-life, compared to only three out of every ten who attend services once a month or less. Similarly, nearly half of the mainline Protestants who attend services once a month or less are decidedly pro-choice, compared to only 30 percent of those who attend more regularly.

The effect of decreasing participation upon attitudes toward abortion varies according to the moral community from which one is becoming unglued. Liberal Catholics who remain active in their parishes, for instance, tend to remain consistently pro-life, while those whose attachment has weakened tend either to privatize their pro-life convictions or to react against the Catholic community by becoming consistently pro-choice. The same cannot be said for theologically conservative Catholics, who remain consistently pro-life even when unleashed from their community moorings. Further, while community *detachment* privatizes the pro-life sentiment of liberal Catholics, community *attachment* cultivates a privatized pro-life stance among mainline Protestants. That is, increased participation in the mainline Protestant community nurtures a tentative pro-life sentiment that is not to be "imposed" upon others. Thus active mainliners may anguish personally over abortion, but they remain neutral or pro-choice in their political identity and agenda. Evangelicals who drift from their community moorings remain pro-life, but not consistently so. They begin to equivocate in either their political agenda or in the personal stand they would take if faced with an "inconvenient" pregnancy.[35]

All of this underscores the tremendous complexity of the abortion dynamic. Keeping in mind that roughly two-thirds of all evangelicals and orthodox Catholics attend religious services once a week or more, compared to only one-fourth of mainline Protestants and liberal Catholics, it is clear that the dramatic disjuncture between conservative and progressive moral communities partially reflects qualitative differences in moral authorities and commitments, as well as differences in levels of participation and integration. Whatever one's community of moral discourse, a heightened level of ritual integration will modify one's moral commitments. And whatever one's level of ritual integration, the differences between moral communities remain dramatic. Indeed, the association between abortion opinion and participation in distinct moral communities is so strong that it prompts one to wonder whether, as a rule, persons can be devotedly pro-life without being religiously orthodox and observant.[36]

In the end, what these clusterings of morally ambivalent opinion—and their relationship to a host of other factors—clearly show is that people's views of abortion cannot be adequately framed in terms of a single dichotomy between those who favor it and those who do not. It is not enough to say one is more or less pro-life or more or less pro-choice. Public opinion on this issue is not one-dimensional. One's attitudes toward abortion can be qualified (and perhaps even contradicted) in various ways by other considerations. Indeed, probing deeper, one is likely to discover still other attenuating factors that shape people's views toward the issue. All of this together adds more reason to deepen public debate.

How Americans *Really* View the Movements

Gaining popular support for treasured social and political ends is invariably tied up in the legitimacy of the movement that advocates those ends. And legitimacy is invariably linked to image. Let us face it: no matter how elevated or well-intentioned the goal, bad public relations can completely undermine the ideals that animate a movement. Here, too, surveys provide insight as to how the pro-life and pro-choice *movements* are perceived in the public imagination.

As one might expect, the most consistent and staunch supporters of the pro-life and pro-choice positions carry fundamentally opposite images of each other's movements. Each of these coalitions views its own activist organizations as being much more concerned about values, morality, and the family. Each also views its own movement as being more compassionate toward the poor and more sensitive toward the interests of women than the opposition. Conversely, even in the greater public, those holding strongly pro-life or strongly pro-choice commitments view the opposing movement as being given to extremism and intolerance.

In the end, though, it is the pro-life movement that shows itself as having the most serious image problem in the eyes of the American public (see Figure 11). Outside of the rank and file of the pro-life movement, average Americans—even the closest allies of the pro-life movement, the secretly and conveniently pro-life groups—tend to view the pro-life movement in the same negative way that the pro-choice constituencies do. The average American is much more likely to view the pro-life movement as unconcerned about women and the poor, and as marked by judgmentalism, extremism, and intolerance.[37] This is a remarkable measure of the success of the pro-choice movement in casting the pro-life movement in a negative light and itself in a positive light, as well as the failure of the pro-life activists to counter these destructive images effectively. Needless to say, the murder of abortion provider Dr. David Gunn by abortion opponent Michael Griffin in 1993 merely confirmed what most

Figure 11

The Public Image

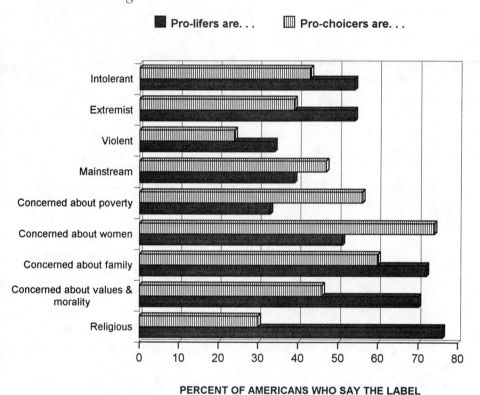

PERCENT OF AMERICANS WHO SAY THE LABEL
FITS "WELL" OR "VERY WELL"

Question: For each of the following phrases, tell me how well you think it describes people who are pro-life? Pro-choice?

already believed. One wonders whether the pro-life movement will ever recover from the effects of this event.

One explanation for this could be found in the moral culture inhabited by the consistently pro-life. As we have seen, the stalwart supporters of the pro-life movement have found moral allies in their cause among the secretly pro-life and the conveniently pro-life. Yet outside of the abortion issue, the conveniently pro-life and especially the secretly pro-life seem to have more in common with the various pro-choice coalitions. This may provide a clue as to why, for example, the secretly pro-life are *secretly* that way. Despite their personal opposition to abortion, they are hesitant to think of themselves or identify themselves before their peers as being pro-life. Clearly the label *pro-lifer* would put them in the same camp with persons who are, in many ways, profoundly different. It only follows, then, that they would regard the pro-life movement with the relative disdain that they do.

The success of the activists of the pro-choice movement in publicly demonizing the pro-life movement, however, is all the more curious when one compares image to the actual beliefs and commitments of ordinary pro-lifers (see Figure 13). When asked to express their degree of concern for a wide range of social issues, individuals who identified themselves as being pro-life were, with but a few exceptions, as concerned as the so-called socially conscious pro-choice groups. On average, pro-lifers were more concerned about poverty, racial discrimination, nuclear war and minority rights than were the pro-choice. Given what we know about the different worldviews of opposing advocates, pro-life and pro-choice individuals undoubtedly have different motivations for their concern and different ideas about how to address them in public policy. But the base concern is there all the same, and at this level, the grass roots of the pro-life and pro-choice movements are not greatly different.

The Problems of the Pro-Life Movement in Making a Convincing Case

Since the overall public perceptions of the pro-life movement are shaded so negatively, pro-life activists acknowledge the urgency of learning which of their arguments is the most compelling in order to regain ground in the battle for public opinion. How do the various pro-life arguments play to the public as a whole? The findings provide even more evidence that pro-life and pro-choice Americans

Figure 12

Burning issues

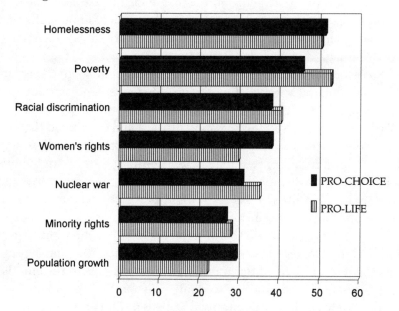

**Percent of "Pro-life" and "Pro-choice" Americans
Who Say They are "Very Concerned"**

Question: "I am going to read you a list of social and political issues that are being discussed today. For each, please tell me how concerned you are personally."

live in different moral universes. In general, those on the pro-choice side of the debate find little that is compelling in *any* of the pro-life arguments. Contentions that all human life, including that of the unborn, should be protected; that every unborn child has a basic right to life; that human life begins at conception, and therefore abortion is murder; that while abortion is sometimes necessary, it is used too frequently as an easy way out—none of these holds much credibility. Pro-choicers do not even find the feminist arguments against abortion (that abortion enables men to take advantage of women; that it promotes a disregard for the value of human life; that it leaves women with emotional scars; and so forth) at all convincing. It is as though they have been immunized.

But what of those Americans who are ambivalent about the issue? It is their opinion, after all, that the pro-life movement is most eager to influence. Which arguments do they find most plausible? A Wirthlin study pressed this question furthest and concluded that the pro-life movement can best shore up support among its allies, and best undermine its opposition, by concentrating on a "rights-oriented" message—emphasizing the rights of the unborn to live and thus make all of life's choices; the right of women to receive counseling and thus make an informed choice; the right of a father to share in the choice of whether his child is aborted; the right of parents to have a choice in counseling a teenage daughter who is pregnant; and so on. Part of this strategy, they suggest, is to reclaim the language of "choice" and, by so doing, rename their opponents according to what they truly promote. Thus pro-lifers are encouraged to call their opponents "pro-abortion," "abortion supporters," and so on, rather than "pro-choice." The conclusion, in other words, is not to rework the old pro-life message or articulate a new message but to adopt the language used by the opposition, infusing it with new meaning that will ultimately lead people to start thinking about the protection of fetal life. In sum, the Wirthlin study shows (and it is supported somewhat by the other surveys) that it is the language of "rights" and "choice" that resonates most broadly in the public arena. Wirthlin's chief advice to the pro-life movement, therefore, was to recognize this appeal and to promote it as the central apologia for the protection of fetal life.

That the language and logic of rights and choice resonate with the majority of Americans comes as no surprise. It plays to both the best and worst aspects of American individualism. But to then conclude that this message should form the principal argument of the pro-life movement in its effort to shore up its support is remarkably ironic and, perhaps, a bit too desperate. The cultural impulse that animates many secular modernists (in the arts, in the gay-rights movement, in multiculturalism, in some forms of feminist thinking, and so on) is derived from precisely this libertarian ideal. To adopt a communications strategy for the pro-life movement that accepts this cultural premise is, for them, to fight a battle by conceding the war. To the extent that this becomes the pro-life agenda for the future, then the pro-choice activists can break out the champagne to celebrate their inevitable victory: the animating spirit of the pro-life opposition will have been neutralized. It is not, as Charles Krauthammer argued (see Chapter One), a consensus among the three branches of government that would have brought about a pro-choice victory, but rather a co-opting of their opponents by having the latter accept the moral vocabulary of the pro-choice movement.

Public Opinion and Public Debate

We have examined the attitudes of Americans on the matter of abortion with some care to illustrate the remarkable complexity of opinion that exists underneath the dualism of public debate. We have seen that the complexity of public opinion is far richer than mere degrees of support or opposition to abortion rights. Rather, very different levels of knowledge, kinds of ambivalence, and styles of moral engagement exist and these relate fundamentally to a person's larger life-world, not least the community of moral conversation in which the person participates.

Such complexity exists underneath the dualism of public debate over homosexuality and gay rights as well. A survey of public opinion in Colorado following the passage of Amendment 2 (a referendum denying protective status to gays and lesbians) showed this clearly.

As one would expect there are polarizing tendencies in the general population. Three-fourths of those who thought of themselves as "very conservative" strongly agreed that homosexuality is morally wrong compared to three-fourths of those who called themselves "very liberal" who strongly disagreed with that position. Likewise, three-fourths of the very conservative strongly agreed with the view that when homosexuals talk about gay rights, what they are really saying is that they want special treatment compared to two-thirds of the very liberal who strongly disagreed. This polarizing impulse played out in views of military policy as well. Of those calling themselves very liberal, ninety percent agreed that homosexuals should be allowed to serve in the armed forces, compared to three-fourths of the very conservative who disagreed with this position.

Yet, as with abortion, the existence of a polarizing impulse in the larger public's attitude is just the beginning of the story. In the Colorado survey, the most religiously committed tended to view homosexuality as morally problematic yet demostrated little of the irrational fear and hostility toward gays and lesbians that we are often led to believe exists. Of the most committed believers, for example, the overwhelming majority agreed that homosexuals are no different from anyone else except in their choice of sexual partners. They disagreed that homosexuals were more likely to sexually molest children than heterosexual persons. They disagreed that AIDS was God's way of punishing homosexuals. They disagreed too that children who have homosexual teachers or a homosexual parent run the risk of becoming gay themselves. As to matters of law and public policy, the most religiously committed were mixed in their views. The majority disagreed that homosexual behavior should be against the law even if between consenting adults and they unanimously rejected the idea that gays and lesbians should be required to wear an identification badge so people who wanted to avoid associating with them would know who they are. As to the matter of gays serving in the military, they were split, though a full half agreed that homosexuals should be allowed to serve. As to public education, two-thirds of the most religiously committed rejected prohibitions against gays and lesbians teaching in the public schools. As to AIDS research, a fourth agreed that more money should be spent on researching this virus even if it means spending less on other diseases.

The picture that begins to emerge is of an abiding moral rejection of homosexuality yet, simultaneously, a fairly substantial and (according to national surveys) increasing acceptance of the legitimacy of homosexuality for others and a recognition of gay and lesbian civil rights, even among the most morally and religiously conservative. Even the majority of liberals in Colorado (according to the Colorado survey) agreed that the average person is not nearly so prejudiced against homosexuals as many gay-rights activists would want people to believe.

Here again, a brief review is only suggestive. Still richer and multilayered patterns of opinion undoubtedly exist underneath the common accusations of "faggot" and "homophobe"; patterns that beckon to be understood and reflected in public argument. Needless to say, the patterns of public opinion are just complex on other matters of public dispute. Such complexity is difficult to summarize in a few words. One thing is clear, however, and that is that there is far less knowledge—and far more nuance and ambivalence—in the views of middle America than activists on either side of the controversy would care to admit.

One might suggest that the general public seems poorly equipped to deal with such controversies, if only because so little is known by the average American about the laws that govern them on these issues. This has not kept people from forming opinions, obviously, but improving what people know about the law is still probably the first way to enhance the quality of public discourse. It is also probably the best way to begin searching for a democratically sustainable solution to this controversy. But we also need to learn more about ourselves as individuals and as a society.

But in the end, surveys are never the last word about public attitudes. They can provide fairly comprehensive understanding of the topography of public opinion, insight into the substance of people's views, but only a glimpse into the foundations of their attitudes. It is in the way that Americans articulate their ambivalence that we see just how equipped we are to engage in a serious and substantive debate. This provides the focus of the next chapter.

— 5 —

The Culture of Ambivalence

What Role Feelings Play in Middle America

The polling data speak to one matter clearly: if we are ambivalent about abortion—or about race, homosexuality, avant-garde art, euthanasia, or the environment—it is in part because we are ambivalent about ourselves. But where does the ambivalence come from? Here the survey findings provide us with little insight. Surveys are at their most useful in providing a kind of topographical map of opinion about a particular issue at a particular time. But having mapped out with a measure of detail *how* Americans view the matter of abortion, the question is now *why* Americans view it the way they do. Or better still, on what grounds do we come to a conclusion about where we fit into this and other controversies?

In what follows here, let us listen to the way some ordinary citizens (in this case, mostly middle-class Americans who are not embroiled in activism on behalf of one side or the other) articulate their views about abortion and the various issues relating to the controversy.[1] What we learn from these conversations derives less from the particular things they say about the matter than from the way in which they say it. Thus it is how people give voice to their views that

122

we gain insight into the nature and sources of the intransigent ambivalence that prevails in the public mind on this matter. Not incidently, what we learn by listening to these individuals will tell us a great deal about the possibility for serious and substantive democratic argument to take place among average citizens.

The Safe Refuge of Labels

Perhaps the first and most striking observation to surface from our numerous conversations with people around the country was how quick everyone was to identify themselves with the dominant labels of the controversy. Typical was Rich Carver, a thirty-three-year-old writer and soon-to-be father from Sacramento, California. When asked how he placed himself in the abortion controversy, "Choice!" was his one-word reply. The ease and certainty with which he stated his response was equally evident in the replies made by nearly everyone else we spoke to: "I'm on the pro-life side," said another; "Oh, I'm definitely pro-choice, a woman should have a choice" was a statement made by a third. For Rich, as well as the many others we talked to, the response carried in it the tone and character of a reflex, albeit a reflex with real emotion. People stated their position with a quickness that suggested both familiarity and reflection with the contours of this issue. So much for ambivalence, we thought to ourselves. At the very least, it became clear to us that the labels *pro-life* or *pro-choice* were flags to rally around. Most of the people knew precisely under which flag they took refuge and made no bones about telling us which one it was.

But if a flag signals a person's loyalty, how well do they know—and how committed are they to—the positions and institutions that these flags represent? When probing just beyond the labels, what we found was not familiarity and reflection with the issue. What we found, rather, was that their stated positions were very often put forward against a backdrop of confusion about the law over which the controversy as a whole has taken form.

When we asked Rich to tell us anything at all about the law over which the controversy centers and within which he positioned himself, his reply was revealing: "Yeah, let's see. I'm going to sort of think out loud here. It has to do with the pregnant mother's right to terminate a pregnancy and the court's subsequent ruling on it. I know the names were changed, but you know what, I forget who the other one was. Let's see, it wasn't *Roe* versus *State*, or it wasn't *State* versus *Wade*, was it? There was another principle that was involved, I think. Well, that's about as good as I can do."

"What about the parameters around what the law actually permits?"

"No, I don't recall," he said. "There are probably some details I would remember if you prompted me, but for now I just don't know."

"Have you heard about the *Webster* decision?"

"That one," he replied, "I don't know anything about."

Ann Plotz, a college-educated mother of a six-week old boy from Colorado Springs, responded much like Rich when asked if she could place herself in the controversy; with no hesitancy at all she replied, "I'm pro-choice!" Here again, though, her knowledge of how the choice to have an abortion related to the particulars of the controversy—any particulars—was shallow, to say the least.

"Can you tell us anything at all about what the Supreme Court decided in the landmark case *Roe v. Wade?*"

"Not very well—no," she said.

"What about the most general thrust of the law?"

"It said you can choose, and that's all I know. I really have no idea about the specifics of the ruling." Ann had not heard of the *Webster* decision, and of the *Casey v. Pennsylvania Planned Parenthood* case that was being deliberated at the time of the interview (but which had not been ruled upon) she said she had heard, "A very little bit. I think they decided that they were against abortion in that one."

It is entirely understandable how someone with full-time responsibility for a six-week-old child could be a bit behind on the news or even have a lapse of memory about the larger legal controversy, but Ann's and Rich's rather weak grip on the nature of the dispute was fairly typical of everyone we spoke to who was not somehow actively involved in the dispute themselves.

This was true as well among those who said they were pro-life. Saundra Ferris, an art history graduate student living in Chicago, described herself as "pro-life, but in some 'mitigated' form." When asked to describe her understanding of *Roe v. Wade*, she replied: "What I would say in real general terms is that I know it was a court case that allowed for public monies to be used—no, you know what, as it comes down to it I don't really know. . . . It's all sort of faded now. . . . *Roe v. Wade* was about allowing abortions, and then *Webster* challenged it in some specific way." Others leaning to the pro-life side of the controversy were more like Chris Thomas. Chris could say that public policy on abortion allowed a woman "a right to choose" but could not offer much beyond that: "I'm not positive. I believe it's legal up until the first trimester, but I'm not sure. I know it's illegal after—I shouldn't say I know—I believe it's illegal into the third trimester."

Clearly some do better than others. One or two of the individuals we spoke to had a pretty good fix on it. A few were like Sylvia Turner, an actress originally from Connecticut, who, while fairly inarticulate about the issue, confessed that she took the label *pro-choice* because "it's shorter than going on and on about what I think and what I believe." In general, though, the insight noted in Chapter Four is reinforced here: popular opinion does not form out of a wellspring of knowledge about the law based upon which people position themselves and voice their opinions. Vague impressions of what the law allows or does not allow are the main tools most people outside of the controversy are working with in sorting out their own place in the dispute.[2]

Seeing the quickness with which people identified themselves in the dispute, contrasted against a slowness or inability to retrieve any useful information or knowledge of the legal dispute itself, made my assistants and me distrust even more those who say that the majority of Americans are "pro-life" or "pro-choice." The labels, it would seem, express a sentiment, not a conviction or even a commitment. And that, as it turns out, is the nub of the matter.

The Language of Sentiment

It was Paul Archer, a forty-five-year-old architect from Annapolis, Maryland, who quite unwittingly showed us how this forms the foundation of the ambivalence people "in the middle" have toward abortion.

We had begun our conversation in his office but decided to continue it over lunch at a small restaurant nearby. I raised the issue of how people's choices should be weighed against a responsibility to protect human life: at what point do we say that a person should not have a right to choose, but rather a responsibility to protect and care? He asked me to elaborate what I meant by this line of questioning, so I began to suggest a number of concrete points in human development—even after the birth of the child—as well as a range of circumstances in which he might imagine the question being relevant. With regard to abortion in the first three months of pregnancy, for example, he thought that a woman's right to choose was preeminent. With regard to late-term abortions, though, he was very uncomfortable. About a child who is born but living with severe medical problems, he said that the parent should have the right to terminate its life; parents, he said, have no right to abandon a young healthy infant. There were other scenarios I posed to him as well. I then asked him *why* a parent or a woman should have a right to choose in one situation but not in another. He replied, "I just can't tell you why."

I pressed further, asking him if he thought it was important to sort these things out, particularly since societies can be very arbitrary about who or what they say is worth or not worth protecting. At this point he was becoming somewhat agitated with me. His reply went to the heart of the matter: "*I just don't want to get into a philosophical or theological wrangling,*" he said. "*I know how I feel, and my feelings are valid.*" He paused for a moment and then continued. "*Look, these feelings are based on experiences that are mine alone, and you can't tell me they are wrong. Other people have other experiences and will feel differently about things.*"

"But . . . ," I began.

I was tempted to push the matter further, but the tensions were mounting. From the look in his eye and the tone in his voice, I decided that to press him any harder might not jeopardize my life, but it would surely violate his sense of civil conversation. I had stepped over some invisible boundary and, in so doing, threatened him.

Much of what he said in the course of our conversation was interesting, but the most striking thing was his begging off from philosophy and theology, even at the most elementary level. Within this move was a tacit rejection of either humanistic or theistic ideals or moral traditions—the languages of conviction—as relevant resources for comprehending the issue or dealing with its complexities. In his case, it was his feelings that guided him ("I know how I feel, and my feelings are valid").

In this, Paul Archer articulated the terms of his understanding of abortion. His ambivalence about abortion was not, it would seem, terribly well thought out. It was, however, deeply *felt*. What he revealed about himself turned out to be true of virtually everyone else we spoke to who was not actively involved in the controversy. In short, *the ambivalence most people have is rooted primarily in the language of sentiment and not in the languages of conviction.*

Our conversation with Barbara Cohen ended up being fairly short, but it was illustrative of the salience of emotion in framing her perspective as well. Barbara, also in her early forties, was highly educated and affluent. She apparently had struggled for years to become pregnant. She was now a new and full-time mother and demonstrably devoted to her young child. When we explained that we were interested in exploring how nonactivists viewed abortion and the abortion controversy, her response was brisk. "Honestly," she stated, "I couldn't see how I could possibly help you. I don't have time to discuss these things. I just know that I'm pro-choice, and I really don't have anything more to say about it." In the spirit of honest persistence, we tried to pry just a bit further. Surely she had given thought to the matter. How did she come to her views? But her patience was being tested: "I have my own personal feelings on these things, and I just know how I feel. But I'd really rather not discuss it."

The emotionality of the issue was perhaps more palpable in this conversation than in many of the others, but the vocabulary of sentiment she employed was (as it had been for Paul) typical of the priority others gave to framing the issue in their minds. "Floating thoughts" was the way another described her views; "shaped by a hodgepodge of influences"—but mainly her life experiences. In the end, she said, "I know how I personally feel about this but really can't say why."

On Abortion Itself

The vocabulary of sentiment, we found, provided the means by which most people we spoke to comprehended (and articulated their views of) the larger issue as well as the particular aspects of the controversy. It was, for example, evident in the way people processed the inevitable tensions, inconsistencies, and contradictions in their views of abortion itself. On this issue, as was demonstrated in Chapter Four, tension, inconsistency, and contradiction are often the norm. While the contradictions people maintain are typically based in a superficial understanding of what abortion law says, this is not even the most interesting finding; not everyone can be a lawyer (thank heaven!), and even technically trained lawyers have been known to get it wrong. What is more interesting, then, is not the fact of the inconsistency but rather the way in which inconsistencies are framed and articulated. No one was more candid about this than Alice Horning.

Alice Horning retired with her husband of forty-one years to Fort Meyers, Florida. In her early sixties at the time of the interview, she had raised five kids, all close in age, and was now in a retirement condominium near the shore enjoying a less hectic pace and the fruits of a lifetime of work as a part-time schoolteacher. She admitted that the issue of abortion was not of immediate concern primarily because, as she put it, "I'm past childbearing, and I really feel like it is not my problem anymore." Her background aside, she said, she still supported a woman's right to choose to have an abortion. When pressed, she qualified her position by stating that a woman's right to choose should only extend through the second trimester of her pregnancy. Later still, she said that she did not like the idea of even second-trimester abortions and would "probably go along with a law that restricted it" to the first trimester.

Curious to know how she was coming to her opinions, I asked her about her views of the abortion procedure and what she thought was being aborted. "If I'm honest with myself," she began, "I would say that the fetus is a human life. But I don't choose to dwell on it and call it human life. I prefer to think of it as human tissue. It may be a copout on my part, but I prefer to think of it as extra human tissue that can be surgically removed because, well, [this way of looking at it] makes me feel more comfortable. . . . At the end of pregnancy, it's much harder not to view [the fetus] as a human being, because there is movement and it has all of its parts. Before the end of pregnancy, though, I guess I rationalize to myself that it is not a human being, but I admit I do it in order to make myself more comfortable."

Consider too Lisa Rodriguez, who was introduced in Chapter One. Maybe because the experience of motherhood was so new to her, the idea of abortion struck her as "personally appalling." Yet even before she was married, her instincts had always made her nervous about abortion. She knew of girls in college who had had abortions—one acquaintance had even had two—but what was so troubling to her both then and now was not that her classmates did not take their abortions seriously (in fact, most of her classmates were troubled by their abortions), but that they would not seriously entertain any other options. The "embarrassment" of carrying a child to term out of wedlock was so great that it was as though her friends did not really have a choice at all. But it was and is important to Lisa not to be "judgmental," so she stayed quiet about her discomfort.

Lisa leans to the pro-life side of the abortion controversy probably more from instinct than from deep conviction. She was raised and married in the Catholic church, and her son was baptized in the church, but she admits that it is not central to her life now. Perhaps she heard distant echoes of a childhood faith as she formed her opinions about abortion. "Look, maybe I'll change my opinion in a few years," she said, "this is just the way I feel about it now." In the end, she confessed: "I don't think a whole lot about [the political] side of the [issue]. God, I mean, being a mom is so great. I guess I want to think it is this good for everyone."

And then consider Louise Schaeffer, a graduate student in her mid-twenties studying at Stanford, who expressed a kindred sentiment about this difficult issue. Like so many of the others, Louise had only the vaguest background knowledge of the abortion controversy. Nevertheless she said that she had a "gut feeling" that at some point and under some circumstances a woman needed the latitude to choose. And the fetus or unborn child? "Sometimes," she confessed, "it's easier not to think about that."

Activists on opposing sides of this controversy might want to claim each of these three women (and the many, many more like them) as generally supportive of their agenda. Yet it is probably more accurate to conclude that these women are in a moral and political category of their own—both for and against each side of the controversy in their own ways. What is distinctive about their ambivalence toward abortion has something to do with the play of emotions as they reflect on the issue. It was important to them to "feel comfortable" or to avoid emotional turmoil in this matter, even if it meant "rationalizing," "copping out," or "not thinking about" the implications of the positions they had taken.

The Role of Empathy

One of the main ways our subjects' feelings about abortion congealed in their minds was through another feeling; that of empathy. It seemed universal. People really wanted to think of themselves as compassionate and for us to see them as such, and so it was that they often related their feelings about abortion in reference to an expression of compassion. This was expressed primarily in terms of an identification with and sympathy for those who suffer. The interviewees projected themselves into the circumstances of others in need and empathized with them. Compassion, in this way, was expressed primarily as a feeling of empathy with others.[3]

Among the activists, of course, empathy falls out along predictable lines: The pro-life identify with the unborn and empathize with its suffering as it is "poisoned or pulled apart and finally killed"; the pro-choice identify with the anguish of a woman in an unplanned pregnancy, "the turmoil of her decision to have an abortion and the terrible danger to her life if she faces an illegal abortion." The most extreme activists on each side cannot or choose not to empathize with the object that generates such empathy for the other side.

But this is not so for most Americans. Part of what places these individuals in the ambivalent middle of this controversy is a capacity to feel for both the unborn child and the woman who wants an abortion. How they place themselves in the controversy in part depends upon the object for which their empathy is greatest, but a feeling of empathy is there for both the woman and the fetus in varying intensity.

The Appeal to Experience

If people *feel* strongly about abortion, and are variously empathetic for pregnant women and gestating children, how are their feelings shaped? Surely there are factors of which these individuals are simply unaware—their social class, their gender, the region of the country they are from, and so on. But our conversations suggest that at a conscious level, it is neither the collective opinion of a community to which they belong nor the imperatives of a tradition of moral reasoning to which they adhere, but rather the field of their own experience that is most formative of their views. It is to personal experience that they make their main appeal. Paul Archer pointed to this when he declared that his feelings about abortion were based on experiences that were "his alone." "Other people have other experiences," he said, "and will feel differently about things."

Karen Pentalla spoke to this as well. A twenty-seven-year-old social worker from the Pittsburgh area and a mother of a ten-month-old child, Karen placed herself "more with the pro-life side than the pro-choice side" of the controversy. She said, though, that she did not believe that groups like Operation Rescue or the National Right to Life Committee spoke for her. The reason, she said, has to do with the filter of personal experience that pro-life organizations simply have no access to: "What I say and what I really feel when I really think about it is different at times. I guess what I want to say is that my feelings change depending on the circumstances. If someone I know has had an abortion, then it becomes more of a reality, and so I have to rethink what I thought before." Most recently, it was the experience of having a baby herself that prompted her to rethink the issue of abortion in the context of the "big questions." This experience, she said, "has made me wonder why anyone is put on this earth. Does a woman really have a right to take that life [through abortion]? Having a baby [that was not planned] might seem like it would ruin your life, but you don't know that really."

Needless to say, the experiences people had were as varied as there were people to have them:

- For Karen Pentalla, it was the birth of her child that crystallized her views, or should I say feelings, on the matter.
- For Alice Horning, mentioned earlier, her views (even now as a sixty-year old) were shaped indelibly by her experience during adolescence. She grew up under the shadow of a very domineering father who, she says, had a quick temper. "If I had had premarital sex, and if I had gotten pregnant—and I thought about all

of these things, as there are many temptations during courting—then I would have had an abortion immediately. I'm just sure I would have found a way to have an illegal abortion without any regard to the risk involved, because it would have been far better to face that than the anger I would have had from my father."

- For Barry Walker, it is living with his daughter, who he describes as "adamantly pro-choice." She was born out of wedlock when Barry and the woman who is now his estranged wife were in college twenty years before. Barry, too, was born out of wedlock. He said that these distant realities, though, did not figure into his views now. One wonders.
- For Kate Beck, it was the experience of seeing young girls die from illegal abortions back in the 1950s when she was a student nurse at the University of Colorado. "I've pumped blood into dying girls who wouldn't tell you who punctured their abdominal aorta rather than their uterus." She is now active in Republicans for Choice.
- For Mark Fielder, whom we met briefly in Chapter One, it was the experience of having to deal with his girlfriend's unplanned pregnancy. She wanted to keep the baby, at least at first, but he pressured her to have the abortion until she relented. "I felt guilty about the whole thing," he said. "After it was all over I knew it was unfair of me to leverage my judgment on her. . . . I'm sure there were a lot of selfish reasons for doing it." Not knowing whether he wanted to marry his girlfriend, he was more than a little relieved when she finally had the abortion.
- For Kelly Gorman, it was no particular experience, but life itself. "I think it has a lot to do with the way my parents brought me up, my religious background, the high school I went to, the college I went to, the people I met there, the books I've read, and so on."

For still other women, it is the experience of their *own* abortion that has crystallized their feelings on the matter. Consider the stories told by Robin Wysocki and Betsy McRae, both women in their early thirties.

ROBIN'S STORY

Robin Wysocki had her first abortion at the age of seventeen during her last year in high school. She was raised in an up-

*wardly mobile, churchgoing (yet not at all strict) Catholic fam-
ily in the Northeast. She was a straight-A student and, as the
oldest child in her family and the first grandchild, a source of
enormous pride to her folks and family. "At the time I found
out I was pregnant," she said, "I didn't think twice about having an abortion. But I never told my family about it. . . . In ret-
rospect I'm sure my parents would have supported me, but at
the time I was so grieved with the thought of disappointing
them that I just didn't want them to know. I just couldn't bear
the thought of telling them. . . . But the boy's parents knew. In
fact, I spent the day I had the abortion back at his house, sleeping mainly, because I was in a lot of pain."*

*While she did not think twice about having the abortion, af-
ter it was over, regret set in. Was it post-abortion stress? we
asked. No, she insisted, it was "downright guilt. . . . I remember going into church and just sitting there through Mass and
crying and crying. My mother didn't know what in the world
was wrong with me, but it was me dealing with a tremendous
sense of guilt." With time, however, the experience became a
distant, if bitter, memory—one that was not lost.*

*Seven years later Robin found herself in New York City
working as a model. One evening she was with a good friend
who was male, but with whom there had never been any
prior romance. As she remembers the evening, "Our passions got the best of us, and we slept together—just that one
night." Alas, she found she was pregnant for the second
time. With the first pregnancy, she says, she could justify it:
"I was young. But this one was different. I had been on my
own. I was a career woman. And from the trauma of the first
one, I knew it was absolutely wrong, and I just couldn't rationalize it." So she decided "to accept the responsibility" for
her actions.*

*However, her roommate at the time, a woman in her early
thirties, "would kind of harp on me about how ridiculous I was
being. 'What was I doing thinking that I would raise a baby?'
she said. 'Could I give it a good quality of life?' You know,
things like that." The day she was going to catch a train to see
her family to tell them she was pregnant, she panicked and had
a change of mind. Instead she caught a cab and went to a clinic*

in Manhattan and had the abortion. "I didn't feel any of the pain this time. I remember waking up and feeling cheated. I thought to myself, 'You're such a pig. You deserve to have been awake and felt that pain and gone through that experience.' The whole thing was just the epitome of selfishness. I was absolutely disgusted with myself."

This second experience, Robin said, threw her into an "emotional, psychological, and spiritual tailspin." The result was a season of deep soul-searching that led her back to an active faith in God and a life intimately linked to the church. She was now very strongly pro-life in her views, even working with teenagers in her church to give them perspective on the problems of growing up, not least those having to do with sex.

BETSY'S STORY

For Betsy McRae, the experience of an abortion was no less troubling, but it did not lead her back to religious faith. A part-time actress living in Culver City, California, Betsy said that she tries to avoid talking about the abortion issue because the memory, she confessed, "kind of haunts me."

It had been seven years earlier. Betsy was twenty-five years old and had been going out with a guy for about three months. "As soon as I knew I was pregnant, I decided that there was no way I am having his child. I never wanted a future with him. There was just no way in hell I would have married him—and yet I stayed with him for two years." She said that she was glad that she did not have his baby right now, but she still felt guilty that she "ended a life."

Like Robin, Betsy was also raised in the Catholic church, migrating as a child from Philadelphia to Richmond, Virginia, and finally to Salem, Oregon. From the time she left home, her attachments to the church quickly waned. Her experience with the nuns in parochial school was, as she recalled, less than inspiring. Now she does not think of herself in any way as a

Catholic. Even so, she says, "I find it hard not to believe in God."

And yet as much as Betsy had distanced herself from the Catholic faith, it still shaped many of her instincts about the issue and her own experience. When asked why she did not want to think about the issue, her reply was, ironically, very "Catholic": "To think about this issue is to think that I'm like a murderer." The tensions of her background and her experience constitute the dominant theme of her story. After all these years she remained pulled in different directions: "This whole conversation is difficult for me because I'm not clear on what I did. . . . My instincts tell me I did the right thing. I'm just so relieved that he [her former lover] is not a part of my life. I can't even tell you how much I've grown since I've left him. But I still have this problem. . . . I guess what I should have done, what I couldn't have done, was to have the baby and give it up for adoption. But I couldn't have done that."

"Why?" I asked.

"Because I know I could have supported it somehow. We both came from families that could have helped. And, it would have been a part of me and I couldn't have given it up. . . . I could have cared for the baby. My life would have been totally different—maybe even better, I don't know. I don't know if what I did was right or wrong, I just don't know. But I like where my life is now. I guess there's the good and the bad."

In the end, she copes by trying to forget the bad. "It's very tough for me."

The stories Robin and Betsy tell are, obviously, only two of literally millions of stories that could be gathered. As my assistants and I listened to these, we could conclude that no one was less moving than any other. How much more moving and even traumatic they must be for those who personally experienced them.

But whether or not our subjects had had an abortion themselves, or knew of someone who had had an abortion, it was "personal experience" that provided the overriding appeal for the shaping of their feelings about abortion. Yet experience was never a good predictor of the direction their feelings would move. Perhaps Paul Archer was right all along: "Other people have other experiences and will feel differently about things."

What About the Languages of Conviction?

The Paul Archers we spoke to were fairly atypical in totally rejecting philosophy and theology as resources to make sense of the issue. For others it was different. One did hear numerous references to the institutions and communities that sustain particular philosophical or religious traditions. Yet except for the strongly pro-life, rarely did we hear an appeal to either the bonds of a community or the authority of institutions as realities that had a clear priority over feelings in their lives. (Indeed, we were repeatedly struck by the general lack of connection these mainly middle-class individuals had to *any* institutions outside of their workplace and perhaps their family.) Typically, then, it was individuals' relationship to a moral community or the demands of their affiliation with local institutions that were reinterpreted in light of their personal experiences and feelings, rather than their membership and rootedness in a community providing an interpretive grid for the experience. This was even true for those churchgoers who leaned toward the pro-life side of the controversy. The languages of conviction tended to be subservient to the language of sentiment and the personal experiences that sustained these sentiments.

Ann Plotz demonstrated this tendency in virtually a single breath. When asked how she came to her views of the abortion issue, she replied that she was influenced by "religious and philosophical beliefs." We wondered what those beliefs would be, and she responded, "Well, I just strongly feel that it's a woman's own body, and it should be her choosing what she does with it." She never did make any reference to a larger system of any beliefs; she could only assert to us how she felt.

Alice Horning provides another, perhaps more eloquent case. Since she told me that she was a churchgoing Methodist, I asked her how her religious faith related to her views of abortion. (Recall that she leaned toward the pro-choice side of the controversy.) She replied as follows: "I don't think about [the connection] very much because it doesn't make me feel very comfortable. I don't feel like I'm totally consistent in this, to be honest. To try to substantiate my views in relation to the Bible, for example, really causes me a certain amount of grief. I have a problem with the Bible, so I keep these things in two different compartments. I guess at my age I have decided to concentrate on making myself feel good. Now, I'm the first to admit that, though I'm not very proud of it. I'm trying to make myself feel comfortable." Could she relate her religious faith to her belief that a woman should have a right to choose? we asked. "I don't think I can answer that," she replied. What is so interesting is that Alice is so conscious of making her commitments to church and faith on this matter subject to the final authority of her feelings.

Even though she has become fairly strong in her pro-life views as an evangelical Christian, Robin Wysocki spoke insightfully about these tensions as well. "The one thing I've learned," she started, "is that you can really feel like you have such a set of principles and values and standards that you say you unequivocally hold to no matter what. But then you are confronted with a real-life decision. All of a sudden it is just a completely different feeling. Over and over again in my life I have seen how shallow I actually am when my deep-rooted feelings of right and wrong are confronted with a real life decision." In Robin's worldview, principles of right and wrong are themselves articulated as feelings rather than, say, obligations.[4] Tested within the crucible of experience, such feelings are prone to change.

Julie Howard was also troubled by the tensions of trying to practice her faith. As a professed Christian, she said that a "child is a child, before birth or after birth." But then she confessed: "I feel like a hypocrite a lot of times because if I *really* believed these children are children, I should be doing more than I am. I mean if I saw a two-year-old drowning in a pool, wild horses couldn't keep me from jumping in to try to save it." But this was not how she responded to abortion.

Most people are not like Alice, Robin, or Julie in honestly facing up to the tensions and perhaps even failures of conviction. Easier than admitting the contradictions are the tendencies to relativize and privatize one's beliefs. For example, Rebecca Darmin, an occupational therapist from Fredericksburg, Maryland, said that she was opposed to abortion but that her opposition was mainly "personal." She insisted that she would never have an abortion, the reason being that the fetus is, in some sense, a human life. Abortion, she said, "isn't murder but it is the taking of human life, or at least potential life." "The problem I have," she noted, "is speaking on behalf of other people. Telling someone else whether they can or can't do that. I take the view, 'who am I to force my views on someone else?' There's an element of judgment when you impose your views on other people, since you don't know the road they have traveled. You don't know where they're coming from, so to speak. It just seems unfair."

But is this really imposing? It would be if she coerced them to accept her views. But why would it be imposing if she simply tried to persuade them of the rightness and even truthfulness of her views, as in a good Socratic dialogue? "I think a person has to be open to the information you're presenting them," she said. "They have to be willing to listen." I was curious why she was so sensitive to this.

The reason, in part, had to do with transitions Rebecca was going through.

Not many years earlier she had been deeply involved in a charismatic Christian church. The last several years, though, were marked by a migration from that world to a much more secular and, in her view, more enlightened way of life. The changes in her biography provided a poignant contrast: "There was a time in my life when I would show pictures of aborted fetuses to friends and say, 'Look at this, isn't this awful, this is murder.'" Even then she was uncomfortable doing this. "I was just part of the bandwagon," she said. The change in her views on this issue came mainly from a change in her faith. She was not much involved in any church, and she reflected, "I don't feel as much of a personal, absolute relationship with God as I used to."

While Rebecca's story is unique to her, the manner in which she articulated her views was not. When asked whether her fundamentalist faith as well as her strongly pro-life views of abortion were right or wrong for her at the time, she said, "They were right for me then, even though I didn't have much depth or understanding as to what I was doing." Her views of abortion and of God and of faith had become quite different and were still evolving. She again retreated to the stock phrase of popular relativism: "I would say my views are true for me, but I can't put that on someone else. I just can't force my truths on other people."

Sylvia Turner, an evangelical Christian who called herself pro-choice, put it this way: "Maybe I'm just wimping out. I have always had this incredible conviction that Christ is the way, the truth, the light—that kind of thing—but that he might not be the way for everybody else. That whole way of thinking is definitely reflective of how I see a lot of issues—like abortion." Scott Allen, a "lapsed" Catholic, conveyed the same theme. He openly argued that the fetus was a "person," but when asked if its status as a person afforded it protection from the choice of the mother to have an abortion, he said, "No, because [the fetus] might not be a person to that mother. . . . It's not for me to say that it is a person to that mother, because she's the one that ultimately makes that decision."

The predilection to relativize and privatize convictions is an underlying theme among many of those willing to be publicly pro-life as well. Take Karen Pentalla. Her views, she told us, were very personal and that she could not speak for others. "I don't know where others are coming from. I don't know how they feel. I don't know how they were brought up to feel." This, for Karen, became the reason why she would not become publicly involved in the dispute. "I'm leery to voice my opinion," she said, "because of other people's feelings. If they know that that's how I feel about this issue, I might offend them in such a way that it might affect my relationship with them." Here, too, feelings reign supreme.

The moral traditions from which the languages of conviction derive have by no means disappeared. Americans will invoke them as personally meaningful, but at the same time they do not view them as publicly binding. Rather they are relativized ("This is true for me") and privatized ("I would never impose my view on anyone else"). As such the languages of conviction, and the moral traditions from which they come, become rather beside the point. Subservient to the imperatives of personal sentiment, they fail to provide any common resources for individuals and communities to sort out the complexities of the controversy.

The Specter of Government

If personal experience provides the main appeal by which people's ambivalent feelings are understood and expressed, it is not the only appeal. People's ambivalence about abortion also draws from an ambivalence toward the government. Mere mention of the word *government* provoked reactions from our subjects that ranged from reticence to outright hostility. Here, too, the medium was a vocabulary of sentiments.

The strongest visceral reaction was among those who thought of themselves as being pro-choice (even if their actual feelings were not entirely consistent with the way they identified themselves). Mark Fielder from Santa Monica, for example, left no doubt about his position on this. "I don't think any government or legal institution has the right to tell an individual what he or she may do. It's like, 'Excuse me, you can't take a pee today because it's Wednesday. The government says that you can't piss until Thursday.' It's the same thing with abortion. It has no business getting involved here." The word *government* prompted a similar response from Kate Beck, the nurse from Colorado. "I think that the government and its laws should simply get out of people's private lives. If it doesn't, people will do what they want to do anyway, but it will all be underground, and in the case of abortion, it will be horrible." Sylvia Turner came right to the point: "I don't know, I guess I have this Big Brother image of the government." While she is "big on paying [her] taxes," she is increasingly aware "of just how much I think they're against us."

Even among those who tended to think of themselves as pro-life, there was a self-consciousness and even defensiveness about the idea of government involvement in this issue. David Ronfeldt, an insurance salesman from Richmond, Virginia, spoke volumes on this in a single phrase. "Hey, being pro-life doesn't mean I'm against choice!" he explained. "I believe that people do have the right to choose on some things. In this case, I just think people have made a choice to engage in sexual activity that can lead to pregnancy. Once you're pregnant, the time of choices is over." The idea of the government, then, touches a nerve, provoking an immediate and typically negative reflex for people. People intuitively understand the great power of the state and are, to say the least, wary of it.

But the issue is more complicated, as everyone we spoke to eventually agreed. All admitted that the government "imposes its will," "sticks its nose into people's business," and "tells people what to do" all of the time, for both good and for ill, in setting speed limits, requiring estranged husbands to pay alimony to their wives, demanding taxes, and so on. Even on the matter of abortion, there was a general sense—when the subjects were pushed a bit—that the government could not completely divorce itself from the abortion issue: it should regulate the medical procedures and conditions of abortion, it should step in "at some point" to prohibit some abortions, and so forth. So how do people sort out what is a proper or improper role for the government to play in their lives, and in the realm of family life and reproduction in particular?

The general agreement among those we interviewed was that the state should step in to regulate abortion practice at the point where life begins. That agreement, while noteworthy, in a way was little more than a banality. The real question was, could a government ever write into public policy at what point life begins? Here the people we spoke to became squeamish once more. "Does [life] begin at conception?" Mark Fielder thought out loud. "Does it begin at birth? Does it begin a year after it's born? Who makes that call? I don't know. *I guess I think it really is up to the woman to make that determination of when a life begins.* An institution like the church or like government should not interfere with the autonomy of the woman to make the determination of when life begins."

Ann Plotz insisted there had to be limits to the practice of abortion. She relied on intuition and a feeling of what would be right. "I don't think that fetuses beyond twelve weeks should be aborted," she said. "They turn into humans. Before that I don't think they are. I really think that the time factor has to be put in [the law]—except if there are medical problems." We asked if there should be actual legal restrictions after twelve weeks that the government enforced. "Yes, I'd feel much more comfortable with that," she said. Five minutes later, though, she baldly asserted her view that "the whole thing with the government being involved and making abortion legal or not, I think that is ridiculous. I just don't think the courts should be in this either."

Rebecca Darmin, among others, also spoke of the need for "some kind of consensus on [when life begins] in order to keep the country intact" but, like Mark Fielder, did not want the government to have any role in forming or articulating that consensus. Betsy McRae thought that life began when it "can exist on its own," and for this reason she found late-term abortions abhorrent. In this she saw it appropriate for the state to step in. But then she retreated from this view, adamant in her hostility to the state's involvement: "I just don't want the government involved at any level."

Barry Walker also thought there should be some limits to the practice of abortion. Though he said he leaned to the pro-choice side of the controversy, he said that the gestating child represents life: "There's no doubt about that!" So when would he say that "life in the womb" should be protected? "Hey, I'm no Abraham. I mean, I don't have the kind of wisdom that it takes to make that kind of decision. I don't know. And I have no idea how you could legislate something like that."

Here, too, the language of sentiment provided the grid through which most people finally responded to the presence and role of the state in this controversy. The emotions, needless to say, pull in different directions.

Rights Talk

In working through the tensions inherent in a discussion about the role of government in this issue, the word *rights* was invoked again and again. This came as no surprise, since the "right to life" and the "right to choose" are the respective rallying cries of the two movements. But even for those in the middle, the word was invoked and then qualified as a means of positioning themselves in the controversy. Here too, though, the word was spoken reflexively. It is only fair to push beyond the reflex to the questions of substance—namely, where do rights come from? And how does one come to say that an unborn baby has a right to life, or a woman a right to choose?

The answers were mixed, as one might suppose, in terms of both substance and sophistication. Among those leaning toward the pro-life position, the answers given were fairly predictable, since all were either churchgoing evangelicals or Catholics. Saundra Ferris, the graduate student in art history from Chicago, was unusually articulate about the matter. She identified herself with what she called a "Christian version of natural law." Though one might find aberrations, she explained, in general there is "a law that's written on our hearts by God." As evidence she argues that "general moral codes that develop seem to develop in every culture and are common to all humans." And it is here that she believes that the right to life, at least at some point, is guaranteed. Susan Alder, who described herself as a "Christian theist," echoed this theme when she spoke of "a transcendent law that is above human laws" and said that it was here where one found a right to life.

Most of those in the middle of the controversy who nevertheless leaned to the pro-life side were more like Karen Pentalla, Marie Tagliano, or Sue Whittle. Sue stated simply that rights "come from God." "From my perspective", she explained, "I feel like the right to life is probably the most important right." One could hear confidence in this, to be sure, but something less than certainty. The assertion, after all, was expressed as a feeling and qualified as merely her own perspective.

This diffidence was reflected in Marie's views as well. When asked about rights and where they came from she said, "Geez, I don't know. . . . I guess basically my whole thought on this is based on Christianity, I guess. To me, I just guess I just feel that that baby does have a right to live. It doesn't have anyone to speak for it, but I think it's just a God-given right to life." What about those who say they have a right to choose? "It's just the way they feel about it—I don't. To me, I don't personally have a right to take that life away. That's just the way I think about it."

Karen conveyed the same sentiment, but in a way that was more ardent if no less precise. As she explained, "People nowadays feel that they have all these rights. Sure, in a lot of things you do, you do have to be able to make choices to make your life go how you want it. I think, though, that people try to carry this too far by trying to plan out every single part of their lives. But they had nothing to do with the creation of life. It's just something that can happen when two people have intercourse. They take that risk. Now they do have a right to prevent [fertilization], but [once that has happened] they don't have a right to end it."

For those leaning toward the pro-choice position, the responses were of a very different cast. On this side, none made any strong appeal to God or to Nature (capital N) as the source or justification of rights. Rights were much more—well, human and contingent. Sarah Cooper, an eighth-grade social studies teacher, was fairly typical of the pattern. When asked where rights (as in the "right to choose" or the "right to life") come from, she offered this reply: "We're social animals. Society created us and constructed these rights. Some people say there's a natural law, that rights are innate. It's not necessarily true. There's no way to know whether there's a higher law out there, that there's a God, that there's a truth with a capital T. I do like to think that there is something heavier and more important about certain rights, like individual rights, but then I think that's totally American; it doesn't apply to other countries. . . . I guess I'm uncomfortable saying that there's a higher law to appeal to."

She was not the only one uncomfortable appealing to a higher law to defend the notion of individual rights or a right to privacy central to the abortion liberty. "I suppose you could say that God gave us these rights," said Kelly Gorman, "but they are implemented by men, so you might as well say that rights come from people or maybe society in the aggregate—laying down what other people should be allowed to do. That's really where they come from."

Most of those who leaned to this side of the controversy responded to the "rights" question a bit less reflectively, simply answering "the government" or "the Constitution" and preferring to leave it at that. Glenda Goetz, a computer analyst from Wilmington, Delaware, was one of these. Given her reply, we asked Glenda to reflect about the nature of these rights. We asked her to imagine the government making abortion completely illegal. Would the right still exist, say, in some ultimate sense? "I guess there's a legal right and then there's a personal right," she said. "Your personal right is the way you feel—what you feel is right to do." If other people do not recognize that right, "there's a legal consequence." "I think you have the ability to do whatever you want to," she went on to explain, "but within the law you don't have the right to." We then asked if she believed she had a personal right, but that it would be okay if other people did not agree. "Yeah. That's why we have the legal system. It's society that comes up with our rights, and then you put up laws to enforce it."

Gary Jones, an executive in a voluntary association based in Washington, D.C., reflected on individual rights and responsibilities in a similar way. "A sense of responsibility to care for others really only exists if someone believes in it and takes it on. Some people do feel that responsibility, and they get active in churches and social work and volunteer agencies and so forth. Other people don't feel that responsibility, and they never get involved in work like that. But God doesn't create that responsibility and say you ought to be doing that, nor does he create rights and say that these rights exist. I don't think that rights come from anywhere inherently except that people who agree on certain rights in a democratic country establish them in law, and then the rights do exist."

Though invoked regularly, there was more than a little vagueness in people's use of the term *rights*. People often spoke of them much as they would speak of "wants"—as the rightful demands of a consumer. More significantly, there was no common understanding of where rights come from or how they might be grounded. For some, rights originated from God; for others, they were social constructions agreed upon by consensus; for others, they were simply privileges conferred by the state; and for still others, rights were strictly personal.

Worry About Overpopulation

Another factor that stirred deep emotions as people related to the abortion controversy was the problem of overpopulation. We never raised the issue in our conversations; it just came up voluntarily, particularly among those who maintained pro-choice sensibilities. Among these, abortion was regarded as a proper response to the problem of overpopulation, particularly among the poor. The emotional connection, however, was mixed.

For some, like Kate Beck, the emotional connection was fear. "If you wipe out all of the moral part of it—God, religion, et cetera—and get right down to dollars and cents, you know, plain economics," she said, "you can see that this country cannot afford to keep on having women on welfare having babies, and that's why abortion needs to stay legal."

For others, it was a sense of compassion. Barry Walker, a forty-eight-year-old black photographer from Denver, put it this way: "I grew up in a very poor environment, where I think a lot of people who, had they had the option, probably would have opted to make their lives a little simpler. The larger the family, the less means there are to support everyone, like giving the kids a proper education. I mean, I come from a place where there are lots of single mothers and welfare and stuff like that. So I think limiting the number of children had by a lot of people that I grew up around would have been a good idea. Their resources could have been directed a little more effectively than they were."

Alice Horning was even more explicit. "You see so many babies that are born to teenage, unwed mothers, ones who have been on drugs, ones who really had a very poor chance in life. I think abortion should be legal in situations like these. I don't think it's fair to the child. They need a fair shake. . . . I just don't think that God wants us to have a lot of underfed babies, starving babies, a lot of children who are in great want for medical services and things of that sort."

For still others, like Betsy McRae, the emotional connection between abortion and overpopulation was a measure of anger. "It seems to be the lower socioeconomic classes of people; they are the ones uneducated and just screwing and having children by the dozens. It's not healthy for the survival of society. There are so many unwanted kids being born, and that's where I see abortion as something that should be able to happen or even suggested to some of these nineteen-year-old street people."

The issue, it becomes clear, is not just overpopulation, but the overpopulation of the country by poor children and minority children.[5]

The Politics of Ambivalence

Surely it is unrealistic to imagine that the average citizen can be fully informed and entirely rational about most public affairs. The amount of information is simply too overwhelming. For this reason alone it is unwise to be too sentimental about the "common person." Nevertheless, even in a society as large and complex as ours, it is not unrealistic to imagine that citizens possess enough knowledge and sophistication to exert pressure upward—pressure upon politicians, special interest groups, and the like to elevate the content and conduct of democratic process. If so, then what is the possibility that such pressure could be generated? The answer, in brief, is this: it is not so much that people are unwilling, but rather that they are ill equipped for such a task.

The problem of the general illiteracy surrounding abortion law bears repeating here: there is simply no agreement about the law over which people so passionately disagree. So the foundation of public knowledge and understanding about the issue is shaky to begin with. As individuals reflect about abortion, the first and instinctual appeal people make to ground their views is to personal experience. There is nothing wrong with this in itself. From the vantage point of what will enhance public argument, however, there is a problem—namely, that each person's experience represents a different empirical base, and from this there is no easy way to predict how a given experience will affect one's views of the controversy. One woman's abortion may lead her to embrace pro-life views, while that of another woman will lead her to a pro-choice position. There is simply no common ground to be found in *personal* experience.

Individuals will appeal to humanistic or theistic traditions of moral reasoning—the languages of conviction—but the appeal is very often weak or qualified as private and personal beliefs. As such, these traditions provide scant resources for people to engage each other substantively over abortion, public policy, the nature of rights, or even the role of government.

And then there is the omnipresent play of people's emotions. This is seen in the strong but often contradictory feelings people have about the act of abortion, about the role of government, about the law, and about the activists, as well as in the tendency for people to frame their views with the vocabulary of sentiment. One might ask, what is the big deal about emotion having such a central play in this controversy? After all, abortion is a deeply emotional issue. The point is not to sever our emotions from this issue or any other. To do so is to dehumanize controversy and the players and events that they comprise. Rather, the deep and conflicting emotions of the abortion dispute are rooted (as they are for all of the particular controversies of the culture war) in categories of moral understanding that have become largely unconnected to any formal or theoretical schemes of moral reflection. The task, then, is to call out those categories into consciousness and into public reflection. Otherwise, upon what else is there to build public argument?

In brief, *without a base of knowledge about the law, without traditions of moral understanding to draw upon, and without cohesive moral communities within whose values, norms, and ideals our lives are patterned, all we have left are our emotions. Public debate among citizens becomes an exercise in emoting toward one another.* Alas, this is just the model of public engagement to which Roger Rosenblatt, in his book *Life Itself* (see Chapter One), would have us aspire.

Clearly all Americans need not become moral philosophers versed in humanistic and theistic traditions of moral reasoning. But if all there is to public understanding is intuition and sentiment, then all we can do is express our mutually opposed sense of revulsion to one another. Surely, as the survey data from Chapter Four make clear, people's sentiments about abortion do tend to derive from latent assumptions and beliefs. The influence of these assumptions and beliefs is much stronger than the people holding them suppose. Yet still, most people are not at all self-conscious about them, rarely make an appeal to them, and cannot articulate the binding authority of these beliefs over their feelings of abortion. They cannot help but respond viscerally to the images and rhetoric of the issue.

We hardly need to be reminded that the political appeals of the interest groups take advantage of this state of affairs. Virtually all of these appeals—whether in direct mail, paid political advertisements, or television sound bites—play to the emotions of people and little if anything else. Such appeals, as was discussed in Chapter Two, are pitched almost exclusively in the distorting language of sentiment. On such grounds alone, it will be nigh impossible to either elevate public debate, or to hold public leaders or the special agenda organizations accountable. Matters are made worse. The practices of a shallow democracy are reinforced; the massive aberrations such practices represent become normalized.

Yet this is not the end of the matter. The deepenings required by a substantive democracy can occur. Central to that coming about are the middle institutions of civil society, institutions uniquely capable of equipping citizens for substantive democratic life.

— PART IV —

Searching Within the Institutions of Civil Society

The Politics of Failed Purpose

— 6 —

The Politics of Civil Society
How Civic Institutions Mediate Conflict

It is a commonplace, though one that is vastly underappreciated, that the founders of the American republic held the democratic experiment as a success only if citizens participated in an informed and enlightened way. "Whenever the people are well-informed," Jefferson wrote once in a letter to a friend, "they can be trusted with their own government; [so] that whenever things get so far wrong as to attract their notice, they may be relied on to set them to rights."[1] To another he implored, "Preach, my dear Sir, a crusade against ignorance; establish and improve the law for educating the common people. Let our countrymen know, that the people alone can protect us against these evils [of tyranny], and that the tax which will be paid for this purpose, is not more than the thousandth part of what will be paid to kings, priests and nobles, who will rise up among us if we leave the people in ignorance."[2] Jefferson was not alone, of course. The necessity of an enlightened citizenry to the vitality of democracy was a theme often repeated by the entire chorus of eighteenth-century visionaries: Washington, Madison, and Adams, among others.

But how are citizens to become "enlightened"—equipped to participate in a just and legitimate ordering of public life, even if only in the most elementary of ways? How is civic competence encouraged? Ironically, it is through participation in public life itself. A vital democracy educates citizens into responsible participation through responsible association and engagement in public affairs. This may not be a terribly efficient way for a government to run, but as the "ancients" understood it, efficiency was not the goal of good government. Rather, good government was that which "best promoted the virtue and intelligence of the people."[3] By so incorporating people into the affairs of public life and tending to the improvement of their character, a vital democracy would be established and enhanced.

Clearly, as Jefferson himself alluded above, public education of one sort or another would be an essential part of the process. But public education is just one of a wide range of institutions that constitute civil society. These are the institutions that stand in between the individual and the state, mediating between private interests and concerns and the functioning of the government: the press, professional organizations, philanthropic institutions, and institutions of faith (churches, synagogues, denominations, and the like). Unlike the special agenda organizations, which stand for one set of interests or another, these institutions exist for all citizens. They are not exclusive but rather exist as a central component of common life, providing either a forum for substantive public debate, a stimulus to it, or a source of information that makes it possible.

This matter is acutely relevant to the problem at hand. If the only just way beyond the stalemates of public controversy is *through* them—in the hard work of substantive public reflection and discourse—then it is essential to appreciate how these public institutions mediate public controversy to the larger body of citizens. My purpose in this chapter is to briefly explore the ways in which a number of these institutions respond to the problem at hand, the controversy over abortion.

The Press

It is impossible to underplay the significance of the press in civil society for the enlivening of democratic experience. Jefferson himself argued that the press was "the best instrument for enlightening the mind of man, and improving him as a rational, moral and social being."[4] Its power remains as strong as it was in Jefferson's day, yet its public character has changed significantly.

From the founding of the republic through the antebellum period, the press was fiercely partisan.[5] This was largely due to the financing of the major newspapers, more often than not, by political parties or partisan organizations. As such, libelous assaults on public figures (Jefferson himself was the target of unparalleled press attacks), vulgar political humor, and blatant lies were the order of the day. Even through the last half of the nineteenth century, as they became independent of parties, newspapers made little effort to impose a sharp line of distinction between news reporting and editorial content. These were the days of the "penny press" and, later, "yellow journalism," a time when sensationalism titillated the public imagination, provoked controversy, and in turn, fueled the expansion of the newspaper industry. Thus newspapers throughout the century functioned, as Christopher Lasch has summarized, as "journals of opinion in which the reader expected to find a definite point of view, together with unrelenting criticism of opposing points of view."[6]

The reform of the press toward a code of professional detachment and objectivity did not come until the early decades of the twentieth century. It was Walter Lippmann who was perhaps most influential in setting this course for modern journalism. Lippmann, in his early years, fully endorsed the Jeffersonian view that only enlightened political participation could serve and sustain democracy and that the press held the high and noble responsibility of enlightening the masses. "The real enemy [of democracy]," he wrote in 1920, "is ignorance, from which all of us, conservative, liberal and revolutionary, suffer."[7] Standing against this, according to Lippmann, was the newspaper: "in all literalness the bible of democracy, the book out of which a people determines its conduct. It is the only serious book most people read. It is the only book they read every day."[8]

Yet Lippmann, caught up in the rising spirit of early twentieth-century progressivism, insisted that the task of journalism was to break with its long tradition of muckraking and turn its commitment to providing the public with reliable information. In polemics like

Liberty and the News (1920), Lippmann wrote of the necessity of "going behind opinion to the information which it exploits, and in making the validity of the news our ideal"; of going "back of our opinions to the neutral facts for unity and refreshment of spirit"; and that "the administration of public information toward greater accuracy and more successful analysis is the highway of liberty." For the press to accept this responsibility, he argued, not only would enlighten the mind of the citizen but would protect for "the public interest that which all the special interests in the world are most anxious to corrupt."[9]

Though his romanticism about the "common man" was to unravel a few years later,[10] Lippmann's polemic against journalistic muckraking fit the mood of the country and of the profession, too, for change in the press establishment did come. Notwithstanding the influence of critical studies on journalistic education, the standard articulated by Lippmann has been handed down to the present as the code by which most journalists are still trained and the ideal that the consumer of news has come to expect.

Understanding the transformation of journalism from a strictly partisan orientation to one of positivist neutrality adds new light to the oft-heard complaint today that the press is biased. The implication here is that in earlier times, journalists were not biased but held a higher standard of professional conduct. Of course, nothing could be further from the truth. But here is the rub: while the nineteenth-century press was partisan, *it made no pretense to be otherwise.* The problem today is just the opposite, that when personal prejudices or class interests find their way into news reporting, they do so under the pose of neutrality and fairness.

The criticisms of journalistic bias we hear nowadays are mixed—it invariably depends upon who is doing the criticizing—but on all sides, conspiracy theories abound. From what remains of the New Left, the complaint continues to be what it has always been: that the press is captive to the interests of the economic or political establishment.[11] (If it were as simple as that, Jesse Helms would never have tried to buy majority stock in CBS back in 1985, and the religious right would not have set up their thriving alternative media empires in the 1980s; there would have been no need.) From conservatives (especially cultural conservatives), the complaint is that the media establishment is essentially captive to the interests of the liberal wing of the Democratic party.[12] (Here again, it is not so simple as this. Otherwise, four out of the past six presidential elections would have gone the other way, the Equal Rights Amendment would be the law of the land, *Roe* would have remained unchallenged, and so on.)

Yet these opposite complaints do not somehow cancel each other out, leaving the impression that the press is neutral after all. Clearly both sets of criticisms make valid points, but the reality of the politics of press coverage is rooted in a much more complicated amalgamation of factors than either set of critics would be eager to admit. The region and constituency for various media outlets, for example, are rarely considered in such generalizations, nor are the individual variations among journalists in particular news organizations. There is also a great deal of variation from issue to issue in the political leanings of the press. The main problem of the criticisms derives from the blanket generalizations they make; invariably the charges are blown out of proportion. In the end, one can only explore how the press mediates public controversy issue by issue.

Covering Abortion in the News

When it comes to the coverage of the abortion controversy, one can find a wide range in the manner and quality of reporting. Individual journalists and editorial writers can be found on all sides of this issue, and within the larger body of work one can find journalism that is studiously evenhanded. It is fair to say that most journalists try to be fair and, indeed, believe they are. But while intentions are noble, on balance, the evidence shows a distinct tendency to report the issue from a position favorable to the pro-choice perspective and agenda. There is no conspiracy and probably little if any calculation in the way this works out. Indeed, charges of *deliberate* bias in abortion coverage are invalid in almost all cases; a product of the overactive imaginations of war-weary pro-life activists. But whether deliberate or not, when the prestige press mediates the abortion controversy to the public, the evidence (anecdotal and systematic) indicates that, as a whole, they do so in a way that portrays the pro-choice agenda far more favorably than the pro-life agenda.

A simple illustration can be found in media portrayals of the leaders of opposing movements. Here again, many of the articles written over the years on these leaders are well crafted and dispassionate in their descriptions.[13] But when bias seeps into the reporting, it does so in the predictable ways.

Of Planned Parenthood's Faye Wattleton, *Time* magazine said (in a profile entitled "Nothing Less Than Perfect") that she was "self-possessed, imperturbable, smoothly articulate ... imperially slim and sleekly dressed ... a stunning refutation of the cliché of the dowdy feminist." The *New York Times Magazine* featured her as well, describing her as "relentlessly high-minded," "telegenic," "immaculately tailored," and "a striking six-footer with an aristocratic bearing."[14] The *New York Times Magazine* also featured NOW's Patricia Ireland. This portrayal was not quite as glowing as the one on Wattleton, questioning, for example, whether Ireland spoke for today's women. Even so, her public style was characterized by "cool grace and humor," her physical appearance was marked by "a winsome smile, a perfectly sculptured pageboy and a sleek wardrobe," and her abilities as a leader were defined by sensitivity, "ameliorative skills" and "logical skills."[15] Describing NARAL's Kate Michelman, *Regardie's* said she was "articulate, personable, and media savvy with an on-camera presence that's always thoughtful and never combative." Other publications ranging from *Newsweek* to the *Boston Globe*, the *Washington Post,* and the *Atlanta Journal-Constitution* simply portrayed Michelman through her own words without editorial comment.

Now, the contrast. In portrayals of Operation Rescue's Randall Terry, there is nearly always editorial comment. He is almost universally described in the major print media as "a former used car salesman." The *New York Review of Books* went further, speaking of him as a "zealot" not going "into the storm of publicity ballasted by much knowledge."[16] A portrayal in *Rolling Stone* was even less generous, saying that "nearly everything about Terry seems adolescent"; that his "quirky, wrinkled intelligence has been only slightly pressed by education"; and that he is one who "knows all of life's answers without condescending to ponder its questions" and has an "expansive ego."[17] The *Washington Post Magazine* profiled American Life League's Judy Brown in 1986 in a similar way, describing her repeatedly as a "true believer" and highlighting her background as a manager with K-mart and her current leadership of a "moral minority" of "absolutists."[18]

The point need not be belabored. One is inclined to conclude from these accounts that pro-choice leaders tend to be intelligent, articulate, and generally impressive people, compared to a pro-life leadership that tends to be common, sanctimonious, and extreme. Reflecting on Randall Terry, a journalist at the *Boston Globe* conceded that "we [she and her colleagues in the media] were [in her opinion] delighted to find out that he sold used cars." The reason, she explained, was that the phrase suggested something "a little unscrupulous . . . not quite trustworthy."[19]

But if this is an illustration of the general unevenness reporters give to their work covering abortion activists, is it at all representative of the way the media covers abortion generally? According to David Shaw, a staff writer for the *Los Angeles Times* who investigated abortion coverage extensively in 1990, the answer, with some qualifications, is yes. He wrote at the start of his series that "careful examination of stories published and broadcast reveals scores of examples, large and small, that can only be characterized as unfair to the opponents of abortion, either in content, tone, choice of language or prominence of play."[20]

Overall, Shaw found, among other things, that the news media consistently used language and images that framed the abortion debate in terms that implicitly favored pro-choice advocates; that the latter were quoted more frequently and characterized more favorably than pro-life advocates; and that many news organizations had given more prominent play to stories on rallies and electoral and legislative victories by advocates of abortion rights than to similar stories that drew attention to the vitality of the pro-life movement.

Take, for example, the way in which the controversy is framed. In this, Shaw explains, there has been a distinct tendency to use language and symbols that are largely favorable to the pro-choice construction of the issue in the way it emphasizes the presumed rights of the woman rather than the rights or the life of the fetus:

When the networks broadcast an abortion story, the backdrop has often been the large word "abortion"—with the first "O" in the word stylized into the biological symbol for female. The networks could just as easily stylize the "O" to represent a womb, with a drawing of a fetus inside. But they don't. When *Time* magazine published a cover story on abortion last year, the cover was a drawing of a woman; when *Newsweek* published a cover story on abortion two months later, its cover featured a photo of a pregnant woman. Neither cover depicted a fetus. . . . When the *Washington Post* wrote about proposed anti-abortion legislation in Louisiana last month, it spoke of the state House of Representatives making a decision on "a woman's reproductive rights." As Douglas Johnson, legislative director for the National Right to Life Committee, pointed out, "In discussing abortion as a matter of 'a woman's reproductive rights,' the *Post* adopts both the paradigm and the polemic of the abortion-rights lobby." When the *Los Angeles Times* covered the same story, it referred to the proposed legislation as "the nation's harshest." That's the view of abortion-rights advocates; it's "harsh" toward women's rights. But abortion opponents regard the legislation as benevolent—toward the fetus. . . . The Associated Press, *Washington Post, Boston Globe* and *Time* magazine, among others, have referred to those who oppose abortion "even in the cases of rape and incest" (circumstances under which most people approve of abortion). But the media almost never refer to those who favor abortion rights "even in the final weeks of pregnancy" (circumstances under which most people oppose abortion).[21]

Shaw also contends that events, issues, and stories favorable to abortion opponents have been sometimes ignored or given minimal attention by the media. "I remember in particular," he recounts, "a story by Bob Woodward [of the *Washington Post*] in 1989 disclosing that two U.S. Supreme Court justices who had played a major role in the *Roe v. Wade* decision had conceded, in private memos, that they knew they were 'legislating policy and exceeding [the court's] authority as the interpreter, not the maker, of law.' If a journalist of Woodward's stature had discovered private memos showing, say, that justices knew they were 'exceeding the court's authority' in the *Webster* decision . . . the media would have swarmed all over the story. Except for a brief mention in *Newsweek* three months later, the major national media didn't touch it."[22]

Along this line, Shaw observed that "newspaper editorial writers and columnists long sensitive to charges of police brutality and violations of First Amendment rights and other civil liberties in cases involving minority and anti-war protests, had largely ignored these questions when Operation Rescue and other abortion opponents had raised them."[23] His observation has some merit. Consider protest at abortion clinics. However else one may want to character- ize these protests (either as a rescue of unborn children or as a ter- rorist attack on women), everyone agrees that the law is being deliberately broken, albeit by nonviolent or civilly disobedient means. Though the circumstances are quite different, the same is true of the protests of the civil rights era. But in the succession of sit-ins beginning in 1960, 3,600 people were arrested. By contrast, 65,000 arrests of anti-abortion protesters were made between 1987 and 1991. Rescues are reported, but their significance is not. Poli- tics aside, abortion protest is civil disobedience, and the volume of arrests is probably greater than that of any other "rights" movement in this century. One might well wonder why the media establish- ment has not explored the similarities and dissimilarities of these cases. The answer would seem to be that most journalists and edi- tors accept the pro-choice interpretation, maintaining that the protests today share nothing at all in common with those of the early 1960s.

The mystery of the media's general failure to explore the sub- stance of abortion protest and counterprotest is deepened when considering the matter of the civil liberties of the protesters. Dozens of allegations have been made in sworn depositions by abor- tion protesters (and are substantiated by witnesses and videotape) of excessive force and police brutality in Los Angeles, Santa Clara (in California), Atlanta, West Hartford (in Connecticut), and Pitts- burgh. In one instance, a seventy-two-year-old bishop was hand- cuffed behind his back and then lifted from the ground, where he was sitting, by billy clubs between his wrists. Both of his shoulders were dislocated. In another case seventeen female college students were required to take their clothes off and were forced to walk in the nude (and, in some instances, crawl).[24] Protesters have endured "pain compliance" technology (in other words, torture), have been denied medical care in jail, and have been held incommunicado in some cases for up to five days. Again, one might imagine that these facts would be of passing interest to journalists, particularly since similar allegations during the civil rights and antiwar period re- ceived great attention, but with one or two exceptions, the journalistic establishment has neither probed the allegations nor even questioned the appropriateness of such police actions.[25] Rather, the response has been one of silence.[26]

Anecdotes are compelling but not entirely convincing. More systematic evidence of an overall tendency to favor the pro-choice construction of the controversy comes from a content analysis of abortion coverage conducted during the first nine months of 1989 (the months leading up to and right after the Supreme Court's *Webster* decision). The study, performed by the Center for Media and Public Affairs (CMPA), showed that the television networks described abortion-rights organizations as "pro-choice" in 74 percent of their references, while they described abortion opponents as "pro-life" only 6 percent of the time.[27] The print media in the study performed much more fairly but were still twice as likely to use the term *pro-choice* than *pro-life*. Evidence of this leaning is seen further in the sources journalists use to document their stories. As mentioned in passing in Chapter Three, most of the sources journalists rely upon on the abortion beat come from the advocacy groups. But according to the CMPA study just mentioned, journalists drew up to 40 percent more often from pro-choice advocates than from pro-life advocates.[28]

Has reporting improved since the years when these studies were published? Shaw himself believes so. Indeed it has, but perhaps less than he might have suspected (and pro-lifers hoped for). A follow-up study of abortion coverage in the months leading up to and immediately after the *Casey* decision in 1992 showed that in both print and electronic media, reporters still quoted pro-choice advocates about 30 percent more than pro-life advocates.[29] (Even when they did quote pro-life sources, they were overwhelmingly likely to quote representatives of one of the most strident pro-life groups, Operation Rescue; when they quoted pro-choice representatives, they were most likely to be from the institutional mainstream of Planned Parenthood.)[30] Though reporters for newspapers learned to use *anti-abortion* and *abortion-rights* most of the time, when they did lapse from the practice they were about twice as likely to use the term *pro-choice* than *pro-life*.[31] Among reporters from newsmagazines and television news, this tendency was even more pronounced.[32] Finally, opinion columns and editorials in major newspapers were five times as likely to be pro-choice than pro-life.[33]

In the end, the most telling confirmation of Shaw's observations came from a woman active in ACLU abortion-rights work. "Well, I wish you hadn't written that," she confessed to Shaw, "but we certainly can't argue with you. We've loved having the media's support, but we've been wondering when someone would finally blow the whistle."[34]

The Much Greater Problem of Superficiality

There is a far greater problem, in my view, that in many ways encompasses but also overshadows the problems of a witting or unwitting bias. This is the problem of superficiality—the failure, or perhaps inability, to explore the deeper issues and implications of the abortion controversy. This is true about the coverage of perhaps all of the controversies of the culture war.

With regard to the dispute over abortion, one must look very hard to find any discussion of the factors that lead a woman to seek an abortion or the agony involved in coming to this choice. One must look even harder to find a discussion of the meaning of a woman's "right to choose" vis-à-vis other parties (from the biological father to the state) who may claim a right as well. Likewise there has been virtually no reporting at all on the debate over the moral status of the fetus. What is being aborted, after all? Similarly, one would be hard-pressed to find any reporting on the factors that lead abortion providers to risk harassment and hardship to end unwanted pregnancies and anti-abortion protesters to risk jail sentences to protect life in the womb. So, too, debate over the role of religion and religious institutions in this realm of public policy is, for all practical purposes, nonexistent. Reporting on the abortion controversy in the national media is, then, remarkable for its superficiality. Its overall failure to penetrate the claims made by each side, and to go beyond the rhetoric, permits whatever public discussion there is to continue at the level of slogans exchanged.

There are at least five interrelated factors that contribute to this. The first is *a predisposition to dichotomize* the subject. Newspapers, radio, and television have long been dramatic media. This has certainly not abated over the years. But intrinsic to the forms is a narrative structure that depends in large part upon the interplay of antagonists and protagonists, heroes and villains, victims and victimizers, and so on. Conflict involving competing interest groups, highly visible litigation, and inflamed partisan rhetoric obviously plays to this predisposition. Yet it is partly in the failure to listen to other voices that do not fit neatly in the grid of rhetorical extremes—the voices of scholars, of people who are genuinely and thoughtfully ambivalent, and of people whose otherwise ordinary lives have been caught up in public dispute—that public discourse becomes more polarized than we as a nation are.

A second factor is *the tendency to reduce controversy to the struggle for power.* Cultural disputes obviously develop a political dimension to them, but the tendency is to frame everything in terms of the question of who has power and who does not. Barbara Brotman of the *Chicago Tribune* admitted as much: "We've gotten bogged down in reporting the political ups and downs of the sides, like we're covering sports, and we've gotten away from reporting the issues."[35] When the cultural, moral, and aesthetic dimensions of controversy are ignored or overlooked in favor of the legal or political, public sensibilities and expectations cannot help but be framed by the zero-sum logic of winners and losers. We come to imagine that what divides us can be addressed merely through administrative manipulation or technical innovation. Thus the possibility of serious, substantive argument is rendered even more difficult.

A third factor, related to the first two, is the *commercial pressure* to make news reporting competitive with prime-time entertainment. The point need not be belabored, but clearly ratings, market share, and advertising dollars create tremendous pressure to substitute style for substance in news reporting. As Eric Sevareid reflected a decade ago about the downfall of CBS News, the trouble began when the news organization began to turn a profit. "People forget," he said, "that television news started out as a loss leader."[36] It was expected to lose money. But when it became clear that each rating point meant several million dollars a year in ad revenue, then the goal was no longer quality but ratings. MTV's entrée into political reporting only accelerates this trend.[37] As MTV becomes "a full-service network," as its officials plan, even the new and improved forms of "infotainment" that exist in the major networks today will increasing look like dinosaurs. Print media, and newspapers in particular, are not exempt from these pressures either, as *USA Today* (and the competition it represents) illustrates.

A fourth factor is the news "beats" themselves, a euphemism for *journalistic specialization.* The increasing specialization of tasks is commonplace in all work and professions in the modern world, but it has particular consequences in covering the culture war. The problem here is that most of the controversies I am talking about typically involve several layers of meaning. The conflict over the funding priorities of the National Endowment for the Arts, for example, does not fit neatly into any particular beat. It isn't arts reporting, religion reporting, legal reporting, or even political reporting, strictly speaking, but a curious amalgam of all of these. Getting to the heart of the issue requires multiple competencies. The same can be said for controversy surrounding sex education in city schools. Is it education? City politics? Legal reporting/civil liberties? Who is sophisticated enough to get at the complexities of this? Without systematic study, my intuition is that most journalists, living with a deadline and not wanting to make mistakes, simply fall back on what they know. More often than not, this means a reporting of the dynamics of power politics in the situation.

A fifth factor is *the culture of the news room*—and here we come back briefly to the issue of journalistic prejudice. In sociology, it is a commonplace that one's location in the social world fundamentally shapes one's worldview. It is no different with the news media. The disproportionately white, middle- and upper-middle-class, highly educated, and secular urban background of most journalists is fertile soil for a liberal modernist worldview, and this cannot help but influence their framing of issues. Let me be clear: I would affirm the sincerity of most journalists in their trade—their effort to be fair. I would also affirm the journalists' ability to transcend their class culture. The problem is often not so much of bias but one of tone deafness born out of class and cultural predispositions. What this means is that a good many journalists are simply unfamiliar with the experiences and subtleties of meaning that people outside of elite, urban culture impute to their lives.[38] As regards to the abortion controversy, the culture of the newsroom simply assumes the correctness of the pro-choice position.[39]

Some journalists David Shaw spoke to admitted as much. A reporter for National Public Radio put it this way, "we [at NPR] just do not cover this issue because we think it has been decided." A producer at CBS echoed his view: "The struggle I have in the newsroom is to get people to admit that there's still a debate."[40] Still another confessed that in the eyes of most journalists, to take a position opposing abortion "is not a legitimate, civilized position in our society."[41] This attitude is reflected in editorial opinion. According to Shaw's investigation, columns of commentary favoring abortion rights outnumbered those opposing abortion by a margin of more than two to one on the op-ed pages of most of the nation's major dailies.

Peter Steinfels of the *New York Times* has mused with great poignancy about the adequacy of a journalism that fails to go beneath the surface:

> If, in fact, the public debate is a lousy debate, is it sufficient for the media to cover that lousy debate fairly? If we thought of a question like nuclear waste and we found out that both sides of that issue were simply shouting at each other, repeating the same things, would we as reporters want to explore some of the aspects of the nuclear waste issue beyond those making their voice heard publicly? Are there critical aspects of [the abortion controversy] that we do not cover because they are not well represented in the public manifestations of the loud voices?[42]

Steinfels' query is not without contention. Some journalists will argue, and perhaps correctly, that newspapers and other modern media are simply not set up to provide moral analysis of this kind. But even if this is true, there is no reason why reporters cannot raise the questions and seek out those who have credentials in the field to report on what they are saying and debating as a way to lay out some of the complexities of the issue.

In all of this, it is too much to conclude that the problem of superficiality is uniform either within or across news organizations. But the structural pressures toward superficiality are beyond doubt. Investigative journalist Carl Bernstein has written that "the really significant trends in journalism have not been toward a commitment to the best and most complex obtainable version of the truth, [and] not toward building a new journalism based on serious, thoughtful reporting."[43] His indictment goes much further:

> For more than fifteen years we have been moving away from real journalism toward the creation of sleazoid info-tainment culture in

which the lines between Oprah and Phil and Geraldo and Diane and even Ted, between the *New York Post* and *Newsday,* are too often indistinguishable. In this new culture of journalistic titillation, we teach our readers and our viewers that the trivial is significant, that the lurid and the loopy are more important than real news. We do not serve our readers and viewers, we pander to them. And we condescend to them, giving them what we think they want and what we calculate will boost ratings and readership. Many of them, sadly, seem to justify our condescension, and to kindle at the trash. Still, it is the role of journalists to challenge people, not merely to amuse them.[44]

Bernstein concludes that the problem is linked to arrogance. "We have failed," he says, "to open up our own institutions in the media to the same kind of scrutiny that we demand of other powerful institutions in the society. We are no more forthcoming or gracious in acknowledging error or misjudgment than the congressional miscreants and bureaucratic felons we spend so much time scrutinizing."[45]

The Obvious Question

"The real value that we have to add as the media is to give people the information they need to make up their own minds."[46] This statement, made by a colleague of David Shaw's at the *Los Angeles Times,* speaks directly to the problem at hand of how citizens become competent for enlightened participation in a democracy. Jefferson could not have said it better. The question her statement implies is pointed: how well can people make up their own minds if the information they receive is, for the most part, both shallow and often tendentious?

It would be foolish to generalize about the conduct of the press from this discussion. Clearly on some issues the press betrays a conservative bias; on other issues it has demonstrated heroic feats of fairness as well as serious, thoughtful, and probing reporting. But on this issue at least, one cannot shake a measure of doubt that the press has not been, as Jefferson put it, "the best instrument for enlightening the mind of man." A journalistic establishment that does not go beneath the superficiality that too frequently characterizes public discourse concerning the culture war will be part of the problem rather than part of the solution (and resolution) of the conflicts dividing us. Is it any better within other institutions of civil society?

Public Opinion

At first blush, it may seem odd to think of the public opinion research establishment as an institution of civil society. What do "bean counters"—however methodical and scientific they may be—have to do with democracy? In principle, public opinion research operates much like the press, by providing information; in this case, information about the attitudes of the American public on various issues. One may dismiss its intrinsic importance, but few would doubt its actual impact on public discourse and public policy-making. For better or worse, it is a sacred crystal politicians dare not fail to consult.

That public opinion research plays such a visible role in political and social affairs comports, at least on the surface, with its founding vision. More than a scientific method for studying popular attitudes and more than a source of information, public opinion research was originally idealized as a tool for enhancing democratic experience. George Gallup, Sr., the founder of the Gallup Poll, gave voice to this high calling in the Stafford Little Lectures at Princeton University in 1939. There, Gallup argued that the new science of public opinion research would help restore for the nation as a whole the model of the New England town meeting, "one of the earliest and purest forms of democracy." Along with the radio and newspaper, he contended, the entire nation is now

> literally in one great room. . . . The newspapers and the radio conduct the debate on national issues, presenting both information and argument on both sides, just as the townsfolk did in person in the old town meeting. And finally, through the process of the sampling referendum [public opinion surveys], the people, having heard the debate on both sides of every issue, can express their will. After one hundred and fifty years we return to the town meeting. This time the whole nation is within the doors.[47]

In actual practice, though, the institution of public opinion research is often little more than a caricature of this ideal.

Part of the problem stems from the fact that the most visible firms—Gallup, Yankelovich, Harris, and the like—are businesses that live and die by the exigencies of the market. The university-based research centers, like the National Opinion Research Center (NORC) at the University of Chicago or the Center for Survey Research at the University of Michigan, operate much the same way. Keeping overhead and operating costs down, generating a steady flow of paying clients, letting clients' needs drive the research, and so forth are as important as the process of research itself. In the end, the business side of survey research provides a context that heavily shapes the nature and quality of the research.

Consider the practicalities: the cost of a national survey of opinion on a topic can be quite high. Each question on an "omnibus" survey, for example, can cost between eight hundred and twelve hundred dollars, and a complete survey of a national sample of Americans using face-to-face interviews over the period of time it would take to really probe an issue well—say, forty-five to fifty minutes—can be, and usually is, well over one hundred thousand dollars (in 1990 dollars). Obviously there are few independent scholars, newspapers or television networks, or advocacy groups willing or able to handle the expense. So a survey is typically limited to just a few questions. Even federally funded national surveys like the annual General Social Survey funded by the National Science Foundation and run through NORC at the University of Chicago asks only a handful of questions on any one issue. The consequences of this are that the few questions that are posed to the general public by public opinion firms typically elicit sharp contrasts at the extremes, rather than shade and nuance that might reveal ambivalence about issues. The example from research on abortion ("Is abortion murder—yes or no?") has been mentioned already and is but one notorious illustration of this.

The context created by the exigencies of the survey business also means that public attitudes about an issue are generally explored in isolation—that is, as though other issues that engage people's minds and commitments were completely unrelated to it. On a typical omnibus survey, market-oriented questions on toothpaste will follow questions about personal religiosity. Thus the contingencies of the survey research industry make it nearly impossible for the actual research to proceed as part of a larger conversation about political and social theory. The cost of operating any other way is simply too prohibitive.

The net effect of all of this is an intransigent superficiality in our knowledge of what Americans really think about most issues. The problem is plain: *survey research that fails to go beyond the superficialities says very little, lending itself to the ideological manipulations of the antagonists of the culture war.* This is precisely how special agenda organizations on opposing sides of many issues can claim that the majority of Americans support their positions. We have seen this played out in the abortion controversy, where both claims can be accurate enough depending on how questions are actually worded. Survey findings on women's issues, gun control, the death penalty, social welfare, and other issues are all similarly vulnerable. Without more substantive research, this is probably inevitable.

In the final analysis, survey research on the abortion controversy has brought us, at best, a mixture of insight and ignorance into the nature of American public opinion on a matter of great importance. Without attention to more substantive issues, though, the idea that the "sampling referendum," as Gallup called it more than a half century ago, could pave the way for a return to a purer form of democracy is implausible at the least.

Professional Associations

Mediating between the state and individuals working in elite occupations are professional associations. Not single-issue organizations whose vested financial interests are directly related to a particular political goal, their political power vis-à-vis various public issues resides in their apparent disinterestedness; their authority, before both the state and the body politic, rests in an ability to speak expertly in a posture of rational detachment, if not objectivity. It is in this capacity to provide an authority autonomous from the state, then, that professional associations also mediate between the government and citizens.

Professional associations played a significant role in abortion reform in the 1960s and 1970s. Leading up to the Supreme Court's

Roe decision in 1973, numerous professional organizations, including the American Medical Association, the American Bar Association, the American Academy of Pediatrics, and the California Medical Association joined the chorus calling for changes in the law. By so doing they created a climate where abortion reform could be seen by the courts as mainstream. This was especially true in the *Roe* and *Doe* cases. For these, *amicus curiae* ("friend of the court") briefs were submitted by more than twenty broad-based organizations, not least among which were the American College of Obstetricians and Gynecologists, the American Medical Association, the American Women's Medical Association, the New York Academy of Medicine, the American Psychiatric Association, the American Public Health Association, and the American Association of Planned Parenthood Physicians. By contrast, what existed of the pro-life movement at that time could only muster four *amicus* briefs from groups whose identity and agenda could only be perceived by the justices as narrowly single-interest in orientation: the National Right to Life, League for Infants, Fetuses, and the Elderly (LIFE), Americans United for Life, and "certain physicians and fellows of the American College of Obstetricians and Gynecologists."[48]

The impression that professionals and their associations are disinterested voices when speaking out on social and political issues, however, does not withstand closer scrutiny. One need not be a Marxist to recognize that the position professionals or their associations take on a political issue may be indirectly related to their own interests. Their politics may be more a reflection of the moral and ideological affinities members share by virtue of their common social background than of objective findings derived from the particular expertise the profession provides. There are numerous illustrations from which to choose; I will offer one from the American Bar Association and another from the academic discipline of history.

The American Bar Association

As the largest professional association for the nation's lawyers, the American Bar Association (ABA) wields considerable clout. Its power, though, is found not so much in any direct influence it may have over public policy as in the legitimacy it bestows or withholds. When the ABA adopts an official position on an issue, it is in effect placing the imprimatur of law, order, and justice upon a social agenda. For it to oppose a policy officially goes far toward undermining that idea's legitimacy. The ABA's power to legitimate or discredit particular policies, then, is unusual. Thus for the ABA to take one side of the abortion controversy would be, needless to say, a significant event in the playing out of the conflict.

Until early 1990, the ABA avoided taking a position on abortion. But in February of that year, during its midyear meeting in Los Angeles, the ABA's delegates passed a resolution that did not mince words:

> Be it resolved: that the American Bar Association recognizes the fundamental rights of privacy and equality guaranteed by the United States Constitution, and opposes legislation or other governmental action that interferes with the confidential relationship between a pregnant woman and her physician, or with the decision to terminate the pregnancy at any time before the fetus is capable of independent life, as determined by her physician, or thereafter when termination of the pregnancy is necessary to protect the woman's life or health.[49]

The reaction to this strong pro-choice resolution was immediate and intense. Within a few months, nearly 1,500 individual attorneys (out of a total membership of 365,000) had resigned their membership, the state bar of Texas (and its 53,000 members) had threatened secession,[50] there was speculation that entire law firms would pull out, and even law faculties (such as that of the Notre Dame Law School) were poised to withdraw their dues and membership if the resolution was not reversed at the annual meeting six months later.[51]

By the start of the August 1990 meeting, coalitions of attorneys both inside and outside of the organization (including such special agenda organizations as NOW, the Illinois Pro-Choice Alliance, Americans United for Life, the National Right to Life, and the Pro-Life Action League) had mobilized to force the issue to another vote. There was a small contingent wanting the ABA to adopt a pro-life resolution, but the principal conflict was between those wanting to maintain the pro-choice resolution passed in February and those who wanted the ABA to replace it with one that pledged neutrality regarding "constitutional, moral, medical, or other questions involved in a decision to terminate a pregnancy."[52] The Pro-Bar Committee for Abortion Neutrality alone had a budget of $100,000. Its chief opposition, the Committee to Protect the Pro-Choice Resolution, was outspent but still committed significant resources to the battle.

On their own terms, the arguments were very compelling; both sides pitched their views in terms of what would enhance or preserve the credibility of the association. For example, resolution supporters urged the ABA to face, not to step away from, this issue. "You have to make hard choices in controversial times," said one spokesperson. "At the point you are afraid to make a hard choice because you are afraid to alienate a large portion of your membership, I think you lose your effectiveness."[53] "Don't be misled," said another, "the motion to rescind will not create neutrality. It would tell the people of the United States that the nation's lawyers no longer support a woman's right to reproductive freedom."[54] But the opponents of the resolution disagreed. "We have never taken a position which has been directly contrary to the moral principles of a large segment of our membership," said one neutrality supporter. "What we have [in the pro-choice resolution] is a serious weakening of the association by affecting its credibility because part of its credibility is the broad spectrum we represent."[55] For the ABA to take a position on abortion or other controversial issues, said another, "is an intrusion by an overly-anxious ABA to be heard on issues where it has no special competence. If we start acting like a political lobbying group, we'll have trouble attracting members; and I think Congress will laugh at us. Credibility is a depleting resource."[56] And back and forth the arguments went.

By the end of the convention, the ABA's board of governors, its assembly, and its delegates voted to adopt the neutrality resolution. But the matter was anything but resolved. The neutrality position was challenged at the 1992 annual convention in San Francisco, and all of the battles of 1990 were reenacted. This time, neutrality was abandoned in favor of a pro-choice position.[57] The exchanges over this were but echoes of 1990. Outgoing president Talbot D'Alamberte asked the assembly for approval, saying, "Are we as lawyers immobilized by our fear of conflict?" Past ABA president John

Curtin responded by saying, "This resolution will not help people listen but will only add to the din—the shouting." And while Hillary Clinton exhorted the crowd to protect abortion rights, Vice President Dan Quayle accused the ABA leadership of being a Democratic party special interest group. The meeting even witnessed a protest by the Bay Area Women's Action Coalition that included several topless women wearing black tape over their nipples, all chanting, "Hey, hey, ABA; vote pro-choice, vote pro-gay!"

Needless to say, the stage was set for the cycle to occur again, and perhaps well into the future.

281 Historians

These tensions are also played out in academia. If there was any place where one might expect to find a striving for objectivity and fairness in the search for truth, it would be here, and to be sure, most academics operate with very high standards in this regard. But when academics come together as collective entities, they face the same sociological pressures as any organized group. They assert a public identity and authority that often reaches beyond strictly professional interests to partisanship on behalf of a particular agenda. The pressures are perhaps greatest in the social sciences, where professional expertise relates to social and political problems.

By far the most fascinating case of this was in an action not of an official association but of 281 professional historians (a number that grew to more than 400) who drafted and signed an *amicus* brief at the time of the *Webster* case in 1989, supporting *Roe v. Wade,* urging continued abortion liberty. Those involved in the brief were keenly aware of the significance of their involvement: "Never before," the brief began, "have so many professional historians sought to address this Honorable Court in this way."[58]

The Justice Department's case against *Roe* had asserted that American history condemned abortion practice and, in support of this argument, had cited James Mohr's *Abortion in America.* But Mohr himself believed that his account had been misused; the historical record was not so clear. Thus aware of the potential uses and misuses of historical evidence, pro-choice attorneys initiated the drafting of the brief "to provide a rich and accurate description of our national history and tradition in relation to women's liberty to choose whether to terminate a pregnancy."[59] Not only "rich and accurate," but also "authoritative": "We submitted the brief," wrote two of the attorneys providing legal counsel to the historians, "because we believed that without an authoritative statement of abortion history, the Court might use bad or simplistic history to decide the case wrongly."[60]

Two major substantive points were addressed in the brief. The first was that the practice of abortion "was not illegal at common law;" rather, that "through the nineteenth century, American common law decisions uniformly reaffirmed that women committed no offense in seeking abortions."[61] Tolerance toward the woman having an abortion, the authors argued, was the message of the American legal tradition in the past, and this in turn was merely a reflection of the beliefs and practices of ordinary Americans. Cases of abortion we know about in the colonial period, for example, "are described as routine and are unaccompanied by any particular disapproval."[62] Even through the nineteenth century, "abortion remained a widely accepted popular practice," only curtailed when physicians placed controls on it. This was done, the brief explains, not for moral or religious reasons as much as to establish and consolidate their sovereignty over medical practice.[63]

The second major point the brief made was that "the moral value of the fetus became a central issue in American culture and law only in the late twentieth century."[64] The authors did acknowledge that concern for the fetus had been expressed by some, yet they insisted that "this concern was always subsidiary to more mundane social visions and anxieties."[65] The problem with this newly articulated value was that it was "not embedded in our history and tradition and therefore cannot justify the costs and burdens imposed on women when abortion is restricted."[66] In this light, they questioned "whether protection of unborn life has become a surrogate for other social objectives that are no longer tolerated"[67] (such as "keeping women in traditional roles"[68]).

The history of abortion is complex, to be sure, and the *amici* were limited to just thirty pages (plus appendices) to summarize their collective wisdom on the subject. All the same, the brief was fundamentally flawed: its arguments were built upon what many of its drafters and original signatories admitted later in public was a selective use of the historical evidence.[69]

The brief's first contention (that abortion was "not illegal through much of the nation's history" and "not illegal at common law") suggests that abortion was, if not exactly legal, then at least tolerated; elsewhere in the brief it is described as a "liberty." The argument, though, ignored evidence to the contrary dating back to thirteenth-century England. This evidence was acknowledged by such common-law commentators as Edward Coke (sometimes referred to as the "father of the common law"), Matthew Hale, and William Blackstone, and it was reflected in nineteenth-century American legal statutes and case law. In all of these sources one finds evidence that abortion was illegal, particularly after quickening, but in some cases even before.[70] To say further that the woman committed no offense implies no criminal liability for the abortion. But these sources show that in fact there was criminal liability, directed most often at the one performing the abortion but sometimes at the woman having it.

The second contention of the brief (that the moral value of the fetus has only become a central concern in American culture and law in recent times) also comes up against evidence to the contrary. In *Abortion in America,* Mohr offers evidence that suggests that accompanying the self-interests of the medical establishment as a primary reason for their campaign to control abortion was a belief that it was indeed immoral. He argues that "most regular physicians" sincerely believed "that abortion was morally wrong," and that the convergence of this belief with their professional self-interest "helps to explain the intensity of their commitment to the cause."[71] In the brief, this fact is acknowledged only in passing. Mohr himself contended, however, that these physicians defended the value of human life from the time of fertilization and were fierce opponents of any attack on it.[72]

Physicians were not alone in their moral outrage concerning abortion. The most prominent nineteenth-century feminists, including Elizabeth Cady Stanton, Susan B. Anthony, Matilda Gage, Victoria Woodhull, and Mattie Brinkerhoff, were strongly and consistently opposed to abortion, believing that it was "infanticide," "child murder," a "woeful crime," and the "ultimate exploitation of women."[73] This fact is explored by Mohr in his own book, but not acknowledged in the brief. Most social scientists would not doubt for a minute the powerful institutional interests of a professionalizing medical establishment in bringing about sharp regulations in the practice of abortion. But perhaps there was a greater consensus of *moral* opposition to abortion in the nineteenth century than the brief let on.

Curiously, drafters and key signatories knew that evidence existed that contradicted the arguments of the brief, but signed the brief anyway. Sylvia Law, lead counsel to the brief, admitted openly that there was a "tension between truth telling and advocacy." To this she offered the example of the failure to deal with the fact that most nineteenth-century feminists opposed abortion:

> We document the misogyny of the American Medical Association and of the state legislatures that adopted these laws, but we do not address early feminist attitudes. There is a rich literature on this issue, and the question is so important that space limits do not justify excluding it. The problem here was that we could not agree on what to say. Each draft attracted more intelligent critique. In the end, we, the lawyers, decided to punt. Again, the silence is distorting.[74]

Estelle Freedman, a historian at Stanford University and one of the signatories, also admitted that at the end of the process she "still disagreed with a few of the major arguments"[75] of the brief. For example, while she agreed that the brief's assertions about abortion in the eighteenth century were accurate in an absolutely literal sense, she felt this characterization did not quite capture the best understanding of that society's attitudes toward abortion. "Although we do have evidence of the use of abortifacients in this period," she said, "I find it hard to argue that abortion was 'not uncommon,' given the economic and religious motives for childbearing within families."[76] Even more troubling to this scholar was the way in which the silence of the law was implied to read as an awareness and even an acceptance of the social practice of abortion: "By implying that abortion is historically a protected constitutional right, the brief relies solely on the argument of 'rights' to support reproductive choice. . . . I want to note that it is tricky to claim abortion as an inherent and original right given that feminists of the nineteenth century condemned the practice."[77]

The problem here is not just flawed history, but a history understood to be flawed in service of a political agenda. James Mohr, whose book became so prominent in the discussion, admitted that he did not "ultimately consider the brief to be history, as I understand the craft. It was instead legal argument based on historical evidence. Ultimately, it was a political document. Those of us who signed it, signed as citizens, in my opinion as well as historians."[78] Law, too, conceded that "the brief-writing project [was] one element in a larger effort to mobilize pro-choice political power."[79] Freedman also accepted the primacy of partisanship over scholarship by admitting that "for the practical purposes of writing this brief, it was necessary to suspend certain critiques to make common cause and to use the legal and political grounds that are available to us."[80]

Trusting the integrity of the brief after admissions like these is not helped by deconstructing the distinction between advocacy and scholarship, yet this was precisely the position adopted by two other counselors to the document. "If all knowledge is socially shaped, and thus political," they said, "the distinction between advocative and objective scholarship becomes difficult to maintain."[81] Scholarship thus becomes little more than political posturing. Such arguments are always compelling on the surface but pose at least two problems. First, even postmodernist intellectuals who believe that all truth (even academic truth) is socially constructed cannot maintain the simultaneous validity of two opposing claims to truth. Moreover, thinking of this sort tends to undermine the foundation of the effort to do empirically based research. If there is no such thing as objective evidence (because all knowledge is socially manufactured), then disciplines like history are exercises in the creation of fiction. If one concedes the possibility of objectively valid evidence, however, then one also concedes the possibility that evidence may contradict assertions of fact. Enough of this.

In the end, the brief was not so much the "rich," "accurate," and "authoritative" history of abortion law and practice its drafters aspired to produce. Rather, it was a historical account that represented, in part, the partisan interests of 400 citizens who happened to be professional historians. When, in 1992, the *Webster* brief was resubmitted to the Supreme Court with minor changes for *Casey v.*

Pennsylvania Planned Parenthood, a large number of the original signatories did not sign, including James Mohr.[82] My assistants and I called many of these historians to ask why. Many did not sign for the simple reason that they were not contacted by the drafters. But others deliberately chose not to sign it again, in part because of an admission that they could not vouch for the validity of the brief. One professor of history from an elite state university in the Midwest put it this way:

> Because I received the *Webster* brief from someone I respected, that swayed me. I decided to sign the *Webster* brief, but I signed with some misgivings. My misgivings stemmed from the fact that I don't know enough about the issue of early abortion law. When the second letter arrived, I knew that I couldn't in good conscience sign it without taking the time to learn more about the issues. When I didn't have the time to research it, I chose not to sign. I simply don't feel that I can be authoritative on this issue. I suppose that it is really a case of distinguishing your personal feelings on a subject from your ability to be an authority. That is the basis for my decision not to sign. I'm comfortable with the decision to take my name off the list.

Another history professor (from an elite university in the West) who is an expert on the subject reiterated this problem. He said he did not object to the mixing of history and advocacy per se:

> I think history and the historical perspective can be very important in advocacy. . . . What I objected to was that historians were signing a document which was making a case for something that they knew nothing about. *Most of the historians signing the thing know nothing about the history of abortion and abortion law in this country.* That coupled with the idea that we would send the Justices the same brief twice—an act which is simply insulting to the Court—was enough to keep me from signing.

The temptation to use, and even distort, historical analysis and interpretation for partisan purposes is surely as great among cultural conservatives as it is among progressives. Clearly the Justice Department, in its own partisan drive to overturn *Roe,* did not get the historical record right either. But this is why a respect for truth—in all of its complexity, subtlety, contradiction, and paradox—is essential, even when it fails to support one's personal or political commitments. Mohr not only spoke for historians but for all professions when he said, "If we lose credibility as open-minded observers, the power of the opinions we have to offer will be seriously undermined."[83]

Historians, though, are by no means the only academics facing the temptations of partisanship. The American Psychological Association, for example, has adopted official resolutions on an entire range of public policy issues, including abortion policy. As one might predict, the APA frames its positions and objectives in language appropriate to the discipline it represents, and the public pronouncements it makes are, in the main, based upon careful review of the scientific evidence. The same is true for its declarations on abortion—statements based upon a review of the evidence on the psychological effects of unwanted pregnancies and of abortion itself, as well as on the emotional stability of teenage girls in deciding how to handle an unwanted pregnancy.

In tone and substance, the association's testimony is tempered and qualified and stays very close to the data.[84] But from these statements, the association moves quickly to political judgment. In this case it has since 1969 taken a very strong pro-choice position, contending "that the termination of pregnancy be considered a civil right of the pregnant woman." As an association it has, moreover, moved into advocacy, aligning itself with the major special agenda organizations of the pro-choice movement—the ACLU Reproductive Freedom Project, the National Abortion Federation, NARAL, NOW, Planned Parenthood, and the Religious Coalition of Abortion Rights, among others.

Though empirical science can and should inform ethical judgment, in no way can science establish the correctness or adequacy of ethical judgments. This is why the jump from careful scientific work to advocacy strikes one as a bit odd. As with the lawyers of the ABA and the historians of the *Webster* brief, the politics of the APA become more a reflection of the shared values and assumptions of its members than the only logical conclusion one can draw from dispassionate psychological expertise. These tensions and temptations are endemic to the times and to the role that professional associations play in public life. They are even played out among associations that seemingly have little direct interest in an issue like abortion.[85]

Missing the Point

In his book *Abortion: The Clash of Absolutes,* Laurence Tribe makes reference to an *amicus* brief submitted to the Supreme Court for the *Webster* case by 885 American law professors and then asks us how plausible it would be that they would fail to recognize as blatant a legal blunder as some say the Court made in *Roe.*[86] His implication is that as professionals in the realm of law and justice, the expert knowledge of these law professors assures us that *Roe* was, in fact, a good decision; as they mediate the complexities of jurisprudence, we should trust them. But his question rather misses the point, for he ignores the sociological realities behind the brief they submitted. Tribe assumes that the judgment of the professors has taken place in a sociological vacuum in which they are only guided by the light of their legal knowledge. The sociologist will want to ask about the social characteristics of the group that might predispose the latter to regard law and the larger world the way it does. Professional competence and association can quite easily be a veil for the personal political values of the individuals constituting the association. For it not to be requires awareness and will and an adherence to the rules of discourse that academic disciplines establish for their protection against such tendencies.

The Institutions of Faith

What about the very prominent role of religious institutions in the abortion controversy? There are some who hold that the constitutional mandate against the establishment of religion—what Jefferson, in private correspondence, metaphorically called "the wall of separation" between church and state—actually means the separation of religion from the affairs of public life. For those who maintain this line of thought, religious faith should remain quietly sequestered in the intimate reflections and private activities of citizens. Never should faith, and the institutions that represent it make claims on how public life should be ordered. This reasoning explains in large part why southern conservatives were upset with the involvement of northern liberal clergy in the civil rights movement, and why northern liberals were upset with the involvement of southern evangelicals (like Jerry Falwell and Pat Robertson) in the political issues of the 1980s. Both conservatives and liberals had the sense that the clergy's respective claims on the ordering of public life somehow violated the "separation" of church and state.

Of course, there was no such violation. Religiously informed values and the people and organizations that articulate them (conservative *and* progressive) always have informed public debate. They continue to do so, both lawfully and legitimately. In the context of the present culture war, difficulties arise in democratic practice not in the fact that religion engages the concerns of public life, but rather in the *way* it does so. This is true as well for the way institutions of faith engage the specific matter of abortion. Here again, it is neither surprising nor problematic that the people and institutions of faith have a partisan stake on either side of this issue. Rather, it is the manner in which they often engage the controversy that the difficulties arise.

Politics as Modus Operandi

The temptation for churches, synagogues, denominations, and other religiously based organizations is to conflate public life with politics. When yielded to, as they all too often are, the pursuit of political power and the wielding of political influence become the dominant way in which religious bodies define themselves and their mission in the social order. In *theory*, all of the major faith traditions—on both sides of the cultural divide—reject the elevation of politics and political influence as the highest form of public witness they can take. In *practice*, though, this is precisely the ethic that is embraced.

Such an affirmation was clearly captured by a press release issued by the public affairs office of the National Association of Evangelicals [NAE] at the association's fiftieth-anniversary convention in 1992:[87] "As we begin NAE's second half-century, our nation is caught in a profound culture war. Evangelical Christians possess the weapons to win that war." What are those weapons? we ask. Prayer and voter participation, comes the reply. "NAE's Board of Administration approved the [Christian Citizenship] Campaign for 1992 to stir evangelicals more fully to meet their civil and biblical responsibilities as citizens, and thus *to strengthen their influence in public life*" (emphasis added). The goal of the campaign, as described in the press release, is to "recruit millions of evangelicals to pray more specifically and knowledgeably for their political leaders, and register one million new voters." The "NAE believes," the statement goes on to say, "that the combination of more intense prayer and increased voter participation can have a significant impact on the cultural crisis in our national life." Here the cultural nature of the conflicts they are in are acknowledged, yet it is politics (along with prayer for political leaders) that is held up as the solution.

The impression that the word *evangelical* is a political, rather than theological, designation is reinforced by groups like Pat Robertson's Christian Coalition. The latter is described by those involved as "a grass-roots coalition of pro-family, pro-life Evangelicals, conservative Catholics and their allies formed to make government and the media responsive to our concerns . . . [by] mobiliz[ing] and train[ing] Christians for effective political action. It is our purpose to reverse the moral decline and encroaching secularism in this country, and reaffirm our godly heritage."[88] For evangelicals, politics is the dominant modus operandi for addressing matters of public concern.

Evangelicals, however, are not alone in this. The same ethic is embraced by mainline Protestant leaders. In a remarkable conference held in the fall of 1991, the most prominent leaders of the mainline denominations gathered to assess the engagement of their churches in public affairs since the 1970s. What was striking was that all invoked political criteria as their measure of success and failure: "access to the President," "access to members of Congress," "congressional testimony," "the submission of *amicus curiae* briefs to the Supreme Court," the "mobilization of constituencies" and "the use of civil disobedience"—all geared toward the influence of specific public policies. And what were the lessons learned from their activism? "To wield influence," one Methodist bishop claimed, "requires preparation, development and readiness," including, as he noted, the use of media consultants, the organization of press conferences, and so on. "Be imaginative," said a one-time leader of the

United Presbyterian Church, "in seeking new ways to achieve an effectiveness of communication with the federal government." Said another, "Do your homework, prepare well, utilize leadership networks, move, if necessary toward civil disobedience." And finally, from a former head of the National Council of Churches, "Learn to tap the grass roots better. It's votes, it's constituencies that count," that will make "the witness of the church felt in Washington and in other state and local centers of power."[89]

The leadership of the Catholic Church in America, particularly as represented by the United States Catholic Conference (representing American Catholic bishops), has demonstrated a similar inclination toward this kind of politicization. An interesting illustration of this is the quadrennial (since 1976) voter guide written by the administrative board of the organization. The 1992 issue, entitled "Political Responsibility: Revitalizing American Democracy," provides a case in point.[90] The document is intended to inform the laity and others of the Catholic view of public affairs. The document acknowledges the right and responsibility "to speak out without governmental interference, endorsement, or sanction," at the same time offering the important disclaimer that they, the bishops, are not posing as merely another religious interest group. "What we seek," the bishops write, "is not a religious interest group, but a community of conscience within the larger society, testing public life on these central values. Our starting point and objectives are neither partisan nor ideological, but are focused upon the fundamental dignity of the human person."[91] Indeed, early on in the document, there is a call for substantive exchange that goes beyond "empty rhetoric or polarizing tactics" to a politics that reflects a search for the common good.

Having said all of this and reflected on the role of the church in the realm of politics, the document then moves to endorse or oppose a wide range of specific policies in a long list of "concerns": abortion, arms control and disarmament, the economy, education, food, agriculture and the environment, health, housing, international human rights, immigration, the mass media, and so on. If the specific and partisan nature of the bishops' positioning on these issues does not reflect an ideological factionalism, it certainly plays to such factionalism. Deepening this suspicion is the way in which these issues are discussed and judged. With few exceptions, the language and appeal make no reference to either distinctly Catholic or even distinctly Christian sources.[92]

These are but indications. One need not perform an extensive review of the engagement of ecclesiastical bodies to note a similar propensity to frame issues and operate via the language and tactics of power politics throughout conservative, moderate, and progressivist wings of all the major faith traditions.

The chief consequence of the elevation of politics is that institutions of faith acquire the identity, in effect, of a political lobby—just one more among many others that seek to influence congressional and presidential decision making. The use of the term *political lobby* is not just metaphorical. Denominations will speak of their "Washington office," but the lobby is the form of organization and activity that religious groups often adopt in order to press their claims in public and to influence national life. Indeed, as the fissures in American public life have widened and the culture war has intensified, the number of religiously based lobbies has proliferated. In 1950 there were just sixteen major religious lobbies in Washington, D.C.; in 1985 there were at least eighty, and the list has grown since then.[93] Abortion has remained one of the central issues over which religious groups attempt to wield influence.

That religious bodies look to politics as perhaps the principal mechanism to engage national life is itself not surprising when we realize that politics is also one of the chief ways used to deal with disagreements internal to their own organizations. Indeed, there is hardly a denomination in America that is not engaged in its own microcosm of the culture war; in virtually all, the quest for institutional power is perhaps the main means for factions to engage each other. Battles to shape national conventions, to control seminaries, and to dominate the agenda of an endless number of task forces are a staple of activity for denominational bureaucracies in most of the religious bodies today. The "Baptist battles" of the Southern Baptist Convention that took place in the 1980s have been only the most visibly contentious.[94] Though the lines are drawn differently, similar battles are fought in the United Methodist Church, the Episcopal Church, the Presbyterian Church USA, the United Church of Christ, and the Disciples of Christ.

In many of these intradenominational wars, abortion is one of the flash points of division. Throughout the decade of strife in the Southern Baptist Convention, opposition to abortion became for denominational conservatives almost as salient a test of one's orthodoxy as commitment to biblical inerrancy. In each of the old-line religious bodies as well, there are large, active, and vocal evangelical constituencies, each of which has taken the denomination's leadership to task for their consistent pro-choice advocacy.[95] As they confront each other, and as they confront the secular world, politics and the pursuit of power are the reigning motif.

The Missed Opportunity

Still another consequence of the politicization of the churches and their public witness is that a large and diverse laity are left by the wayside of public life. Allen Hertzke, whose study of the presence and role of religious lobbies in the American polity is the most complete to date, has argued that religious lobbies can be an important component of American political representation, providing a voice for people whose views otherwise might not be heard. On many issues this is in fact the case; on abortion, however, it is not. Conservative religious lobbies take a much more pro-life position than their constituencies, and progressive religious lobbies take a much more pro-choice stance than theirs. There is particular irony on the progressivist side of this, as Hertzke points out: whereas conservative denominations represent their *most* committed members by taking a pro-life stand, when liberal denominations (such as the Episcopalians, United Methodists, Presbyterians, and American Baptists) take a strongly pro-choice position, they articulate the sentiment of their *least* active and *least* committed members.[96]

The problem, in the end, is not that religious bodies are themselves flawed democracies.[97] Matters of moral and religious truth have not historically been, and still are not typically, subject to prevailing democratic pluralities. Leaders of faith traditions, in this light, have the obligation to apply their tradition's understanding of truth to the affairs of society. The problem is in the application: there is a failure of vision and of education.

Consider all of this in light of the evolution of "ecumenism" in twentieth-century America. Ecumenism can be understood as the effort among people of different religious faiths to forge alliances and unity where once there was tension and conflict between them. The great ecumenical efforts in the 1950s and 1960s were primarily theological, liturgical, and institutional in nature. In practice this resulted in the historic ecumenical dialogues among leaders from various Protestant denominations and between these Protestants and the Catholic hierarchy (as well as leaders in Judaism). Conferences were held, joint worship services conducted, position papers drafted, pledges for continued cooperation shared, and in a few cases, denominational unity achieved.

But though once highly touted, one rarely hears of this older version of ecumenism anymore. The reason, in part, is that it has been displaced by a political ecumenism—a forging of strategic alliances among religious groups who share common political interests and a common political agenda. Accordingly, this ecumenism is delimited by the boundaries of position. The preponderance of ecumenical activity, in other words, takes place among groups with a progressive agenda or among groups with a conservative agenda, but rarely if ever *across* the cultural and political divide.

The problem is that churches, denominations, and other institutions of faith are not political institutions, at least not principally. They are institutions of faith, meaning, tradition, and community—for all practical purposes, alone in their capacity to articulate a transcendent moral vision of human society, shared obligation, and an understanding of the human condition. The Jewish and Christian traditions are mines rich with resources for addressing these fundamental matters in their totality. Different communities obviously approach these traditions with fundamentally different hermeneutics, but the essential resources, the texts, and the broader history are the same. Finding within them elements of common and transcending moral understanding from which to approach particular public concerns becomes a possibility. Put differently, what institutions of faith seem to be uniquely qualified for, but show little interest in pursuing, is a *cultural* ecumenism toward the forging of a common vision for the common good. The zero-sum stakes of political activism obviate the very possibility of such an effort.

But vision is only one part of the problem. The other part is education. In practice there is a general and widely acknowledged failure of religious leaders to bring their congregations along with them, educating the laity (still nearly 90 percent of the American population, in one form or another) into the doctrines, teachings, and moral reasonings of the faith traditions. In Chapter Four we came to see that such traditions, or communities of moral discourse, are the single most important factor in shaping opinion about abortion (and the many other issues of the culture war). Yet we have seen, in Chapter Five, that most ordinary citizens have no facility with the languages of their own communities, what I call the languages of conviction. They are "moral stutterers," as Alasdair MacIntyre has put it, resorting chiefly to their current feelings. Institutions of faith are in a position to equip their laity with resources greater than political slogans or emotivist rhetoric, but they generally fall short of this task. Sam Hawkins, the pastor from Columbus, Ohio, echoed the complaint of many church leaders: "We don't make any effort to educate the laity—or the media or anyone else for that matter! And how can we? We [the leadership of churches] are neither comfortable nor confident dealing with conflict within our own ranks, much less dealing with conflict in the larger world. . . . We end up simply being a voice on one side of controversy or the other."[98] To the extent that institutions of faith and their public witness are politicized, they fall short of mediating public controversies in the way they are uniquely capable.

A Final Word

Of course, neither people nor institutions are perfect. But, like most of the controversies of the culture war, abortion is an enormously sensitive, complex, contentious issue, and precisely because of that, the institutions of civil society bear a special responsibility to mediate the controversy carefully and fairly. Far too often, as we have seen, they have not done so. Rather than penetrating the interests and distortions (or, in the case of religious institutions, transcending them) they are very often complicit in perpetuating them. Rather than mediate controversy, they all too typically mimic the dominant ideologies and factions (conservative and progressive) and reinforce

the political forms of engagement. In this sense, rather than protecting individuals from special interests, as Jefferson described
them, they often become de facto special interest groups themselves. To the extent that these developments become normative
practice, the possibility of substantive democracy taking root seems
even more remote.

— 7 —

The Education of Citizens
What Multiculturalism Really Accomplishes

Mediating public controversies is just one role the institutions of civil society play toward the end of enlightening citizens and revitalizing democratic practice. Certainly as important is their role in helping us come to terms with *the differences underlying such controversies*. Given the intensity of the struggle over abortion and the entire range of entrenched disputes in America as well as the prejudice and even bigotry that exists on each side of these contests, a mutual understanding of our underlying cultural differences would seem essential to even the possibility of substantive argument—the kind that would allow us to move beyond the moral and political deadlock we have today. How, then, do we as a society make sense of and deal with the cultural variety that exists in America? In our own circumstances, how are we as citizens equipped to deal with the fundamental diversity we confront in everyday life and that is at the root of the issues of the culture war (not least among them the conflict over abortion)?

The principal way pluralism or diversity is understood and promoted today is through the ideas and programs of *multiculturalism*. There is much one can say about multiculturalism, but already there exists a voluminous literature describing and critiquing it. Most of the commentary and criticism, however, is political in nature, concerned with the political agenda—hidden and otherwise—of those who advocate multiculturalism. This matter of politics can be put to rest quickly: both advocates (particularly the more strident voices) and critics agree that the political agenda of multiculturalism is, finally, recognition and empowerment. Multiculturalists wish to increase the recognition, power, and legitimacy of various minority groups, in part through a delegitimation of an "oppressive" mainstream American culture.[1]

For the purposes of this essay, the political implications of multiculturalism are, for all practical purposes, irrelevant. Delegitimating "a Eurocentric American mainstream culture," as some advocates of multiculturalism put it, may or may not be a legitimate political end. Conservatives say it isn't; progressives say it is—it is not my concern. My concern, rather, is with the way in which cultural differences are thought about and dealt with. In short, *does multiculturalism equip people to come to terms with the cultural differences underlying public controversy in a democracy?*

The promises of multiculturalism to enhance democratic life in this way are bold. As one proponent put it, "Democratic pluralism will remain forever an abstraction unless our youngest citizens experience in their lives the awareness of other cultures and other peoples within our society."[2] "It is," as another argues, "concern for each as a brother-sister that provides the cornerstone of real democracy."[3] Multiculturalism is designed to foster the respect for cultural differences that makes such ideals realities.

In this chapter I explore the adequacy of this educational movement for equipping children and young adults to deal with the diversity underlying controversy. It will seem to take us far afield from the particular controversy over abortion, but the reader should be patient. What we learn about multiculturalism tells us much about the possibility of serious and substantive argument over this issue, and indeed all of the critical issues of the culture war.

Democracy and Diversity: How We Are Taught to Face the Challenge of Pluralism

Pluralism or diversity has been a fact of American life for quite a long time. Strategies for dealing with it are also nothing new. Such strategies have long been centered within one institution in particular—the public school. This is true of multiculturalism, too. What is striking about these strategies, though, is not where they take institutional expression or how they are implemented, but rather the message they actually communicate to children and young adults. When looking at this message over time, one is initially struck by the dramatic changes that have taken place. But there is more to this comparison than first meets the eye. As a context for understanding multiculturalism, consider some of the strategies employed in the past for dealing with the matter of pluralism.

From "Americanization" . . .

The waning years of the 1800s and the opening decades of the 1900s formed, as is well known, the single largest wave of immigration into the United States in its history. But before 1885, most (up to nine out of every ten) of the foreign immigrants of the nineteenth century were from the mainly Protestant countries of northern Europe. As such most of these new settlers shared customs, habits of living, and moral ideals similar to those of the earliest settlers and, except for the Germans, tended not to segregate themselves into their own enclaves. By 1905, however, three-fourths of all immigrants were coming from the countries of southern and eastern Europe and were predominantly Roman Catholic, Greek Catholic, and Jewish. These new immigrants tended to cluster together in ethnic enclaves in the major cities and formed institutions to serve those communities. By 1918, for example, there were 1,800 foreign-language newspapers, with a total circulation of 10 million readers. What is more, according to the census of 1910, millions of the foreign-born were unable to speak, read, or write English, and millions more were illiterate altogether. Of the teenagers and adults in these numbers, fewer than 1 percent were in school. All combined, then, there was a new diversity in America that was now visible and striking—and threatening to the identity and ideals of the established majority.

The response to the challenges of this new pluralism was the so-called Americanization movement. According to Frances Kellor, the movement's most zealous proponent, Americanization was to be the "science of racial relations in America, dealing with the assimilation and amalgamation of diverse races in equity into an integral part of its national life."[4] In practice, it was a far-reaching educational and civic movement, involving private and voluntary agencies, state and town agencies, and the federal government, designed to win newly naturalized immigrants over to "the American way of life," to increase patriotic sentiment, or to engender "American" attitudes and beliefs toward nation, life, and leisure.

Programmatically, the movement involved conferences, pageants, prize competitions, speeches, and newsletters, but most of all, it centered on education. Colleges around the country established programs that would teach teachers and social workers how to educate the immigrant properly. Night schools were established that focused on teaching English as a foreign language. Moreover, by the early years of the 1920s, the movement had been fully institutionalized within the educational establishment. In 1919, for example, the National Education Association recommended that Congress require a year of "compulsory civic, physical, and vocational training" for all young people in the United States. For anyone in America, young or old, it requested "legal provision for compulsory classes in Americanization."[5] In 1921, the NEA had established its own department of immigrant education.[6] During the war years, educators around the country eliminated German from the curriculum (believing it to be an unpatriotic language) and even extended grading on the report cards of children to their classroom citizenship.[7]

The Americanization movement, with its design to assimilate the great hordes of immigrants through education, sounds antiquated to say the least. In its own way, though, it was based upon progressive ideals. As opposed to those who wanted to restrict the inflow of foreigners, the Americanizers believed that immigration was good for the nation. As the National Americanization Committee put it, they wanted, among other things, to create "the desire of immigrants to remain in America, have a home here, and support American institutions."[8] And against the continued presence of ethnic distrust and prejudice, the Americanizers wanted "the abolition of racial prejudices, barriers, and discriminations," as well as "the discontinuance of discriminations in housing, care, protection, and treatment of aliens."[9] Kellor herself, along with her supporters, insisted repeatedly that assimilation occur "with equity," defined in her own words as "impartiality among the races accepted for the blend, with no imputations of inferiority and no bestowal of favors."[10]

The overall effect of Americanization was probably greatest on immigrant children. Evidence suggests that the political socialization of children through civics classes and the like was indeed acculturative.[11] For the adult immigrant population, however, this movement had at best only marginal consequences.[12] The inefficiency and ineffectiveness of the wide range of programs is well documented. For example, in most cities and states where immigrants were concentrated, like New York and Massachusetts, typically less than one out of every ten attended the free night schools, and fewer still ever completed courses of study.[13] As one observer summarized as early as 1919, the institutions and programs of the movement "through no particular fault of their own, have failed to Americanize the adult foreign-born population of the United States."[14]

Yet as Michael Olneck has pointed out, the significance of the Americanization movement was not so much in its actual impact on the attitudes and conduct of the great hordes of immigrants as in its effort to define symbolically American civic culture. It was through the effort to win the immigrant to "American ways" that the Americanizers were able to idealize the values, beliefs, and cultural practices worthy of respect, admiration, allegiance, and imitation.[15]

Perhaps the principal way in which the movement established its own ideals was, as Olneck puts it, in its "delegitimation of *collective* ethnic identity." As the National Americanization Committee saw it, it was racial and ethnic "colonies" and immigrant "sections . . . which keep people in America apart."[16] Ethnicity, race, and religion could be affirmed as the characteristics of individuals, but not of groups. Or, to put it differently, cultural differences were relevant in terms of private reality but not as a public or political reality. To this end, particularistic identifications and bounded ethnic communities were stigmatized as divisive, isolating, and backward, and they were denied symbolic existence.

The delegitimation of collective ethnic identity meant that "there would be no 'German-Americans,' no 'Slav movement in America,' but that we are one people in ideals, rights and privileges and in making common cause for America."[17] Woodrow Wilson echoed this view when he told a body of new citizens, "You cannot become thorough Americans if you think of yourselves in groups. America does not consist of groups. A man who thinks of himself as belonging to a particular national group in America has not yet become an American."[18] Rather, it was the ideal of the autonomous individual that was celebrated. The Bureau of Education made this clear to its readers in one of its publications: "It should, however, not be forgotten that the government of the United States and the spirit of American democracy know no groups. They know only individuals. . . .Not groups of any kind but free men, women, and children make up the people of the United States."[19]

In this understanding, the idea of community did not exist as a "prior organic moral entity," but rather "through the mutual association and actions of previously unrelated individuals."[20] Interests would be the glue of association. "In America," Frances Kellor argued, the plurality of people "are held together largely by their sense of opportunities and their hope of reward."[21] So much for the legitimacy of ethnically-based community organizations.

The same judgment was made about religion and religious institutions, which sometimes were inextricably linked to ethnic identity. In the Americanization literature, churches and synagogues were discussed mainly in terms of the public functions to make good citizens, to educate, to inspire, and to motivate. Moreover, as institutions, they were presented primarily as organizations with which individuals, whose personally held religious convictions happened to coincide, choose to affiliate.[22]

In the end, this was also why learning English was emphasized by the Americanization movement and its sympathizers. It was, in part, a utilitarian concern to have everyone speak the same language. Secretary of the Interior Franklin Lane in 1928 argued that English would widen opportunities for the immigrant, rather than his being "bound and fettered by the language he originally speaks."[23] But this was not all: privileging the English language was even more symbolic of the desire to create national unity in the face of the possibility of disintegration into warring ethnic factions. To abandon one's mother tongue and embrace a new language was to abandon primary political loyalty to one's ethnic group by embracing a new and higher loyalty. As Kellor summarized it, "The English language is a highway of loyalty; it is a medium of exchange; it is the open door to opportunity; it is a means of common defense."[24]

In sum, Americanization built upon a recognition that differences of national culture were indeed greatly divisive. But rather than acknowledge and confront this pluralism directly, the diversity was downplayed and delegitimated. The end of this was the reaffirmation of a common culture and common identity of utilitarian individualism that also happened to be most compatible, if not of a fabric, with the dominant ideals and sensibilities of white, Protestant America.

. . . to Multiculturalism

On the surface, multiculturalism exists in stark contrast with Americanization, but only on the surface. But there are clear lines of continuity with the older model.

Between the heyday of Americanization in the early decades of the twentieth century and the present, particularly between 1935 and 1950, an alternative model called "interculturalism" was proposed and institutionalized in the public education establishment.[25] Here, too, the ideals and intentions were noble: to reduce interracial, interethnic, and interreligious tensions by promoting mutual understanding and a respect for the differences found among citizens. The model's backers also condemned ethnocentrism, parochialism, and the politicization of religious or ethnic group identity. Unlike the Americanists, however, who sought an unqualified assimilation and conformity of the immigrant population into the mainstream of American culture, the interculturalists tried much harder to acknowledge the depth of diversity in American life and even to celebrate it. Consider the advice teachers were encouraged to share with their students:

Let me plead with you to appreciate your own background, and never be ashamed of it. . . . If your parents speak Italian or Polish, or any other foreign language, don't answer them in English; learn to speak the language yourself . . . just as your parents are learning English. Learn what it stands for and what the people of that country have brought to America.[26]

A central assumption of intercultural education was the idea that diversity was largely attributable to the different circumstances, conditions, or environments in which people were born and with which they had to cope. For this reason, cultural practices of different people had to be judged on their own terms. At the same time, interculturalists downplayed the idea that these cultural differences were either permanent or immutable. Rather, they insisted upon the essential anthropological similarity of all people. At bottom, their understanding and teaching about pluralism in America was also guided by an assimilationist vision of national unity, made possible by a single dominant culture, comprised of some diverse elements.[27]

It is from the noble ideals and programs of interculturalism that the agenda of multiculturalism evolved.[28] In light of the high-minded intentions of the past, one might wonder what is exceptional about multiculturalism today. "Recognizing and celebrating diversity," "shedding ethnocentrism," "fostering understanding," "sensitivity, tolerance, and acceptance of different perspectives," "validating traditions other than one's own," "building the self-esteem of minorities," and the like—these are the phrases commonly invoked to describe the goals of the movement. Albert Shanker, of the American Federation of Teachers put it this way: "If only we understood where other people were coming from—if only we had more sensitivity to their cultures—we might not be so wedded to our own points of view and we might have a better chance of avoiding the conflicts that come from ethnocentrism."[29] The New York State Board of Regents embraced this sentiment and translated it into one of their goals for global education. "Each student," their statement read, "will develop the ability to understand, respect, and accept people of different races; sex; cultural heritage; national origin; religion; and political, economic and social background, and their values, beliefs, and attitudes."[30] The District of Columbia Board of Education struck a similar chord:

> Although the ethnic diversity of our city is growing, many students misunderstand and fear newcomers rather than appreciating their characteristics and contributions. Such ignorance and fear often breed ridicule and hostility toward recent immigrants and people of different ethnic groups.
>
> If we teach young people to truly value their own history, culture and achievements as those of other races, religions and ethnic backgrounds, we turn them away from alienation and aggression toward a sense of pride in their own heritage, respect for others and a stake in their shared futures.[31]

So, too, the California Department of Education wrote that "diversity is a source of strength and balance. We add to our lives when we appreciate and accept the cultural and ethnic differences in our society."[32] And so it goes.[33]

In all, we hear echoes from the past. Indeed, in the history of pluralistic education, the stated goals hardly seem distinctive at all. But there is something distinctive about multiculturalism's stance on the nature of diversity. The theorists of multiculturalism have crafted a vision of pluralism that, at the least, takes diversity much more seriously than any previous efforts of its kind. Perhaps the most obvious way we see this is in the openness toward bilingual and multilingual education. To no longer force children to abandon their mother tongue and no longer make English the only language of instruction is to create an environment much more conducive to the formation of group identity. Such policies suggest, symbolically, that national unity cannot be forced at the sacrifice of a child's loyalty to his or her national heritage.

Beyond this, the expressions of multiculturalism's seriousness about diversity are really quite varied. In its more genteel forms, a multiculturally sensitive education requires the inclusion of various groups and traditions (typically those outside of the mainstream) in an understanding of the life and history of the nation—women politicians, astronauts, and construction workers; African-American soldiers in World War I; immigrant inventors; and so on. The objective is to show children that the nation's minority populations have played a role and made contributions to national life in the same manner as the majority population.[34] In these versions, a sense of common life made possible by a commitment to common democratic ideals is affirmed.

In its more strident forms, however, the idea of national unity is rejected outright. As proponents of this vision of pluralism will sometimes say, "We are no longer an American melting-pot, nor do we want to be."[35] Thus a "single national culture is no longer acceptable as a feasible concept for educational processes and interpersonal behavior."[36] Indeed, the common ideas and ideals all Americans are supposed to share are in fact the ideas and ideals of a white, male-dominated European civilization and proof of the continuing effort to subordinate those outside of the mainstream society.[37] Racism, sexism, and heterosexism are just three of the main expressions of this Eurocentric culture. This "uniculturalism" has been forced upon non-European minorities with great harm, for it fundamentally denies the humanity of major groups of people and denies true equality.

Thus, for some, African-Americans are really "African persons in America." The notion of a mainstream or "common culture" is just code for male, Eurocentric culture.[38] Proponents of this understanding of diversity in America typically advocate a "centric" (as in Afrocentric) approach to multicultural education. In this model, the history, culture, and identity of a particular group become the fixed point of reference in teaching. How that group has related to other groups in the past is a part of the curriculum, but no common "mainstream" is represented. It simply does not exist as an authentic amalgamation of the various and equally valid histories, perspectives, and identities of those who inhabit America.[39]

In this vision of diversity, then, there is a conscious and clear break from agenda of the Americanists who wanted to celebrate the mainstream Anglo-Saxon cultural identity while ultimately undermining the authenticity of racial, ethnic, religious and gender *group* identities. Multiculturalists reverse the formula. They are concerned to delegitimate "mainstream American culture" as oppressive and to increase the power and legitimacy of minority groups. In this strategy, group identity rooted in ethnicity, gender, sexual orientation, and the like is, in principle, paramount over all other sources of identity.[40]

Though there are different understandings and approaches to the reality of diversity in the broader multicultural movement, one can find clear tendencies in application. In the lower grade levels, the more genteel versions of multiculturalism prevail. As one moves up the ladder of educational achievement, however, one will find the more strident and separatist versions. Moreover, it is to this more aggressive vision of diversity in America that the most vocal theorists of multiculturalism subscribe.

The Unintended Consequences

This brings us back to the original question of this chapter. Does multiculturalism equip people to come to terms with the cultural differences underlying public controversy? Though it seems that multiculturalism approaches pluralism and diversity more seriously than previous efforts, the program actually promotes a vision of pluralism in which differences are flattened out. Ironically, then, the official story is one of celebrating diversity, but as a consequence of its method for understanding culture, the subtext of multiculturalism in all its expressions is one in which the differences among cultures are finally reduced to "sameness." This subtext of sameness is generated by at least three factors.

Trivializing Culture

The leveling out of cultural differences is first promoted through a trivialization of the idea and reality of culture. How so? We begin with an understanding of culture itself. *Culture is nothing if it is not, first and foremost, a normative order by which we comprehend ourselves, others, and the larger world and through which we order our experience.* At the heart of culture is a system of norms and values, as social scientists are prone to call them. But these norms and values are better understood as *commanding truths* so deeply embedded in our consciousness and in the habits of our lives that to question them is to question reality itself. These commanding truths define the "shoulds" and "should nots" of our experience and, accordingly, the good and the evil, the right and the wrong, the appropriate and inappropriate, the honorable and the shameful. Accordingly, culture involves the obligations to adhere to these truths, obligations that come about by virtue of one's membership in a group.

Against this is multiculturalism's approach to culture, which by comparison is rather frail. Within multiculturalism literature, culture is essentially reduced to life-style (choices about how one lives) or, at best, customs (practices that have the sanction of tradition but are not insisted upon as inviolable) or possibly collective experiences.[41] Thus a multicultural curriculum, particularly for younger children, will focus on foods, clothing, recreation and holidays, styles of art, folklore, and dance of various peoples, as well as the different forms in which marriage is found, the different ways caring is expressed, different ways to communicate, and so on. These practices, children are taught, can be imitated, shared, and sometimes even experienced.

Implicit in this is a rendering of culture to the ethic of individual choice. Taste in food, clothing, art, music, and the like are just the obvious ways in which an individual can express this choice. "Because of cultural differences," says one textbook for young teens, "people eat a variety of foods prepared in different ways. . . . A caring person respects the cultural food preferences of others. An open-minded person will try new foods when offered and often likes them."[42] Multiculturalism, though, extends this logic to all aspects of culture. Even religious faith and ethnicity are implicitly presented in these terms. How? Take religion, for example. When multicultural education strives to "understand individuals within the context of their cultural group experience"[43] or "recognizing . . . each person in the context of his/her cultural background,"[44] group attributes like religion are presented as significant by virtue of how they contribute to an individual's unique and personal identity. Thus religion may be something in a person's "background," and yet the implication is that they can choose to embrace it or choose to reject it, perhaps in favor of another way to understand life's mysteries. By the same logic, ethnicity and race may be something one can either choose to feel good about or be ashamed of, depending on whether one chooses to identify with and embrace one's ethnic and racial inheritance. And indeed, multicultural education universally encourages children to participate in, identify with, and adopt the practices of other groups, as though culture was a wardrobe one could put on and take off as one chooses. As one multiculturalist put it, "Rather than forcing all students into the majority culture mold, the educator, with great care and sensitivity, *can help children live in more than one culture*."[45]

The problem with this perspective, of course, is that it assumes a historically specific understanding of the self, one free and independent from culture, unencumbered by moral commitments defined by virtue of one's membership in a community. But culture is much more pervasive, powerful, and compelling than is allowed for in the liberal understanding of the self. By virtue of their birth into a community and a culture, people are bound by moral ties and obligations that are, as Michael Sandel has said, "antecedent to choice."[46] People, then, are rarely freed from the sanctions of custom and tradition and inherited status. By reducing culture to a product about which individuals may choose, multiculturalism further renders culture as a trifling matter.

Also contributing to the trivialization of culture is the selectivity by which cultural practices of different people and groups are presented. For example, multicultural curricula are careful not to talk of the hostile attitudes and strongly punitive practices of many cultures toward homosexuality, or the severe inequalities between men and women in non-Western cultures generally (for example, the practice of clitoral circumcision by some African tribes, the beating of women for misbehavior in traditional Islamic culture, and foot binding in traditional Chinese culture), or the deep sense of superiority over other races maintained and justified by, say, Japanese culture or Chinese culture. These practices are certainly real, and they are engaged in because they are rooted in a normative order that makes such practices "normal" and "right" and "as things should be". Failing to even mention such beliefs, attitudes, and practices is to fictionalize and sugarcoat the presentation of the multiple cultures we seek to understand. Failing to comprehend how such beliefs and practices are normal and true within different cultures is, in the end, to fail to understand the differences at all.

In all of these ways, multiculturalism domesticates, homogenizes, and trivializes culture and the differences among cultures.

Relativizing Culture

Sameness is also promoted through multiculturalism's relativization of culture. This underlying relativism derives in part from presenting aspects of culture in terms of its function. Beliefs, values, and customs may be different around the world, multiculturalists will say, but they function very much the same way. "Students understand," as one declaration put it, "that the differences in various cultures represent different answers to basic human questions that confront all peoples of the world, including their own."[47] This breaks down into the various components of culture. Of the world religions, for example, one textbook explains that they "are ways through which people try to make sense of life and find meaning. . . . For many people, religious beliefs are important to their spiritual well-being and mental health."[48] Or take compassion:

> Caring is a value practiced and demonstrated among people around the world. But caring is shown in very different ways, depending on the culture and its beliefs. In many European and Latin American countries, caring between friends may be openly demonstrated through hugging and holding hands. It makes no difference if the friends are male or female. In American culture people compliment one another to show they care. Many Asian cultures believe that Americans compliment one another too much. They doubt the sincerity of our expressions.[49]

Or take marriage: "Everywhere in the world, families are the basic unit of human living. Everywhere families nurture their young, preparing them for adult life. In this way, families are alike. Family structure, [however], differs among cultures."[50] Or, finally, take attitudes about sex: "For some people [sex] is only for having children. . . . For others, sex is just another way of feeling good—sex for fun, no ties, no commitments. . . . Or sex can be a way of expressing a deep sense of caring and intimacy."[51] In all, the differences we see are simply variations of universal practices.

Since cultures are alike in the way they function, one may surmise that no one culture can be shown to be better or worse than another, no particular values or specific moral ideals can be assumed to be more estimable than others, and so on. The content of all cultures needs to be respected, valued, affirmed, and accepted. Multiculturalists are often explicit about this in wanting to teach students "that no one culture is intrinsically superior to another,"[52] that they should "respect and accept people of different races; sex; cultural heritage; national origin, religion; and political, economic and social background, and their values, beliefs and attitudes;[53] that students should learn to "validate traditions other than one's own," and so on.[54] Multicultural education wants to develop "an American society . . . where [among other things] cultural differences are respected, without the implication that one culture is better or worse than another."[55]

The relativism of multiculturalism also derives from seeing culture as a reflection of a group's environment and/or its physiological characteristics. This is seen in the equation between one's gender, race, ethnicity, or sexual orientation and one's cultural commitments. To be a white male is to look at the world in a particular way, to be a woman is to look at the world another way, to be black in America is to operate within a different culture, and so on. Surely a person's race, gender, class, and sexual orientation influence the way he or she experiences the world, but the implicit assumption within multiculturalism takes it further—that these factors are determinative of culture, and cumulatively so. Human beings, then, socially construct their worlds of meaning in interaction with others out of the crucible of the physical and material conditions of their existence. Since everyone's environment is different, then their cultures will be different. Culture therefore can only be relative to time, place, and circumstance.

It should be said that the propensity in multiculturalism to view culture as a reflection of environment, and its function within that environment, derives from the formidable traditions of academic anthropology.[56] Especially in its classic (late nineteenth- and early twentieth-century) articulation, anthropology assumed the existence of universal features of human life, even though they found expression in vastly different ways around the world. "Behind the seemingly endless diversity of culture patterns," said Ralph Linton at midcentury, "there is a fundamental uniformity."[57] The universals that transcend culture are seen to derive from a common species membership—the fact that we share a common humanity.[58] The particularities of culture derive from the unique and distinct environments within which people have had to forge their existence and history. Thus much of the classical vision and practice of anthropology was oriented toward penetrating the particularities of other cultures in order to understand how these particularities evolved and how they related to universal human traits.[59]

In this, anthropology shattered the evolutionary ideas prevalent in the nineteenth century—popularized by everyone from Auguste Comte to the social Darwinists—that the differences of cultures in history and around the world could be best explained by their different stages in a linear development toward a higher plane of human existence. Classical anthropological study trashed such evolutionary schemes, sending them to the intellectual landfill. Different cultures were now seen as representing different solutions to the same problems: all were worthy of respect and tolerance, and all were equally valid.

The intentions of this pedagogy, whether from anthropology or multiculturalism, are to undermine ethnocentrism. But the *effect* of this educational ideology is to teach children, albeit implicitly, not to take their own culture (or anyone else's) seriously. What Paul Rabinow says of anthropology can be applied with equal force to multiculturalism. Within this general frame of reference, says Rabinow,

> all cultural differences have been both preserved and destroyed. First, difference is emphasized, the uniqueness of each culture; then it is reduced to the Same. They are all doing the same thing. All these value systems are the same insofar as they are world views, or ethoses; their content differs but there is no way to choose between them as long as they survive. The role of anthropology [and, one could easily add, multiculturalism] is to describe the plurality of these meaningful life worlds. Each way of life is worthy of respect because ultimately each is equally untrue. The being of man is all that we can affirm. This is everywhere the same. Ultimately Difference (although praised) is suppressed: the Same is triumphant.[60]

If all cultures in the final analysis are really the same, then the particular truth claims or value positions cannot really be taken at face value. As Rabinow says, they are all "equally untrue." The particular truths children have been socialized into, and the institutions that embody and communicate these truths, then lose their authority.

They no longer are capable of compelling action and obligation. In the end, children and young adults simply come to view knowledge and truth primarily as instruments of power. Needless to say, this is just how many multiculturalists view the nature and functions of knowledge, too.[61]

Sentimentalizing Culture

The subtext of "sameness" in the pedagogy of multiculturalism is reinforced by the moral imperatives of "self-esteem" and positive feeling. The language of sentiment and emotion is ubiquitous in the multicultural literature. A task force created by the New York State Board of Regents published a report in 1987, entitled "A Curriculum of Inclusion," whose findings were fairly typical of this commitment: "African Americans, Asian Americans, Puerto Ricans/Latinos, and Native Americans have all been the victims of an intellectual and educational oppression" that has had "a terribly damaging effect on the psyche of young people." The multicultural program the task force recommended, though, would remedy this for minority youngsters, who "will have higher self-esteem and self-respect, while children from European cultures will have a less arrogant perspective."

The California Department of Education draws a similar connection: "California is characterized by unprecedented ethnic, racial, and cultural diversity. We continue having the opportunity and challenge to create a truly multicultural democracy. We benefit ourselves and our society by growing in our self-esteem to the point where we are able to welcome and feel comfortable with persons of all backgrounds."[62] We hear much the same from other quarters: in an open learning environment, cultural differences become a source of pride, self-respect, and self-esteem; no one is an outsider; students feel they belong; and so on. "To ignore or invalidate this living experience for any individual is, in effect, to distort and diminish the possibilities for developing that person's potential."[63]

But why do proponents of multiculturalism place such a premium upon feelings and self-esteem in particular? In theory, if one feels good about oneself, one is likely to be a good person, to be responsible and self-controlled, to be tolerant of others, to perform well in school, and so forth. From these mental and emotional states comes a sense of control in one's life. As a former state education commissioner in New York put it, "We know that if children are to achieve they must trust their teachers and feel good about themselves."[64] Enhanced self-esteem, then, is a crucial building block toward economic and political equality.

In sum, children are taught that whatever differences may exist between them, deep down they are all the same by virtue of their common emotions and their common need for recognition and esteem. Thus the expression of our feelings of mutual respect is the tangible way that we see our common humanity. Through cultivating such emotions as sensitivity, empathy, appreciation, and the like, people become confident and proud of themselves and their heritage, and harmony among culturally different individuals becomes possible.

The intentions behind all of this are, needless to say, good and beyond dispute. Self-respect, a sense of belonging, and self-worth—these are all important to cultivate among children, adolescents, and young adults. Such ideals are reinforced, as Charles Taylor argues, by the Enlightenment ideal of universal dignity—that all human beings are worthy of equal respect and esteem.[65]

The problem is in the *net effect* of making self-esteem and the like a central emphasis of multicultural programs.[66] The net effect of this explicit linkage is a glossing over of Difference. By emphasizing that what really matters is our sense of mutual esteem, an understanding of cultural differences quickly becomes subjugated to the imperative to make people feel good about themselves. For all its worthy intentions, the priority given to sentiment in this scheme reinforces the idea that differences really don't matter; we need not take them seriously. Once more, Sameness triumphs over Difference.

The reduction of culture to sentiment, then, also has the effect of leveling out our differences. The language and logic of emotivism reinforces the idea that "we're really not so different after all."

The Denial of Difference and the Triumph of Sameness

In sum, for all of the emphasis on diversity within this educational movement, multiculturalism fares no better than previous efforts to educate citizens into pluralism. Multiculturalism simultaneously—

and altogether unintentionally—trivializes culture and denies the essential differences among them. What is more, by relativizing culture in the ways described above, multiculturalism undermines the authority of cultural norms and cultural institutions, unwittingly teaching students that culture should not really be taken very seriously.[67] When, on top of all of this, multiculturalism elevates emotional expression as the essence of our common humanity and good feeling as a moral and political imperative, the fundamental differences among cultures are leveled out. Culture is homogenized.

A direct consequence of this is that moral judgement becomes not only inappropriate, but impossible. Since the substance and content of culture (its truth claims) are, for all practical purposes, hollowed out, we are left with no standards by which we can judge good from bad, right from wrong, excellent from shoddy—except the standard that no one's feelings are hurt. Indeed, as some proponents of multiculturalism will contend, *academic excellence* is a code word for Eurocentrism; *quality* a code word for oppression. This is in part what is behind the National Education Association's long-standing distrust of standardized testing. Such tests, one NEA resolution put it, "have historically been used to differentiate rather than to measure performance and have therefore prevented equal educational opportunities for all students, particularly minorities, lower socioeconomic groups, and women"; for this reason, tests should not be administered when they are either "biased" or when they are "potentially damaging to a student's self-concept."[68]

The bottom line is that one cannot hope to understand culture without understanding its central and commanding truth claims. But these claims imply standards, and standards imply the moral judgment that we are *not* the same and not on the same moral plane. Such standards and judgments violate the central lesson multiculturalism wants students everywhere to appropriate—that "I am as good as you."

And What About Abortion—Among Other Matters—in All of This?

Given the contentious nature of the abortion controversy, one would suppose that advocates of multiculturalism would want to increase the mutual understanding of the cultural differences underlying this dispute. It is, after all, difference in moral community that creates the central fissure among people in this controversy and all of the controversies of the culture war. *These* differences, though, are ignored altogether.[69] By multiculturalism's own assumptions and logic, this issue and the underlying differences that fuel it *must* be ignored. The reason is that each side of this controversy asserts irreducible and irreconcilable truth claims about the rights of women, the ontology of the fetus, the ethics of the procedure, and so on. Thus, *to assert the claim that one value* (say, protecting a woman's autonomy) *is better than another* (say, protecting the life of preborn children)—*or vice versa*—*is to assert a Difference that cannot easily be "appreciated" or "validated" or "accepted" or "celebrated."* By extension, this also holds true across the spectrum of conflicts making up the contemporary culture war—the contests over homosexuality, the arts, school curricula, church/state, and so on. All imply truth claims that are irreducible and irreconcilable.

These are Differences that cannot easily be trivialized or relativized or framed in terms of self-esteem. These are Differences that are, for both sides of cultural controversy, real and immutable, harsh in their implications, morally judgmental, and fundamentally offensive—not only to opponents in the controversy, but to the very notion that we are all ultimately alike. In the dispute over abortion as in all of the disputes of the culture war, "self-esteem" quickly becomes beside the point.

The inability of multiculturalism to even address the abortion controversy, much less the particular cultural differences underlying it, is just the most obvious way in which the movement fails to equip Americans to engage each other over this matter. The same, again, can be said of the other disputes. Even indirectly, in the general framework that multiculturalism provides, it fails. The reason is that multiculturalism denies the very category of Differences that constitutes the friction point between cultures—the substantive and, in this case, contradictory imperatives asserted by and embodied within different moral communities.

Are We Really Tolerant?

Prejudice and bigotry of all kinds have not disappeared, by any means. The effort to combat them, however, has gone far in this country, certainly as measured by any global and historical comparison. The desire to minimize them even further is an essential social and political goal for American democratic life. The question is, does the moral culture of civil society articulated through multiculturalism promote this? Does multiculturalism promote the mutual understanding and tolerance necessary to sustain democracy, particularly since this program coincides with the unfolding culture war?

In all of this, it is worth remembering one of the most rudimentary distinctions: *democracy* is, in its practical manifestations, a political term, not a cultural one. So, too, is *tolerance*. There is, then, a subtle but crucial distinction between treating all people and their communities with equal respect and viewing all cultures as essentially equal. The test of tolerance is not so much "accepting" and "validating" all cultures different from one's own, but rather living at peace with those with whom one disagrees most vehemently, cooperating with those whose claims we may detest, and defending the rights of those whom we regard as fundamentally wrong.

Yet in multiculturalism one finds, at the least, a certain confusion over what one is to be tolerant: sometimes it is the individual, sometimes it is the group of which the individual is a part, and sometimes it is the culture itself. Often enough, the political meaning of democratic tolerance is superseded by the cultural meaning. Thus, instead of the political idea that all individuals and groups should be treated equally under the law, multiculturalism asserts the normative idea that all cultures are in fact equal. No moral differences are allowed, for to suggest that one culture is better, more virtuous, and more excellent, and others are worse—why, this would be "undemocratic." To suggest that some cultures, values, beliefs, or ideals are more true, more healthy, or more humane—this would be "ethnocentric" and "intolerant".

But is this leveling of all differences really tolerance? Surely one demonstrates neither respect nor toleration for that which is trivialized and relativized and, in some instances, ignored altogether. So long as we treat culture the way that we do, we will not only fail to understand anyone else, we will be ill equipped to understand and reflect upon our own beliefs and values. Serious and substantive argument over the issues that divide us will be impossible. One need not gainsay the noble intentions of its advocates. But intentions are not enough. As it is presently articulated, *multiculturalism simply does not go far enough.*

A Shallow Defense for Democracy

The institutional denial of difference in multiculturalism is problematic for yet another reason. Such an approach leaves us ill equipped to defend the very democratic framework within which pluralism exists and controversy takes place. For example, are we, in the name of appreciating diversity, really prepared to view the sending of young boys across mine fields (as Iran did in its war with Iraq) as an acceptable practice deserving of "admiration" and "approval"? Are we prepared to view clitoral circumcision, as practiced in many African tribes, as a "valid tradition", "worthy of attention, consideration, or regard", "as positive, not inferior"? Are we prepared, in the name of open-mindedness and sensitivity to difference, to respect the system that sponsored the genocide of Jews by Hitler, the gulags in the Soviet Union, or the racist ideas that have for generations fueled government-sponsored apartheid in South Africa? Most Americans, of course, are not. But on what grounds do we say that these cultural practices and the political systems that embrace them are not acceptable, not valid, and not to be respected?

When the truth claims—the imperatives—at the heart of culture are hollowed out, when their substance cannot be defended or criticized, there is little left besides "feeling": the moral language and moral imperatives of sentiment. Of course, multiculturalism did not create a culture of emotivism, but it does reinforce it both ideologically and institutionally. Its effects will be especially great for a younger generation being socialized by it. Needless to say, sentiments constitute very shaky ground for sustaining democratic ideals. Unfortunately, though, this is right where multiculturalism (as educational ideology and program) presently leaves us. Shallow democracy is only capable of producing a shallow self-defense.[70]

PART V

The Democratic Imperative

What Democracy Requires

— 8 —

The Futile Quest for Political Solutions

Where the Search Leads

The search for the foundations of a substantive democratic response to these challenges has taken us down different paths and led us to different findings.

Among the special agenda organizations—those groups that participate in the controversy most visibly and audibly—we found a discourse distorted both by the form of rhetoric employed and by an array of unacknowledged interests. The differences in the opposing positions and the uncompromising resolve on each side to realize its own agenda in public policy are intense enough to make substantive argument difficult. But these additional factors, built into the truncated way positions are articulated, virtually guarantee sustained polarization.

Among average citizens, we found more ambivalence than apathy. The range of ambivalence within the general public, however, is mind-boggling. Surely there is no real majority anywhere in this controversy. Yet while the ambivalence is wide-ranging, it is remarkably superficial. Americans would seem to venture onto the seas of this controversy without much ballast of knowledge. Indeed, legal illiteracy and misinformation are the rule, not the exception. And while people feel strongly about abortion and the abortion controversy, they are not capable of articulating much beyond their feelings. The reason, in part, is that they have at their disposal few resources to draw upon besides their own intuition and experience. As a consequence, emotivism reigns.

But the institutions in democratic societies that alone can provide the resources for people to become meaningfully engaged citizens, equipping us to grapple with the differences underlying controversy, have in the main recapitulated the tendencies in other areas. On the one hand, many of the institutions that would mediate the controversy in fact engage the controversy superficially and often tendentiously as partisans. Key civic institutions—among them certain professional organizations, religious associations and even the media—fail to penetrate or transcend the superficialities of this engagement and, in this, serve the special interests if not become de facto special interest groups themselves, in effect carrying out the political agendas of one side or the other. On the other hand, the civic effort to educate the public into the differences underlying conflict fails to acknowledge the nub of Difference at all. Rather than educating people into the depths of diversity, civil society ends up denying central differences and reinforcing the emotivism and subjectivism found in the public at large. The tendencies inherent within other realms of democratic life, then, are reinforced rather than challenged.

In this set of circumstances the very possibility of serious and sustained moral reflection and argument, the kind democracies require to remain vital, is undercut—at least on this issue. However one would choose to name this expression of democracy in action, it is a caricature of what one might expect in the world's most powerful representative of the form, and at least not what one would hope for.

Of Parties and Politicians

What about the possibility of politicians and the parties pointing the way? As the controversy has unfolded over the decades, party involvement has tended to reinforce the artificial character of the controversy. Indeed, despite differences of opinion and position within parties (for example, pro-life Democrats and pro-choice Republicans), such differences tend to be suppressed and publicly unacknowledged; public debate in the parties themselves is hardly tolerated.

The national conventions of the 1992 presidential race provide a window into the workings of the parties in this regard. Of course, the platform of the national Democratic party has been officially pro-choice since the early 1970s, but the position has been put forth more stridently since the 1989 Webster decision. During the primary season, all five of the major Democratic presidential candidates appeared together at a NARAL banquet to identify themselves with the activist wing of the pro-choice movement. The lines hardened up. Thus, when Governor Robert Casey of Pennsylvania (a Catholic and very pro-life) proposed that the platform committee add the clause that "Democrats do not support abortion on demand and believe the number of abortions should be reduced," the governor's aide who made the proposal was booed and hissed and finally cut off as she defended her motion.[1] As Casey complained: "This is the party that's supposed to be tolerant, open to dissent. Now we have a litmus test: if you're pro-life, you're out."[2] Other pro-life Democrats (including roughly one-fourth of all House Democrats in 1992) complained of being "isolated" in the party, treated like "neanderthals," because the Democratic Party had become "the party of abortion."[3] Casey himself was denied the opportunity to speak at the Democratic national convention because of his pro-life views.

The platform of the Republican Party took the abortion issue to the other end of the continuum by calling for a human life amendment, an amendment to the U.S. Constitution that would make abortion illegal even in the cases of rape and incest. In this it also supported legislation that would make "the Fourteenth Amendment's protections apply to unborn children." Pro-choice Republicans who dissented from this position were effectively silenced. At the end of the platform writing process Ralph Reed, executive director of the Christian Coalition, declared: "We are here to celebrate a victory. . . . Within the past hour, the Republican Party passed a pro-life, pro-family platform! The feminists threw everything they had at us! We won and they lost!"[4] A small number of pro-choice Republicans were permitted to speak at the convention, but they were not featured prominently because of the anticipated strong pro-life position of the party. It is little surprise, then, that pro-choice Republican women running for Congress made a prime-time appearance en masse at the Democratic national convention, along with Kate Michelman of NARAL.

In short, the official positions of each party have come to reflect the hard lines of the activist organizations. In itself, this is not a problem. The problem, rather, is that neither party offers anything more than the slogans of solidarity for the already committed. Political parties act as though there are no arguments to be made, only the recapitulation of the symbols of partisan identity.

The incentives for politicians themselves to stay in line with their constituencies in this context are compelling, to say the least. More often than not, they fail to offer anything beyond the standard slogans of the activists. To be sure, the campaigns and administrations of the major candidates for public office to date have done little more than appease partisan interests. Politicians who have tried to move independently, or to state their pro-life or pro-choice positions in a way that will respond to the concerns of all their constituents, struggle against overwhelming obstacles. In this research, my assistants and I spoke with a number of national and regional politicians (Democrats and Republicans) about this, and time and again we heard of the frustration of trying to provide leadership in this context.

None of these politicians denied the legitimacy of special interest organizations and their place in the political process. They are, as one put it, simply "a fact of political life in America." Their effect on the political process, however, is not always salutary from their point of view. A one-time Democratic candidate for the U.S. Senate from Kentucky was labeled as someone who "waffled" on the abortion issue but in fact was trying to articulate some middle ground. As he reflected on his own defeat he conceded, "The special interest groups can make it very difficult for those of us trying to be reasonable." The Democratic attorney general of a midwestern state ran for the governorship and had a similar experience and perspective: "In my campaign I had hoped to get people to sit down and find a common ground, but on issues that are as emotional as, say, abortion or gun control. . . . I found it to be impossible."

A Republican who had spent ten years in the U.S. Congress lost his bid for reelection in 1990. He was pro-life on the abortion issue and, not surprisingly, found himself on the NARAL hit list. "The politics of single issue groups is to divide and conquer. They are extreme, and it's wrong for the country. . . . There will not be any compromise. No compromise is possible, and I'll tell you why. Groups like NARAL make a living off of this stuff. They are employed by this controversy. If there were to be a compromise, they would lose their position, status, and career. This is an issue of money. People aren't going to accept a compromise and be out of a job. And, of course, compromise is not possible for the other side, either."

In the view of one Democratic senate candidate, "politicians are going to have to have the courage to say that the middle ground is the better ground." A pro-life incumbent state representative in California, was also on the NARAL hit list. He did not waver in his views, and as it turned out, he also was defeated. He echoed this perspective: "What we need to see more of is politicians that can hold to their convictions. Politicians need to stick to their strongly held feelings on an issue and not be swayed by every public opinion poll. They need to be firmly grounded in what they believe."

All of the politicians we spoke to also cited the complicity of the press in making their position difficult to maintain. As the former state representative from California reflected, "The campaign was about more than just abortion, but the press kept making abortion *the* issue. It got way more attention than it should have." A Republican politician defeated in the late 1980s in the race for the governorship of a southern state agreed: "Out of the whole panoply of things the press could have covered, they chose to magnify the abortion issue to the exclusion of almost everything else. The press ignored all the other aspects of the campaign. . . . The special interest agenda can loom way too high in the electoral process, especially when the press picks up that agenda. It's pretty much undisputed that the press is pro-choice."

Another politician spoke of the media's role in a slightly different way. "The media always label compromise positions as 'waffling on the issue.' The media label those who are looking for some sort of middle ground as being 'all over the waterfront.'" The midwestern candidate for governor was caught in a similar bind. Ten days before he announced his candidacy, he flipped his position from being pro-life to being pro-choice, and the press pounded him. Reflecting on the experience, he said: "I had to be honest. My views had changed. The press called it an issue of integrity, but I was being honest. There's a lot of peer pressure out there that makes compromise difficult." With more than a tinge of resentment, one politician summarized it this way: "When you are a candidate and you don't have press support, you get your brains beaten in every day. They [the media] don't play fair."

And it is not just abortion that is caught in this deadlock, but the range of contemporary policy issues. Announcing his retirement from office in 1992, Senator Warren Rudman of Vermont lamented, "We have been so polarized by single-issue groups, special-interest groups, lobbyists and the rest that it's not easy to get together any-more . . . and it's not easy to contemplate continuing in this vein."[5] Rudman described the institution of the Senate itself as "an increasingly partisan place . . . a place where fundamental issues are not being addressed." He spoke for many more than himself.

How can one make sense of this state of affairs? The temptation to point fingers at one or another group or one or another set of interests is great. The truth, though, is that the problems besetting political leadership in America have many sources. The special agenda organizations are given to demagogy; the media can be (and often are) lazy and superficial, lacking any self-consciousness of the institution's own cultural predispositions; and politicians are sometimes venal, self-seeking, and hypocritical. But one is remiss if one ignores the failure of responsibility borne by the average citizen in all of this. The public is generally ill informed, unreflective, and too easily fatalistic and dismissive about its own ability and responsibility to exert pressure upward on politicians, the media, and the special interests as a means of making them accountable for their actions. Millions upon millions of Americans, after all, do not even bother to vote. In the end, it is fair to say that we have in democratic practice what we have put into it. Despite the fashion of denigrating Washington and the politicians who give the city its reputation, the reality, it would seem, is that Americans *are* represented in Washington.

The Futile Quest for Political Solutions

Working as they do within the realm of power politics, the efforts of politicians would seem doomed from the outset. Task forces and commissions, policy recommendations, and even the redistribution of funds to deal with such problems create the impression of change, but the kind of change required to deal with the knotty and interminable conflicts of the culture war cannot really be brought about through manipulations of the machinery of the state.

Power Politics

The problem is that all of the major players engaged in cultural conflict tend to operate in the same frame of reference as politicians; all are given to understand and seek resolution through the framework of power politics. The most obvious are the special agenda organizations themselves. In their first resort to lobbying and litigation and their unwillingness to engage the underlying arguments of opponents except through systematically distorted public discourse, they operate entirely in the realm of power politics. The democratic imperative to sustain robust debate becomes but a gloss over the win-at-all-cost agenda they have embraced.

The judiciary has not helped matters. Though by its very nature it is immune from democratic process, it is still capable of providing a highly visible forum for an elevated public moral debate, one that links competing legal reasonings and judgments to the rich moral and philosophical (even if opposing) presuppositions upon which they are based and upon which most citizens implicitly ground their own views. The tendency of judicial action over recent decades, however, has been to divorce legal reasoning and judgment from moral argument altogether.[6] Here, too, power is wielded without meaningful connection to the various cultural traditions reflected in democratic pluralism.

The media's role in this is seen in its unwillingness (perhaps its organizational incapacity) to deal with the controversy in any other way than the political. The cultural and moral dimensions of this controversy are largely ignored or overlooked. It is inevitable, under these circumstances, that public sensibilities and expectations would be oriented toward a political mode of conceptualizing the issue. In the predisposition of some professional organizations to lend their legitimacy to one side of the controversy or the other, even when there is no clear and intrinsic relationship between expertise and advocacy, the situation is further politicized.

Among religious organizations, the pursuit of power is seen in the tendency to elevate ideology over theology. Indeed, religious organizations have shown themselves to be far more interested in organizing boycotts, registering voters, mounting "rescues," creating picket lines and other demonstrations, sending out press releases and direct mail, and lobbying Congress and state legislatures than in proclaiming theological truths, making persuasive arguments, and educating their laity. Here, as with other institutional players, legal and political objectives (amendments, acts, resolutions, and so forth) define the priorities in their public agenda.

The problem, of course, is that when politics is framed as the only (or primary) solution to public disagreement, the only practical question people ask is about who is in control. Is it "our" party, "our" candidate, "our" side—or "theirs"? In this situation, policies inevitably change with changes in personnel: a new administration, a new Congress, a new Supreme Court, and so on. Indeed, the quest for political solutions permits people to avoid or deny altogether the human side of controversy, as though cultural controversy could be formulated as a technical problem permitting a purely technical solution.

Negative Politics and the Will to Power

The problem, though, goes deeper. Not only do all the major players tend to embrace a framework of power politics, but all seem inclined toward a particular *style* of power politics. Even the most casual observer can see that cultural conservatives and progressivists alike (including, prominently, pro-life and pro-choice advocates) are far better at articulating what they are against than what they are for. It is not unfair to describe the nature of political exchange under the present circumstances as a negative politics—one that is oriented first and foremost toward delegitimating and discrediting the opposition. Insofar as this is true, the culture war is not so much a conflict of cultures but a competition of *anti-cultures,* for rarely does one ever hear articulated an integrated, coherent, and affirming moral vision that encompasses the nation as a whole in all of its glorious and irreconcilably messy diversity.

The appeal to politics for resolution, and in particular a politics predicated upon the deprecation of the opposition, suggests once again that what we call democratic practice in America today is the expression of shallow democracy—a "soft imperialism," as Lyotard put it, where words are weapons and debates are occasions to intimidate if not verbally bludgeon one's opponent. What we call democracy in this light may be little more than a comforting fiction idealizing what more nearly resembles the competing "will to power." It is a bitter if not dangerous parody of the ideal we hold in our minds.

We should not miss the irony here. Inasmuch as they accept and work within the framework of power politics, Christians (including, if not especially, conservative Christians), Jews, and humanists— those who would otherwise find Nietzschean ethics anathema—are as Nietzschean as they can be. All too often, in the name of their respective faiths, Christians, Jews, and humanists alike, in practice deny their own rich ethical heritages and come to represent, unwittingly, power-oriented anti-cultures.

Skeptics might suggest that democracy in America has never been anything but a veneer for the competing will to power, but this should offer us little solace. Even if this were the case, there is an edge to the dynamic of power politics today that is at the very least unsettling but, in the end, not altogether surprising. When the shared moral bonds that make community life possible are weakened, when the traditions that make these bonds sacred and inviolable are rendered implausible to vast numbers, what else is there left to order collective life but the exercise of power? The quest for political solutions to all problems is a natural outcome. In the final analysis, though, the exercise of power will never in itself provide a democratically sustainable solution to the controversy over abortion or to the controversies of our postmodern condition.

Substantive Democracy

In the final analysis, the predisposition to force political solutions to the controversies of the culture war is a measure of two things. First, it is a measure of the underlying urgency almost all Americans have about the need to find resolution to these ongoing conflicts. We intuit the dangers at stake, and so we are naturally impatient to reestablish common cultural agreements about the public good; politics becomes a shortcut. At the same time, the predisposition to force political solutions is a measure of the hollowness of democratic practice in American life today in bringing about those ends. A system of formal democratic institutions and procedures remains, to be sure, but it is not buttressed by the substantive participation of citizens in the process of political will formation. The void, as we have seen, is filled by the subtle but nearly ubiquitous institutions and dynamics of power politics.

But, alas, the exercise of power will never provide solutions to controversies that are cultural at heart. The answer can only be cultural as well, in the middle ground between personal sentiment and political action: the realm of moral vision and commitment, filtered through the prism of our real-life social obligations. It is the moral nature of these disputes that make the controversies so intractable, yet rarely if ever are deep cultural realities addressed or engaged on their own terms, in the context of serious and substantive public argument.

The long-term solution, then, can only be found in an enlarged and deepened debate—a debate that is *pre*-political in nature (even if it has practical political ramifications). The long-term solution can only be substantive democracy. Under present circumstances, the idea that political vitality is sustained by substantive reflection and engagement on the part of many and in the context of their communities may sound radical, if not a bit farfetched. But in fact it is not new at all; indeed, the idea reflects a theme central to distinguished traditions of political theory. Such notions were certainly embraced by Jefferson and Madison. It comports, in many respects, with Rousseau's formulation of popular sovereignty. It extends back to Aristotelian notions of citizenship in the *polis:* informed and reasoned participation in the common life of small democratic communities.

Objections

Despite the pedigree, many contemporary observers are nervous about the actual realization of these ideals in contemporary American life. The communitarian political theorist Benjamin Barber ably guides us through the thicket of objections.[7]

Certainly the most persistent complaint is that an enlarged public discussion is tedious, inefficient, and in the end, unlikely to bring about great results. Yet this criticism depends upon a somewhat cynical view of the public as simpleminded masses.[8] The decisive difference is to operate with a *normative* ideal of the public as citizens in community. In Barber's words, "Masses make noise, citizens deliberate; masses behave, citizens act; masses collide and intersect, citizens engage, share, and contribute. At the moment when 'masses' start deliberating, acting, sharing, and contributing, they cease to be masses and become citizens."[9] It is important to emphasize that citizenship in this normative sense does not envision isolated yet omnicompetent individuals, but rather individuals made competent for civic life primarily through membership and participation in distinct moral communities. It is here where individuals find a voice—even if their voice is, in the end, represented by elites in these communities.[10]

Another criticism one can anticipate is that genuine participation will not be possible until the significant economic and social inequities that exist in American society are lessened. Intergenerational poverty and institutional prejudice and racism set up barriers between people and thus are particularly inimical to active citizenship. Clearly the criticism hits the mark; yet what is the alternative? Is not the only way to keep these structured inequities from undermining democracy to make certain that democracy is vibrant and substantive enough to finally undermine the inequities themselves?

Still another criticism issues from the fear that an enlarged and substantive democratic life may actually threaten, if not destroy, hard-won liberal freedoms and institutions. It is far better, the argument goes, to restrict this kind of engagement lest the "ignorant masses" eventually "repeal civil rights laws," "reimpose prayer in schools," and so forth. Needless to say, there are always risks in a democracy, but Barber is probably correct when he argues that a much more worrisome risk is that liberal representative institutions will so thin out meaningful participation that democracy is reduced to "the politics of special interests, the politics of neopopulist fascism, the politics of image (via television and advertising), or the politics of mass society."[11] (In the context of our search, these very illiberal risks sound all too much like realities.) A further threat from a thinned-out version of representative democracy is that it can foster a widespread popular cynicism that undermines the legitimacy of liberal democratic institutions themselves. As Barber summarizes: "To be free we must be self-governing; to have rights we must be citizens. In the end, only citizens can be free. The argument for strong [and, I would add, substantive] democracy, though at times deeply critical of liberalism, is thus an argument on behalf of liberty."[12]

Obligations

More serious than these objections, however, is a sense of cynicism that any meaningful change can take place in the nature and functioning of public life. Such cynicism comes packaged as sociological realism, and its effect is always to make the suggestion of meaningful change sound idealistic, if not naive. As a sociologist, I am professionally inclined to accept such determinisms, but as a citizen I see no choice but to hope against them. The obligation to hope becomes all the more poignant when one is reminded of all that is at stake.

— 9 —

Beyond the Culture War
What It Will Take

We Americans would like to imagine ourselves to be somehow above and beyond the possibility of serious civil strife. The very idea of the civil unrest that has torn apart nations like Yugoslavia, Ireland, and Lebanon happening here jolts the mind. Total nonsense, we are inclined to say; we are much too civilized for that sort of thing.

Perhaps so, and perhaps we think this with good reason. I, for one, am disinclined to believe it will happen myself. But then the idea burrows into the mind, suggesting some uncomfortable parallels. Here, as there, nonnegotiable claims about the ordering of public life are in conflict. Here, as there, the claims made (even if thought of as secular) are religious in character, if not in substance—they emerge out of our ultimate beliefs and commitments, our most cherished sense of what is right, true, and good. Here, as there, the conflicting claims trace quickly back to competing ideals of community and national identity. Finally here, as there, a culture war with deep historical roots has festered just barely beneath the surface of public life. Our discomfort is not assuaged when an ob-

227

server like George Kennan tells us that the population has become too large, that pluralism in America has become too intense and the polity too complex for the central government to coherently hold it together; that perhaps the best solution is to divide the nation into semiautonomous republics.[1] Kennan is not alone.[2] The secessionist impulse (as seen in Kansas, Alaska, northern California, and other areas) often seems to be intensifying. Suggestions along these lines may not amount to the balkanization of America, but it comes very close. Perhaps in form this is our postmodern Bosnia after all.

However implausible such speculation may sound to us, surely we are unwise to minimize the significance of the challenges our culture war presents to American democratic life and institutions. The challenge is not just the potential volatility of particular controversies. The challenge is internal as well, in the ways the normative ideals that democracy itself depends upon have been weakened. The sociological and political realities of the culture war have a centrifugal effect, fragmenting the very normative framework that would provide a rational and non-coercive way of dealing with the conflict. The "center" can no longer hold; the older faiths—Judeo-Christian and Classical—that once amidst great diversity provided a set of common, if not always coherent, assumptions for the ordering of public life (seen most visibly in Western law, literature, arts, and the like) no longer play. And those imagining that we can recreate and reimpose these older "traditional" agreements are simply deluding themselves.

Yet absent some common assumptions, some common metaphysical dream of the world, is it possible to think of people as deeply divided as we are living together in relative peace for very long into the future.[3] Where, now, is the new *unum*, capable of binding together a *pluribus* that seems ever more fragmented? The central premise of this essay is that in a democratic society the unum cannot be imposed from the top down but must be generated from the bottom up, in the dialectical process of generating new working agreements out of a serious confrontation with our deepest differences.[4]

If this argument is right, even approximately so, then on a practical note it becomes clear that there is no quick and easy solution to the abortion controversy, the controversies over homosexuality, the arts, race, church/state—or to the culture war as a whole. Anyone hawking such a solution (see Chapter One) most assuredly has another agenda that, in the final analysis, comprises a bypass around the democratic imperative in favor of the heavy hand of power politics.

As democrats, then, we are stuck. Consider the case of abortion again; even as that controversy evolves, the central issues underlying the politics of reproduction promise not to disappear anytime soon. The same can be said for the controversies surrounding race, gay rights, the arts, euthanasia, fetal tissue research, multicultural education, and the like as they evolve: the core underlying debate will not go away. But the point is, *neither should such controversy go away—not until we have faced up to our deepest differences over these matters directly and substantively.* Democracies that live up to the name would seem to have no other alternative. But how is this possible?

Substantive Democracy: Modesty in Politics

As Daniel Bell once put it, "The thought of Puritan theocracy is the great influential fact in the history of the American mind."[5] Some very small numbers in America today still maintain such hope literally, but the perfectionism implied in the notion of "puritan theocracy" has survived its secularization. Thus the spokeswomen at the National Organization for Women are every bit as much the puritan perfectionists as the spokesmen of Operation Rescue; the impulse driving the attorneys at the American Civil Liberties Union in New York City is every bit as much millenarian as the impulse driving the churchmen and women at the American Family Association in Tupelo, Mississippi; and so on. If there is a national character, millenarianism is certainly one of its defining characteristics. Democrats, independents, and Republicans; conservatives, libertarians, and liberals; religionists and secularists—we all still want America to be "a city upon a hill." We cannot shake it; Bell was right.

The particularly knotty part of this perfectionism, though, is the underlying conviction that all institutions, and especially the state, can and should embody an idealized vision of social life in full historical measure. Our politics so often becomes a means by which we seek some inner purity. Latent in our political imagination is the idea that if we can realize abstract principles and ideals in our political institutions, we can achieve a measure of salvation. Thus, when institutional realities do not conform to the ideal (that is, with an *idea* of reality, untempered by historical experience), the basic legitimacy of the institution is called into question.

What is even more problematic about this underlying utopianism is that it operates upon what Max Weber called an "ethics of ultimate ends."[6] In this ethic, the ends always justify the means. What are the means of which he speaks? Weber, dogged realist that he was, said that "the decisive means for politics is violence." The ends, in other words, always justify forms of coercion.[7] Caught in the logic of this ethical perfectionism, it is easy to see how it is that liberals eventually become quite illiberal, Christians eventually act in quite un-Christian ways, humanists eventually behave inhumanely, conservatives eventually become insensitive to the traditions they espouse, champions of tolerance become intolerant, and so on.[8]

Clearly there is a need to temper the expectations built into this tenacious exceptionalism. It does not take Aristotle to remind us that *any* social order forged, in whatever part, through democratic processes will be inherently flawed, unstable, and ideologically impure. This is because social and political processes are inherently more complex and intractable than the realm of abstract principle. What is possible in theory is usually less than probable in experience.

The call, then, is for modesty about our political objectives. For one, this means a recognition that America will never really be a city upon a hill, and if it is, it will be by necessity a city whose walls are crumbling and always in need of repair; America will never be a beacon, except one that is not so bright and that is periodically prone to go out. Modesty, then, means a recognition that America will always be flawed. For Christians and many Jews, this is not compromise but a frank recognition that the world will always be marred by sin, and that the believer's true citizenship is in heaven. For the secular humanist, this is not compromise but an honest (perhaps even scientific) appreciation for the inherently frail nature of the human condition, and the fact that human progress is an extraordinarily long-term commitment. Such modesty does not require the abandonment of one's ideals, however utopian, narrowly defined, and/or partisan they may be, but rather their interaction with what Weber called an "ethics of responsibility." This is an ethical orientation that acknowledges consequences, intended and unintended, of human actions. It is an ethics that acknowledges that tragedy is interwoven in virtually all human activity, but especially political activity, however well intended.[9] Once again, without abandoning one's ideals, the credo changes. No longer is it "today, we will remake the world"; rather, it is "today, we will try to make the world just a little bit better."

Such modesty in politics, necessary to the cultivation of substantive democracy and essential to the task of moving beyond the tensions of the culture war, can be pursued through at least three strategies. These are outlined below.

Redefining the Public

When people use the terms *public debate,* or *public square,* or *public life,* they almost always refer to that which is most "public"—as in most visible or audible or consequential to the largest number of people. In most cases, then, *public* refers to that which is national in its scope, impact, or character. In this way, "public" debate tends to mean discussion that is filtered through the national media to the general population of Americans; the "public" square is the national politics and jurisprudence; and "public" life is the experience one has within, or the contribution one makes to, national political affairs. As it works out, the more "national" and "public" an idea or position is, the more simplified and clichéd it becomes. Subtlety and particularity are lost; the public becomes conflated with the political, and as a consequence, issues become polarized into mutually exclusive ideologies. So it is with abortion and most of the issues of the culture war.

The problem with conceiving the public arena in this way, of course, is that there exists a vast territory of social life between national culture and individual meaning and existence. This area of social life is either trivialized as unimportant or, more likely is overlooked altogether. The "public" in public debate does not have to mean national debate. It can and should mean local and regional debate—*among* people who live and work in relative proximity to each other and who care about their common neighborhoods and communities, towns, cities, and regions; and *within* institutions that are prominent and integrated into the communities where these people live. As Tocqueville observed on his trip to America, democracy flourishes in small-scale (that is, decentralized or local) settings. In such settings, local institutions and elites can play a genuinely mediating role, for there is, by the very circumstances of the collective life, accountability to each other and to others.

It is, perhaps, too easy to be cynical about redefining the "public" to a more human scale, but a commitment to substantive democracy would obligate us to work toward this end. The idea, in fact, is not a dreamy utopianism; it has been practiced in rare occasions and the experiments have achieved measurable success.

Consider the case of abortion once more. In St. Louis, Missouri, for example, the director of Reproductive Health Services invited the chief pro-life attorney to talk with her in the hope of finding "common ground." This was the start of a series of meetings oriented toward helping women and children. "It was shockingly easy to identify issues we agree on," she said, "like the need for aid to pregnant women who are addicted to drugs, the need for better prenatal care and the need to reduce unwanted pregnancy. . . . Neither side wants women to need abortions because they don't have the money to raise a child."[10] The conversations have even taken tangible results. As reported in the *New York Times,*

> when a pregnant 10-year-old came to the abortion clinic, but decided to carry her pregnancy to term, Jean Cavender, the clinic's director of public affairs and a participant in the common-ground talks, called Ms. Wagner [of Missouri Citizens for Life] for help.
>
> She told Ms. Wagner that the girl needed to stay in bed because the pregnancy was medically complicated but that because her mother worked there was no one to care for her during the day. Ms. Wagner then raised enough money in anti-abortion circles to pay for an attendant and found a woman willing to go into the girl's dangerous drug-infested neighborhood. The baby was later put up for adoption.[11]

Reproductive Health Services and Missouri Citizens for Life also cooperated in sending up legislation to pay for the treatment of pregnant drug addicts. Both sides admit, however, that they are "a long way from any major joint projects."[12]

In Wisconsin, a similar group met over a period of many months. One of the outcomes was a joint recommendation on sex education in public schools offered to the state legislature. "This comes as a great relief to the legislators," said one participant, "because they've been caught in the middle for so long, getting beaten up whatever they do." Of the larger effort to find common ground she said, "We haven't any idea where this will go but we want to see it evolve. For 20 years we've been butting heads, and it hasn't worked, so it was time to try something else."[13]

In Bridgeport, Connecticut, a city and state that are both highly pro-choice, the Catholic diocese has initiated a program to help women of all faiths work through their feelings over having had an abortion.[14] Church officials there do not in any way deny the sinfulness of abortion, but the emphasis is not on theological judgment, nor is it on church politics or social activism. Rather, Project Rachel, as it is called, offers group therapy and one-on-one spiritual counseling to women who "feel like shit," who have "got pain and guilt and depression coming out of every pore in [their] body," who never had "a chance to grieve" over or because of their abortion.[15] Monsignor Martin Ryan, who oversees the diocese and started the local chapter, insists that the church set an example of generosity, believing this to be a precondition of the larger society paying attention: "In a Catholic state we want to show we love the sinner and hate the sin."

What is equally interesting in all of this is that in Bridgeport, much of the church's work is accomplished in conjunction with the Bridgeport Adolescent Pregnancy Prevention Program, a coalition that includes (besides the Catholic church) city social service agencies and even Planned Parenthood. The coalition is tenuously held together, to be sure, working in large part because of the existence of separate tracks for different kinds of clients, yet still there is cross-fertilization among the groups; discussions are held, information is shared, and so on.

It is worth noting in all of these illustrations that *the people most receptive to the idea of talking and even working together are those who deal with women facing unplanned pregnancies on a day-to-*

day basis—either those who run abortion clinics or homes for pregnant women. Those who work in advocacy groups toward legal and political change seem to be the *least* receptive.[16] This makes sense in light of all we know of the special interest organizations.

Yet even in these practical contexts, the situation remains tense. There is, for example, pressure for these individuals *not* to come together. Activist associates are very often "horrified" by the meetings, feeling that "they give credibility to the enemy."[17] Yet neither side has compromised, nor should they necessarily. They are, however, learning to come to terms with each other in the same social space. "No one is ever going to convince me that it's all right to kill unborn babies," said Loretto Wagner of the Missouri Citizens for Life. "And I'm going to go on working to make abortion illegal. But that doesn't mean we need to demonize each other. If this is not to become the Vietnam of the 1990s, we have to learn to sit down and talk to each other."[18] An abortion clinic director and pro-choice advocate echoed this sentiment: "It has become very clear to me that the polarization I have engaged in for years has not served the women in my community, has not helped to resolve anything and was a self-indulgence."[19]

Alas, success (if the word is appropriate at all) is not measured in political terms but in social terms: in the de-escalation of tensions, in the development of a small measure of mutual understanding, and in the outcomes of real people's lives. A similar effect can be found in smaller-scaled mediation dealing with controversies surrounding text-books, church-state matters, the arts, multiculturalism, and so on.

Redefining the "public" in public debate—by downscaling it—is certainly a crucial strategy for finding a democratically sustainable solution to the abortion controversy and any others. By itself, however, it will never be enough. A second strategy entails recovering the languages of public argument.

Recovering the Languages of Public Argument

It is undoubtedly naive to idealize or sentimentalize "the public" or "the common person," even if (perhaps especially if) one carries certain populist sympathies. As we have seen, average citizens are not so much disinclined from serious engagement in public affairs as they are ill equipped. Yet most have neither the time nor the ability to sort through the massive amounts of information necessary to make informed judgments on any particular issue, much less care about the panoply of issues that make up the contemporary culture war. Most are content to operate in the easy lexicon of superficial slogans that quell psychological tensions and create a sense of identity and even belonging with others. And while passions exist in abundance in contemporary public culture, passion guided by serious moral reflection that reaches beyond one's own personal experience is a rarity. The Jeffersonian ideal of a democracy sustained by an enlightened citizenry would seem, then, to be hopelessly inadequate to an information-bloated, hyper-emotivist mass society.

The obvious line of questioning is, is this really necessary? Why not let people's moral and religious idealism recede into the background of public discourse and then encourage them, alternatively, to embrace the ways of pragmatism? Would we not be better off if people just dealt practically with the facts and consequences of their life circumstances?

Pragmatism offers important insights (ones that I affirm shortly), yet as a comprehensive strategy it falls short. Foremost, such a strategy denies or at least mutes, rather than acknowledges, diversity—the rich variety of communities that make up pluralism in America. In the final analysis, community is always particular, and the particularism that gives identity to different communities has long been defined principally by religious and philosophical traditions, ideals, and practices. Besides, pragmatism (so central to liberal modernism) is just one of the particularisms making up contemporary pluralism today. To imagine it is any more universal than, say, Christianity or Judaism as a language of public culture today is either philosophical naïvité or ethnocentric arrogance. As we have seen, the conflicts of the culture war take shape precisely in these communities of moral discourse. Whether or not people recognize it or can articulate it, it is their attachments to these communities of moral discourse that fundamentally shape their views. People, then, should be brought to a point where they are equal to it. Not only is pluralism acknowledged and affirmed in what I am suggesting, but given where citizens are in everyday life, such a strategy is, finally, the pragmatic one.

But is this conceivable?

It is, again, very easy to become jaded about the possibility of "equipping" a larger number of Americans (not least its political and civic leadership) with the resources for serious reflection and argument: the capacity to see how opposing positions on issues are rooted within different traditions of rational justification. But if words like *democracy* are not just empty verbiage, then we have no choice but to try to recover the moral, philosophical, and even theological languages that make a higher level of public reflection and argument possible. But how?

Educating people in the differences that underlie controversy requires an education into the substance of culture—the truth claims, the traditions of moral understanding within which these truth claims are elaborated, and the ways these are enacted in communities. Despite the noble intentions behind them, the current programs for accomplishing these ends, subsumed under the rubric of multiculturalism, contribute to just the opposite, at least as they are currently formulated. They gloss over what is at the heart of multiple cultures by discrediting the very idea of binding (albeit competing) truths, ideals of the good, standards of virtue, and so on. To continue to ignore these differences and their significance for public life is to maintain the status quo. The Differences must be confronted directly.

Public schools and universities certainly have a role in providing "moral education" of this sort. The minimalist approach would be to simply acknowledge that these differences exist; a maximalist approach would be to teach (carefully) young people what these differences are and their significance in the course of human affairs. Perhaps even more significant for the recovery of these resources are the revitalizations of the particular moral and religious communities which are the natural constituencies of the pro-life and pro-choice movements—the evangelical and mainline Protestant, conservative and liberal Catholic, Mormon and religiously observant Jewish and humanist communities. Here, too, *before* disputes enter the realm of politics or litigation, substantive argument needs to take place.

Again, the possibility is not totally farfetched. The "Social Statement on Abortion" of the Evangelical Lutheran Church in America provides one illustration of the way one mainline Protestant denomination, wracked by division over the abortion issue, addressed the controversy.[20] Most significantly, political and legal judgments were minimized in the document. For example, the use of the language of rights (of either the fetus or the woman) in an absolutist way was rejected as unhelpful. Rather, the issue was placed in the context of church life, and then the entire matter was framed in theological language: life in all its phases is acknowledged as "a mysterious, awesome gift of God" and therefore has "intrinsic value, worth, and dignity"; the sin of failing to respond to poverty, oppressive social relationships, sexism, and racism—the factors that dehumanize women and often lead them to consider abortion—were confessed; ethical guidance regarding unintended pregnancies was offered; and so on. It is in this theological frame of reference that pro-life and pro-choice advocates in the denomination discover their commonalities. The document affirmed, in conclusion, that

> the church's role in society begins long before and extends far beyond legislative regulation. It seeks to shape attitudes and values that affirm people in whatever circumstances they find themselves. Its pastoral care, compassionate outreach, and life-sustaining assistance are crucial in supporting those who bear children, as well as those who choose not to do so. Through these and other means the people of God seek to be truly supportive of life.[21]

A similar effort was pursued by the Presbyterian Church USA.[22] As described by the chairman of the committee studying the matter, the majority report sought to avoid a "win-lose" situation by finding areas where abortion foes and advocates of abortion rights could agree. The report describes abortion as an option of "last resort" not to be used "casually, or as a repeated method of contraception." It further described the practice as "morally acceptable" in the difficult circumstances of rape, incest, and so forth. While it also advocated that sex be limited to married couples, the report called for universal health care, affordable day care, and other social services that would make it easier for low-income women to choose to opt out of abortion. In assuming its own responsibility, the report argued that Presbyterian churches should consider offering adoption programs, homes for pregnant women, and other services that would ease the pressure to have an abortion.

My point is not to endorse the particular outcomes of these statements with regard to abortion. One may agree or disagree. My point in highlighting these statements is to call attention to the non-political manner in which controversy in these communities was addressed. In both of these cases, sharp disagreements clearly remain, but not, it would seem, at the expense of the common life of the church. Such efforts illustrate first steps by which the education of the laity into moral and theological life of the churches (and the disagreements that will always be there) is rendered possible.

Such efforts can be duplicated and applied with great fruitfulness to the wide range of controversies that exist in moral communities and in the nation as a whole. In the end, it is only in the context of the moral and sociological communities we inhabit over the course of our lives, and not the public environment defined by direct mail, electronic sound bites, or paid political advertisements, that public debate will have integrity with various but shared biographies. It is only in the context of revitalized communities, where obligations and rights are balanced against each other, that persuasive arguments can have lasting effects.

Reviving the Art of Argument and Persuasion

Reviving the art of argument and persuasion certainly depends upon a conducive environment and the linguistic capacities that give vitality to coherent cultural expression. Just as important would be an affirmation by all parties of certain ground rules for civil but principled engagement. Walter Lippmann provided a compelling rationale for such guidelines that is probably more relevant today than when he penned it at mid-century:

> If there is a dividing line between liberty and license, it is where freedom of speech is no longer respected as a procedure of the truth and becomes the unrestricted right to exploit the ignorance, and to incite the passions, of the people. Then freedom is such a hullabaloo of sophistry, propaganda, special pleading, lobbying, and salesmanship that it is difficult to remember why freedom of speech is worth the pain and trouble of defending it.
>
> What has been lost in the tumult is the meaning of the obligation which is involved in the right to speak freely. It is the obligation to

subject the utterance to criticism and debate. Because the dialectical debate is a procedure for attaining moral and political truth, the right to speak is protected by a willingness to debate.[23]

The most cogent effort to articulate a framework for public argument to emerge in recent times came as part of the celebration of the bicentennial of the Constitution, in a document known as the Williamsburg Charter.[24] Within its reaffirmation of the genius of the First Amendment of the Bill of Rights, four guidelines for conducting civil public debate were set out as a central part of the mutual compact implicit in democratic pluralism.

First, *those who claim the right to dissent should assume the responsibility to debate.* This combination implies that "the characteristic American formula of individual liberty complemented by respect for the opinions of others [will] permit differences to be asserted, yet a broad, active community of understanding to be sustained." Second, *those who claim the right to criticize should assume the responsibility to comprehend.* This suggests a critical difference between a "genuine tolerance" and a "debased tolerance." As the charter puts it, "Genuine tolerance considers contrary views fairly and judges them on merit. Debased tolerance so refrains from making any judgment that it refuses to listen at all. Genuine tolerance honestly weighs honest differences and promotes both impartiality and pluralism. Debased tolerance results in indifference to the differences that vitalize a pluralistic democracy." Third, *those who claim the right to influence should accept the responsibility not to inflame.* When ultimate principles are at stake in public life, it is both natural and very easy for each side to incite the other to defensiveness and hostility. After all, what one side of the cultural divide views as a desacralization, the other views as a constitutional right, and vice versa. A commitment to both the social and moral bonds of democratic civility would seem to require a caution and respect (based in common citizenship) in the manner in which ideas and agendas are put forward. Fourth, *those who claim the right to participate should accept the responsibility to persuade.* Among other things, this means that arguments for public policy "should be more than private convictions shouted out loud. For persuasion to be principled, private convictions would be translated into publicly accessible claims. Such claims should be made publicly accessible for two reasons: first, because they must engage those who do not share the same private convictions, and second, because they should be directed toward the common good."

As Os Guinness, one of the drafters of the charter, put it, these guidelines can constitute a set of "Queensbury Rules" for public discourse—ideals that go beyond a mere proceduralism to provide a usable framework wherein the terms of common life can be forged and reforged.

But the incentives against working toward this form of substantive and principled discourse are great. As an attorney for the American Civil Liberties Union (ACLU) put it when reflecting on the very principles mentioned above: "I don't disagree with the Williamsburg Charter in substance, but it's not in our interest for it to succeed. The ultimate strength of the ACLU is that we have more lawyers than anyone else."[25] Make no mistake, there are many on the other side of the cultural divide who, to different ends, would voice a similar view. But if we agree that a more substantive form of public debate is a requirement of a truly just democratic order, and not just the stuff of wistful utopianism or late-night nostalgia, then *how* we contend with each other must be as important to us as *what* we contend for.

One illustration of this art in practice was a statement published at the time of the 1992 Democratic national convention in the *New York Times*. Entitled "A New American Compact: Caring About Women, Caring for the Unborn," its signatories included women and men; Jews, secularists, Catholics, and Protestants; Democrats, Republicans and independents, and liberals and conservatives.[26] The document leaned strongly in the pro-life direction; for example, it called abortion a "violent act, not against 'potential life,' but against a living, growing human being—a life with potential." At the same time, the statement acknowledged and responded to contentions raised by abortion-rights advocates concerning the need for legal abortion. It further proposed "a new compact of care" in public policies "that responsibly protect and advance the interest of mothers *and* their children, both before *and* after birth." "Such policies," the compact read, "would provide maximum feasible legal protection for the unborn and maximum feasible care and support for pregnant women, mothers, and children." Beyond this, the document reaffirmed the importance of debate, recognizing that "there

are disagreements about what is possible and even desirable."
Whatever one may think of the substance of the statement or the
position it takes, it embodies the spirit of civility and exemplifies the
art of persuasion. It is a public document that invites a response in
kind from those who, for whatever reason, disagree.

The potential for reviving the art of persuasion can be enhanced
along a quite different path by moving away (albeit carefully and
strategically) from the duality of unchallengeable and nonnegotiable principles and to practical moral problems that arise in real-life
circumstances. This is not to abandon debate at the level of pure
principle, nor to apply pure principle to hypothetical hard-case situations; but rather to work through moral and cultural debate
through the dilemmas arising in the real-life circumstances of actual
human beings. Albert Jonsen and Stephen Toulmin have written in
defense of this kind of "casuistry":

> In morality, as in law and public administration, the assumption that
> all practical decisions need to rest on a sufficiently clear and general
> system of invariable rules or principles has, from a theoretical point
> of view, a certain attractiveness. But in the actual business of dealing
> with particular real-life cases and situations, such rules and principles
> can never take us more than part of the way. The real-life application
> of moral, legal, and administrative rules calls always for the exercise
> of human perceptiveness and discernment . . . and the more prob-
> lematic the situations become, the greater is the need for such dis-
> cernment.[27]

Again, public moral exchange does not abandon general principles of moral reasoning but rather seeks to integrate them with wisdom, discernment, and discretion as they are applied to real-life
circumstances. In this way, deadlock does not disappear but is put
on the shelf, as it were, in the effort to solve particular problems
justly. This, in many respects, is precisely what has gone on in Missouri, Wisconsin, and Connecticut—as noted earlier.

Revitalizing Politics Within Its Limits

As we have seen, the politicization of cultural controversy and of
the various institutions of civil society as they attempt to mediate
these disputes has aggravated divisions that are already intrinsically

quite deep. And while the mere exercise of power will not resolve cultural controversy or even ease the tensions, the answer cannot be in the abandonment of politics. To imagine that we could de-politicize these controversies at this point would be sheer illusion. At the same time, it is easy to be disparaging of politics altogether, and the temptation to retreat wholly into the realm of private life is great. Cynicism and renunciation is a bit too easy. But if democracy is an experiment worth continuing, then it is central to come to terms with the limitations of political engagement and to work toward the revitalization of politics *within* its proper boundaries.

To the end of revitalizing democratic politics within the practical boundaries of its sphere of activity, it would also seem essential to multiply, not lessen, the tensions inherent in controversy. The objective here is not to increase tension in some artificial sense or to increase it for its own sake. Rather the objective is to increase tension by deepening it, through facing up to the differences inherent within such tension. It is only in facing up squarely to the differences implicit within a pluralistic society that the full humanity of all our controversies is made tangible, and that the dialectic central to democratic governance is made vital.

Naturally, this is far from easy. As Lippmann recognized, "What men will most ardently desire is to suppress those who disagree with them and, therefore, stand in the way of the realization of their desires."[28] But the consequences of *not* allowing the give-and-take of the dialectic are potentially disastrous. Again, Lippmann saw it clearly: "Once confrontation in debate is no longer necessary, the toleration of all opinions leads to intolerance. Freedom of speech, separated from its essential principle [of genuine confrontation], leads through a short, transitional chaos to the destruction of the freedom of speech."[29] This is what the political correctness—barely below the surface, yet so ubiquitous and urgent—on both sides of the cultural divide continually guarantees.

Through a heightening of the tensions, we are continually reminded of the limitations of political action. We are reminded that politics, in the final analysis, is primarily effective in dealing with administrative tasks. It is not able to deal with the collective search for shared meanings, the formation of public philosophies of public good, or the organic generation of civic obligations, responsibilities, and trust among the citizens who inhabit a community or society.

Beyond the Culture War

In all of this, not only is modesty required, but realism as well.

Realism first implies that the conflicts are acknowledged for what they are and for all that is at stake. Abortion and the like are only one source of divisiveness. The problems of the underclass, urban public education, the deficit, racial and ethnic tension, and the like are equally if not more volatile. Here again, a mere tinkering with public policy will not be enough. Cultural resources are crucial to resolving these matters as well—but what will be their nature and content? Here we are forced again to confront the central problematic of the contemporary culture war: on what terms (that is, the truths, values, ideals, and moral commitments) will we order our lives together?

Realism also implies that the democratic process is acknowledged for what it is—that the actual practice of democracy is intrinsically messy, difficult, and never entirely satisfying work. Complacency, then, is the enemy.

Democracy must be reinvented in every generation and for the circumstances in which each new generation finds itself. If democracy itself is not to be just a slogan but a substantive reality, there is no other choice but to strive cautiously, even modestly, to such ends. In it lies the possibility and hope that conflict, even the very rudimentary conflict of the contemporary culture war, will be transformed.[30] It is the transformation of conflict that must be the goal.

In such a transformation, it is possible that most Americans will find they are uncomfortable with the stark alternatives between individualism and collectivism, egalitarianism and hierarchy, rights and obligations, and so on that mark the contemporary culture war. Are the alternatives really so stark? Perhaps in litigation and in political discourse, but perhaps not in the substantive give-and-take of people living and drawing from different cultural traditions.

Perhaps in the renewal of democratic life, institutions, and practices, we will discover that the rhetoric of current "debate" is artificially polarized. In the special case of abortion, we may discover that the question is not about women versus unborn children, but about what kind of society is it that creates this kind of forced selection to begin with. The choice between alternatives may, in the end, be a false choice. The same, of course, holds for all of the conflicts America endures at the end of the twentieth century: they may all reflect false choices. It is only in the renewal of substantive democracy, however, that we will find out.

NOTES

Prologue

1. See Michel Foucault, *The History of Sexuality, Volume I* (New York: Vintage, 1990).
2. Philip Rieff, "The New Noises of War in the Second Culture Camp: Notes on Professor Burt's Legal Fictions," *Yale Journal of Law and the Humanities,* 3, no. 2 (Summer 1991), 324.
3. As my colleague G. W. Sheldon has written, "If we wish to continue flattering ourselves as 'the nation of Jefferson,' every generation of Americans is obliged to determine how well its society and values measure up to Jefferson's hope for the new American republic" G. W. Sheldon, *The Political Philosophy of Thomas Jefferson* (Baltimore: Johns Hopkins University Press, 1991), 147. This book is written in the spirit of that obligation.
4. The letter was unpublished and was unacknowledged. He wrote again three weeks later with a copy enclosed. In his follow-up he said, "The purpose of this letter is to establish for the record that you did in fact receive the first letter. For if I do not receive an answer to this letter, it is fair to assume that you did." Percy received no reply. The original letter and his follow-up note are published in Walker Percy, *Signposts in a Strange Land,* ed. Patrick Samway (New York: Noonday Press, 1991).
5. Laurence Tribe, *Abortion: The Clash of Absolutes* (New York: Norton, 1990), 58. Several endnotes in his text have been deleted here for the sake of readability.
6. Tim Stafford, "In Reluctant Praise of Extremism," *Christianity Today,* 26 October 1992, 18–24. Some pro-life advocates *would* sanction violence. The response of some grass-roots pro-life supporters to the

murder of David Gunn was chilling in this regard. "Obviously, not all killing is murder," said one woman from Grants Pass, Oregon. "The Bible is full of instances where God told people to kill other people. . . . Griffin did not shoot Mother Teresa; he shot a mass murderer no different from the likes of Hitler or Saddam Hussein. I do not rule out the possibility that when a government refuses to stop mass murders, God raises up people who will." Said another, "Even President Lincoln realized that God demands a price from a nation that prizes such 'national offences,' and that . . . price is war and death, not love and peace." (These statements were taken from the letters-to-the-editors section of *World,* 17 April 1993, p. 5. The letters were all in response to an editorial by John Seel entitled "Killing the Baby Killers.")

7. Andrew Sullivan, "Washington Diarist: Losing Ground," *New Republic,* 14 December 1992, 46.
8. Rieff, "New Noises of War," p. 354.
9. Marcus Aurelius Antoninus, from his *Meditations,* Book IX, 29 (Indianapolis: Hackett Publishing Company, 1988), pp. 92–93.

Chapter 1.

1. Kristin Luker, *Abortion and the Politics of Motherhood* (Berkeley and Los Angeles: University of California Press, 1984).
2. The nature of this problem is driven home when considering the comparison between Europe and America. In most European countries, the controversy does not exist, even though the actual practice of abortion is much the same. In Europe, as in the United States, most abortions (approximately 90 percent) occur within the first trimester of pregnancy. The crucial difference is the law's symbolic message; the point at which law and moral meaning converge. As Mary Ann Glendon has shown, public policy in most European countries "communicates" that fetal life should be protected if at all possible and that abortion is a serious matter that governments have an interest in regulating. According to her study, slightly more than half legally disapprove of abortion except where circumstances amount to a justifiable cause. In France, for example, abortion is available in the first ten weeks of gestation if the pregnant woman considers herself "in distress," and then only after she undergoes mandatory counseling. After ten weeks, abortion is possible only if two physicians certify that the pregnancy is likely to pose a serious danger to the woman's health or that the child is likely to be born with a serious medical condition. In other European countries (such as Austria, Denmark, Greece, Norway, and Sweden), abortion is permitted on demand through the first trimester but forbidden after twelve weeks, except again in an emergency or for the most serious of reasons.

The policy in Sweden provides the best illustration of all because though Sweden's law is the most permissive, even there abortion is not permitted if the fetus is likely to be viable (except, of course, in the case of an immediate threat to the woman's life or health). Until eighteen weeks, a woman may have an abortion at her request (though after twelve weeks a counseling session with a social worker is required). After eighteen weeks (but again before viability), abortion is permitted but only with authorization by the country's national board of health and welfare. This message is further communicated by the generous social benefits offered to mothers, married or unmarried, in many of these countries, which make alternatives to abortion more feasible. American law during the years of *Roe*, by contrast, has said that at no point is fetal life worthy of protection by the state; a woman's interest—her right to an abortion—outweighs all other considerations. Moreover, this message is reinforced by a rather stingy social welfare policy toward mothers. As Glendon concluded from her review, American policy on the issue of abortion is "in a class by itself, at least with respect to other developed nations." Mary Ann Glendon, *Abortion and Divorce in Western Law* (Cambridge, Mass.: Harvard University Press, 1987).

3. It would seem, equally unsurprisingly, that both sides are "right" in their own way. The difference in these interpretations of the law comes down to the difference between principle and practice. In principle *Roe* may present a compromise, but in practice it has failed to do so.

   In 1973, Justice Harry Blackmun wrote the majority opinion for the Supreme Court, arguing that a woman's decision to terminate or continue her pregnancy is a fundamental right, part of a "right of privacy." This right would allow her to have an abortion at any time and for any reason up to viability (between twenty-four and twenty-eight weeks), the only restrictions being those that protect the health of the pregnant woman. The Court argued, however, that the "fundamental right" to an abortion is not an "absolute right" for all nine months of the pregnancy—as the lawyers and many of the *amici* advocated. There was a point at which the state might have an interest in protecting potential life. As Blackmun wrote:

   With respect to the . . . interest in potential life, the 'compelling' point is its viability. This is so because the fetus then presumably has the capability of meaningful life outside the mother's womb. . . . If the State is interested in protecting fetal life after viability it may go so far as to proscribe abortion during that period except when it is necessary to preserve the life or health of the mother. [*Roe v. Wade*, 410 U.S. 113 (1973)].

   In this sense, *Roe v. Wade* was clearly a rejection of abortion on demand, at least for pregnancies in their third trimester.

The problem has come, in large part, in trying to translate the reach of *Roe* in actual policy. In *Roe* itself, abortion was proscribed after viability, yet after viability (measured typically at the end of the sixth month) states must permit abortions that are necessary to preserve maternal life or health. In *Roe's* companion decision, *Doe v. Bolton,* the court defined "health" as "all factors . . . relevant to the well-being of the patient—including emotional, psychological, familial [factors] and the woman's age." The *Doe* ruling also held that states cannot outlaw abortions simply because the women who seek them are nonresidents and that states cannot require abortions be performed in specially accredited hospitals, or that abortions be approved by hospital committees or other physicians. Subsequent decisions not only reaffirmed *Roe* but extended its interpretation, overturning virtually every effort to restrict the practice of abortion. In *Planned Parenthood v. Danforth* (decided in 1976), the Court denied the right of the father to have a say in the decision and also empowered women to prevent a husband (or the biological father) from restricting the abortion. The decision also prevented a young woman's parents from exercising an absolute veto in a decision to abort (*Planned Parenthood v. Danforth* 428 U.S. [1976]). In *City of Akron v. Akron Center for Reproductive Health, Inc.* (decided in 1983) the Court required that any parental consent rule for minors must also provide for an alternative form of approval, usually by a judge, for those young women or girls who show themselves to be sufficiently mature to make the abortion decision on their own. In this decision, the court also struck down a city ordinance mandating a fixed waiting period for a woman seeking abortion, as well as a requirement that all second-trimester abortions be performed in a hospital (*City of Akron v. Akron Center for Reproductive Health, Inc.,* 462 U.S. [1983]). In a series of cases culminating in *Thornburgh v. American College of Obstetricians and Gynecologists* (decided in 1986), the Court struck down state laws requiring informed consent—detailed information on fetal development, on the physical and psychological risks of abortion, and of public and private assistance available to women who decide to give birth (*Thornburgh v. American College of Obstetricians and Gynecologists,* 476 U.S. [1986]).

What was so unique about this evolving law was that it forbade *any* state regulation of abortion for the sake of preserving the fetus until viability. Even after viability there would be no federal regulation oriented toward protecting the fetus until birth. Though constitutional protections for the fetus were "theoretically" permitted after viability, abortion would be sanctioned when necessary to protect the life and mental, emotional, and physical health of the mother; in case after case, efforts to fashion more restrictive regulations of this kind at the state level all came to naught (Mary Ann Glendon, *Abortion and Divorce in Western Law*, Cambridge, Mass.: Harvard University Press, 1987, p. 59.) In Justice Burger's dissent from the *Thornburgh* decision, he wrote that "every Member of the *Roe* Court rejected the idea of abortion on demand. The Court's opinion today, however, plainly undermines that important principle." He concluded that at this point, protection for potential life after viability was "mere shallow rhetoric." (*Thornburgh v. American College of Obstetricians and Gynecologists*, 476 U.S. 747 [1986]) In practice, then, a pregnant woman could get an abortion at any time during pregnancy if she desired it and if a single doctor (who might be the one performing the abortion) judged the abortion necessary to preserve her health (broadly construed to include a notion of well-being).

In sum, *Roe* was a "compromise." It did not technically permit abortion on demand for the full nine months. On the other hand, by defining abortion as a "fundamental right" and striking down efforts "to protect the developing fetus" in challenges subsequent to *Roe*, the Supreme Court did provide a foundation for the practice of abortion on demand for the full nine months.

4. As James Miller writes, summarizing the challenge posed by Nietzsche, "There is no Aristotelian mean, no Platonic idea of the good, no moral compass implicit in our ability to reason, and no regulative ideal of consensus that could smooth away the rough edges of competing forms of life and enable us to reconcile their incommensurable claims." James Miller, *The Passion of Michel Foucault* (New York: Simon and Schuster, 1993).

5. Foucault puts an edge on this, saying that "the unity of society is precisely that which should not be considered except as something to be destroyed." Quoted by James Miller, "Foucault's Politics in Biographical Perspective," *Salmagundi* 97 (Winter 1993), p. 38.

6. As Robert Cover of Yale University once put it, "For every constitution there is an epic, for each decalogue a scripture." See his "Nomos and Narrative," *Harvard Law Review* 9714 (1982), p. 4.

7. Max Weber, "Politics as a Vocation," *From Max Weber: Essays in Sociology*, ed. Hans Gerth and C. W. Mills (New York: Oxford, 1946), p. 78.

8. Charles Krauthammer, "Abortion: The Debate is Over," *Washington Post*, 4 December 1992, p. A31:6.

9. See Alissa Rubin, "The Abortion Wars Aren't Over," *Washington Post*, 13 December 1992, p. C2.

10. Clarke Forsythe, "Winning with Our Backs Against the Wall," unpublished paper, 30 November 1992, p. 1.

11. See Rubin, "Abortion Wars," p. C2.

12. Jonathan Imber cogently lays out the future of abortion policy in light of medical advances in his article "Abortion Policy and Medical Practice," *Society* 27, no. 5 (July/August 1990), pp. 27–34.
13. Quoted in David Van Biema, "But Will It End the Abortion Debate?" *Time,* 14 June 1993, p. 52.
14. Ibid., p. 49.
15. Laurence H. Tribe, *Abortion: The Clash of Absolutes* (New York: Norton, 1990).
16. Roger Rosenblatt, *Life Itself* (New York: Random House, 1992).
17. Roger Rosenblatt, "How to End the Abortion War," *New York Times Magazine,* 19 January 1992, 6, 26:2.
18. Rosenblatt, *Life Itself,* p. 71.
19. Rosenblatt, "How to End the Abortion War," p. 56.
20. Tribe, *Abortion: The Clash of Absolutes,* p. 228.
21. Mary Ann Glendon, "Intra-Tribal Warfare," review of *Abortion: The Clash of Absolutes,* by Laurence H. Tribe, *First Things* 5 (August-September, 1990), p. 55.
22. Rosenblatt, *Life Itself,* p. 9. Here he says, "Every woman in America, in my opinion, ought to have the legal right to choose an abortion, and abortion ought to be funded by the government so that poor women are not put at an additional disadvantage. I do not believe that any satisfactory practical compromise may be applied to this position."
23. Ibid., p. 179.
24. Ibid., p. 45.
25. The bias is summarized by Michael McConnell in his review of Tribe's book:

> The footnotes at the back of the book and the acknowledgments at the front say it all. Tribe cites over thirty scholarly books and articles, and three amicus briefs, by proponents of abortion. He cites no anti-abortion briefs and only four anti-abortion scholarly works. Even that number exaggerates the book's coverage of pro-life arguments. . . . The footnotes thus reveal that Tribe made almost no attempt to acquaint himself with the pro-life position as it has been articulated by anti-abortion ethicists, scientists, historians, and constitutional lawyers.
>
> In the acknowledgments, Tribe expresses thanks to a number of individuals who read the work in draft form and made comments and suggestions. . . . When writing a book designed to discover 'common ground' between contending positions, it would be especially helpful to consult individuals who take a position contrary to the author's. Apparently, Professor Tribe had no such person to call upon. . . . Tribe thanks four scholars in the field. All of them are at least as committed to abortion rights as Tribe is himself.
>
> If the footnotes are an indication of Tribe's reading list and the acknowledgments are an indication of Tribe's conversation partners, it is no wonder

that he was unable to write a book dealing fairly with the issue of abortion. (pp. 1183–1185 in Michael W. McConnell, "How Not to Promote Serious Deliberation About Abortion," *University of Chicago Law Review* 58, no. 3 [Summer 1991], pp. 1181–1202.)

26. Let me say, first off, that Rosenblatt's use of public opinion data is no worse than most, but it is certainly no improvement over other efforts either. The main problem with his rendering of the survey data, as it is so often with others, is in the presentation of discrete findings—that is, citing a percentage of people responding a particular way to a particular question in a particular poll *without* cross-comparisons (say, of findings within polls), measures of statistical significance, or multivariate analysis—as the basis of a reading of the public mind on this matter. For example, Rosenblatt repeats several times in his book the fact that according to one poll, 73 percent of the American public are in favor of abortion rights, yet according to another poll, 77 percent regard abortion as murder. But even with his seven-page appendix elaborating upon various statistical findings from various other polls, we are left completely confused by the "inconsistencies" and "discrepancies". Further analysis does not make all of the problems of interpretation disappear, but it does go a long way toward understanding the complexities of public opinion on this issue.

27. For example, Rosenblatt speaks of pro-life people as "often, ironically, pro-war and pro-capital punishment people too" (p. 119). First of all it is not clear that pro-lifers are any more "pro-war" or "pro-capital punishment" than most other Americans (see Chapter Four). Secondly, his cavalier portrayal suggests that they are so just for the sake of it, as though their views of war and capital punishment are not related to (if not grounded in) fairly complex traditions of moral reasoning. To the extent that pro-lifers are conservative on such issues, one would think it relevant to know why—to know how it is that they come to their views. The problem is in not taking the moral claims of either pro-life or pro-choice individuals seriously by using dismissive caricatures.

28. For example, Rosenblatt characterizes a tradition of Calvinist theology on sexuality and on sin as "the odd notions of Puritanism" (p. 128)—odd to him, perhaps, but not to the Puritans in their time or to those who continue on in that legacy. Consider, too, his suggestion that most Americans in the nineteenth century "except for those obsessed with Calvinistic self-recrimination, did not seriously believe that a night of making whoopie led straight to hell" (p. 127). Besides being an overstatement of what the religiously orthodox (Protestant, Catholic, and Jewish) believed about the spiritual consequences of "making whoopie," the general characterization of orthodox religious belief on such mat-

ters as a psychological and emotional pathos is secularist ethnocentri-
cism at the least, if not vulgar intolerance. The narrowness of Rosenblatt's perspective is reinforced by his reference to traditional sexual
mores institutionalized in various states' legal codes long ago as "sav-
age and inquisitorial laws" (an uncriticized use of a quote from H. L.
Mencken on the subject of American sexual norms), contrasted by the
idea that anyone who might have an "urge to remove [such laws]" as
"enlightened" (p. 126). And then there is his allusion to the impact of
religious reflection and teaching on abortion (one would assume
Catholic and Protestant) as a "simplistic, doctrinaire word from a
church or other authoritarian source" (p. 111).

My point here is not to defend the religiously orthodox or the pro-
life. My point, rather, is to suggest that his appeal for tolerance in this
controversy would have had much greater credibility if he had not
been so derisive about what his opponents take seriously. Indeed, the
general point is that *any* appeal for mutual tolerance can only happen
if players in the controversy take the claims, and experience, of their
opponents seriously.

29. Rosenblatt's view of morality, and indeed culture, suffers in the same
way as that of the multiculturalists discussed in Chapter Seven. He
trivializes them by reducing them to the language of preference and
sentiment: *values, feelings, life-style,* and so on. As any sociologist or
anthropologist will say, a culture is first and foremost a *normative*
structure of "commanding truths"—commanding, in the final analysis,
because they derive from an understanding if not an encounter with
the "sacred" (Emile Durkheim's word), or in a slightly less loaded
term, what Paul Tillich called the "orienting principle" of one's life.
The moral codes that people live by, and certainly the ones at stake in
this dispute, are very much antecedent to choice.

30. Rosenblatt, *Life Itself*, p. 52.

31. Ibid., p. 47.

32. Ibid., p. 45.

33. Ibid., p. 179.

34. Ibid., p. 47. This theme is echoed in another remarkable passage in the
book. Speaking of women before *Roe,* the unborn after *Roe,* of this
country's treatment of African Americans, its dubious role in Vietnam,
and so forth, he says, "However often the country has been involved in
the massacre of innocents, it is also aware of its guilt in such matters.
The guilt reflects its good side, the massacres its bad" (p. 118).

35. Compare ibid., p. 176, 178.

36. This is not an exaggeration. Quoting Rosenblatt himself, his "book . . .
suggests that *the very discussion of our private feelings on abortion*

may constitute a resolution of the problem. Since the abortion issue can never be resolved completely—since, logically, there is no common ground on which those who condemn the practice as murder will stand with those who do not, or who will accept "murder" in this context—the resolution, it seems to me, lies in learning to live with the irreconcilable. That may begin to be achieved *by saying what we feel, in all its emotional contradictions" (Life Itself,* pp. 5–6, emphasis added).

37. Tribe, *Abortion: The Clash of Absolutes,* pp. 80ff, 109–110.
38. Ibid., pp. 193.
39. Ibid., p. 222.
40. See the discussion of the meaning of a "technological fix" to this issue later in this chapter.
41. R. C. Sproul, *Abortion: A Rational Look at an Emotional Issue* (Colorado Springs, Colo.: NavPress, 1990).
42. This statement is taken from the back cover of Sproul's book.
43. Sproul, *Abortion: A Rational Look at an Emotional Issue,* p. 7.
44. Is it possible that the marketing division of NavPress advertised more than the book honestly was supposed to deliver? The author himself admits that his purpose in writing the book was to convince the "undecided" that pro-life is the proper ethical option. Ibid., p. 123.
45. See ibid., pp. 81–91.
46. Part II of Sproul's book (chapters 7–10) is devoted to "An Analysis of Pro-Abortion and Pro-Choice Arguments." Advocates of a liberal abortion policy, however, would likely find his characterizations made of straw.
47. *The United States Law Week,* 6-30-92, p. 4804.
48. Ibid.
49. Ibid.
50. First, the Court was just as divided as it was before *Casey:* "vacillation" over the long term would be virtually guaranteed by the inevitable change and circulation of justices through the Court. Both sides of the controversy have recognized this and have shown themselves prepared to do whatever is necessary, within the strict rule of law, to keep their opponents out and to put allies in the Supreme Court. Secondly, the new standard of "undue burden" means that all of the challenges to regulate *Roe* made in the 1970s and 1980s may need to be rescrutinized and redecided. The measure of "undue burden" is itself determined by the whim of those who happen to sit on the bench. The last thing that either side of the abortion controversy will do in these circumstances is to step back from the argument and simply accept whatever the Court decides on this matter.
51. See S. M. Lipset and William Schneider, *The Confidence Gap* (Baltimore: Johns Hopkins University Press, 1987).

52. See Peter L. Berger and Richard John Neuhaus, *To Empower People: The Role of Mediating Structures in Public Policy* (Washington, D.C.: American Enterprise Institute for Public Policy Research, 1977), p. 4.

53. Jurgen Habermas, *Legitimation Crisis* (Boston: Beacon Press, 1975).

54. The best recent summary of this predicament is stated by Adam Seligman in his book *The Idea of Civil Society* (New York: Free Press, 1992):

> "These beliefs, in Godly benevolence and in natural sympathy, are no longer ours to share, and we can no longer use them to construct our models of the social order. After Hume's attack on the Scottish Enlightenment view of Reason, and after Hegel's (and, following him, Marx's) attack on the 'naturalist' premises of eighteenth-century thought, we are left with the problems but not with the solutions.
>
> The assumed synthesis of public and private, individual and social concerns and desiderata, upon which the idea of civil society rests, no longer holds. The social as well as the philosophical conditions for this synthesis have changed drastically, and a return to more classical formulations will not suffice, not in East-Central Europe and not in Western democratic societies." (pp. 205–206)

55. See, for example, Stephen Lukes, *Power: A Radical View* (London: Macmillan Education Ltd., 1974); Pierre Bourdieu, "Symbolic Power," *Critique of Anthropology* 4 (1979), pp. 77–85; Pierre Bourdieu, "On Interest and the Relative Autonomy of Symbolic Power," working papers and proceedings of the Center for Psychosocial Studies, Chicago, 1988.

56. The phrase is Bourdieu's (see note 55).

57. Michelle Lamont and Annette Lareau, "Cultural Capital: Allusions, Gaps and Glissandos," *Recent Theoretical Developments in Sociological Theory* 6, no. 2 (Fall 1988), pp. 153–168. See p. 159.

58. Habermas and Lukes, of course, were mainly concerned about the way capitalist interests exercised power against those who labored in their behalf, but the principle applies here as well as to any dominant collection of interests. In all such cases, the democratic process is fundamentally subverted.

59. Jurgen Habermas, *Toward a Rational Society: Student Protest, Science and Politics* (Boston: Beacon Press, 1970), see chapter 6; this point is made on p. 112.

60. The point is made by Jean-Francois Lyotard in his exchange with Richard Rorty, (in "Discussion entre Jean-Francois Lyotard and Richard Rorty," *Critique* 41: 581–584). In fact, Lyotard cites Kant in arguing that "democracy is necessarily despotic."

61. Certainly this is the spirit of the religion clause of the First Amendment to the Bill of Rights. "Congress," it reads, "shall make no law concerning the establishment of religion or inhibiting the free exercise

thereof." The amendment speaks explicitly of "religion," but the intent of the amendment (reaffirmed in case law) is clearly to protect people's most cherished beliefs, commitments, and ideals, whether religious (in a technical sense) or not. Needless to say, secular beliefs and commitments are as inviolable as theistic ones.

62. Benjamin Barber, *Strong Democracy* (Berkeley and Los Angeles: University of California Press, 1984), p. 174. My debt to Barber's cogent argument in this book, particularly as I work through the possible resolutions to the culture war in Chapter Eight, is enormous.

63. Ibid., p. 173.

64. This idea of common ground is akin to the idea of "the public sphere" described by Habermas. As with the "public sphere," the common ground of which I speak is that area of social life created for public use. Rules prevail, but all citizens have access. It is institutional space as well as the political/cultural environment in democratic societies that no individual, group, or faction owns or controls. It is available, in principle, to all. The government is the executor of the common ground, but it is not a part of it. The government is subordinate to what transpires there. In America, of course, we have the freedom to associate and the freedom to express our opinions, but if there is no forum in which to associate or to be heard, these freedoms are nearly meaningless. So in democratic societies we create the forum—the public space, the common ground—where, again in principle, citizens may express and publish their opinions, and ultimately agree or disagree. Through most of human history such common ground has not existed. This is obviously still true in many parts of the world; the very idea is unique to modern democracies. The question is, where in American public life do we now find this common ground?

65. Cf. George Weigel, "The Requirements and Limits of Civility: How We Contend," paper presented at the Williamsburg Charter Conference, "Commitment and Civility: The First Amendment Religion Clauses and American Public Life," Charlottesville, Virginia, April 11–14, 1988; Steven Tipton, "The Church as a School for Virtue," *Daedalus* 117 (Spring 1988), pp. 163–175; and *The Williamsburg Charter*, Williamsburg Charter Foundation, Charlottesville, Virginia.

66. What do I mean when I talk about special agenda organizations? It is perhaps best to think of them as a particular kind of voluntary association. What makes them distinct from other such associations is their particular aim to remake society, or at least a part of it. The identity of one of these groups does not derive directly from its pursuit of a specific economic interest (as in a corporation or labor union or professional organization), nor does its identity derive from the fellowship of individuals pursuing a similar pastime (as when stamp collectors or

Civil War buffs get together). Rather, its reason for being is to enact a specific social or political agenda, or cluster of agendas, in society as a whole.

67. Alexis de Tocqueville, *Democracy in America* (New York: Anchor-Doubleday, 1969), p. 190.

68. Ibid.

69. James Madison, "Federalist #10," in A. Hamilton, James Madison, and John Jay, *The Federalist Papers* (New York: New American Library of World Literature, 1961).

70. de Tocqueville, *Democracy in America*, p. 193.

71. Quoted in Norma Graebner, "Government Without Consensus," *Virginia Quarterly Review*, pp. 648–664.

72. Quoted in Thomas Jefferson, *Democracy*, selected and arranged by Saul K. Padover (New York: D. Appleton-Century, 1939), p. 133.

73. Again, see Graebner, "Government Without Consensus," pp. 656ff.

74. The best recent work on the concept of civil society is Adam Seligman, *The Idea of Civil Society* (New York: Free Press, 1992). Other important reflection on the matter can be found in several important essays: Charles Taylor, "Modes of Civil Society," *Public Culture* 3, no. 1 (Fall 1990), pp. 95–118; Michael Waltzer, "The Idea of Civil Society," *Dissent*, Spring 1991, pp. 293–304; and Daniel Bell, "American Exceptionalism Revisited: The Role of Civil Society," *The Public Interest* 95 (1989), pp. 38–56. The term can be and often is used synonymously with democracy. I prefer a slightly narrower definition that regards it as a *sphere of public life* that is both independent of the democratic state and yet intimately related to its functioning and legitimacy. This approach is primarily social scientific in nature (following Seligman's distinctions). As a sphere of activity among citizens, it implies the structural manifestations of the freedom of belief, expression (suggesting alternative sources of information), and association, free and fair elections, and the like. It also implies a complex of highly generalized values and ideals binding individuals (as free agents) to their political community. The institutions of civil society—a free press, public schools, churches and synagogues, professional and philanthropic organizations—are those concrete institutions that both express and secure the practical workings of democratic life.

Chapter 2.

1. We conducted formal interviews with representatives from the National Organization for Women, Planned Parenthood, the National Abortion Federation, the Religious Coalition for Abortion Rights, Catholics for Freedom of Choice, the National Right to Life, Opera-

tion Rescue, the Christian Action Council, the American Life League, Missionaries to the Preborn, and the Virginia Society for Human Life. We also had informal conversations with representatives of Americans United for Life. The only organization that would not speak to us was the National Abortion Rights Action League. We tried no less than twelve times over the course of six weeks, but to no avail.

2. Take Helena, an employee of Planned Parenthood, as an example. She was, as they say, a "scream": very busy, harried, upbeat, and fun-loving— one might say very New Yorkish. When she learned that the project for which we were seeking an interview would be academic and sociological, she immediately chimed in, "God, sounds boring!" When told that we would be speaking to lots of different people with different perspectives, she responded wryly, "Don't tell me you have to talk to those anti-choicers, too?" Bob, of the Christian Action Council, is another example. Unlike Helena, he was calm and even tempered; perhaps even "square." As he walked us through his organization's new, well-lit offices in Falls Church, Virginia, he remarked without a trace of self-consciousness, "Isn't it amazing how well the Lord has provided for us." And as the interview began, he brushed off our assurances of fairness, saying, "Frankly, I'd grant you an interview even if you told me you were adamantly against us. We want people at least to hear our side of the story."

His earnestness was something shared by Susan of the Religious Coalition for Abortion Rights. In her early thirties, she exuded enthusiasm and pride in being a part of what she calls "the monumental struggle for women's rights and religious freedom." From the beginning to the end of the interview, she expressed an eagerness to help in any way she could, with contacts, recommendations for books, and so on. Dorothy, of Concerned Women for America, hardly seemed like an activist at all. She was more of a grandmother figure, articulating her beliefs about the state of the family and nation with sincerity if not nostalgia. It is easy to see how she has become so popular as a radio show host and a celebrity among conservative women.

And then there was Pete, a leader in the "rescue" wing of the pro-life movement. Intelligent, learned, and articulate, throughout the interview he illustrated his points with references to St. John Chrysostum, Basil the Great, and the other great fathers of early Christian thought. He used sophisticated methods of Old Testament exegesis and Biblical hermeneutics. He was anything, then, but the breathless, uncouth, Bible-thumping fundamentalist he and his compatriots are usually caricatured to be. In addition, Pete had, shall I say, an arresting sense of humor. At one point in our interview, we could hear someone in the background in another room receiving a package. Pete stopped for a moment, looked over his shoulder, and shouted back, "Make sure it's not a bomb!" He turned back adding with a chuckle in his voice, "Just kidding; I said that for your benefit."

3. Much of Habermas's larger corpus is directly or indirectly concerned with the nature and functioning of modern democratic regimes. His special concern is on the ideological uses of science and technology, though his insights into the problems they create could be extended easily to the role of special agenda organizations. On this particular point three of his articles are especially helpful: "On Systematically Distorted Communication," *Inquiry* 13, no. 3 (Autumn 1970), 205–218; "Towards a Theory of Communicative Competence," *Inquiry* 13, no. 4 (Winter, 1970), 360–375; and "The Public Sphere," *New German Critique* 1, no. 3 (Fall 1974), 49–55.

4. In our hourlong interview with a spokeswoman for Planned Parenthood, this statistic was mentioned no less than a half dozen times.

5. Pro-life advocates believe that she spontaneously aborted through miscarriage. The county coroner declared her death to be of a massive infection most likely caused by an unsterile abortion. Speculation abounds, with no possibility of certainty.

6. Planned Parenthood Federation of America, full-page ad entitled "Why, God? Why Did My Daughter Die," *Time*, 3 December 1990, p. 93. The statements that follow are quoted in David Haase, "Parents Retell Daughter's Story," *Indianapolis News*, 1 August 1990.

7. Quoted in the *Washington Times*, Thursday, 3 August 1983, p. 3C.

8. These were the words of Congressman Christopher Smith of New Jersey, who commended the Mann story to his colleagues. See his comments admitted to the *Congressional Record*, vol. 129, no. 114, 4 August 1983.

9. Pro-choice placard.

10. Pro-life placard.

11. Pro-choice placard.

12. Pro-life placard.

13. Pro-choice placard.

14. Planned Parenthood Federation of America, full-page ad entitled "Caving In to the Extremists AT & T Hangs Up on Planned Parenthood," *New York Times*, 5 April 1990.

15. Randall Terry of Operation Rescue.

16. Religious Coalition for Abortion Rights, informational brochure, undated.

17. Randall Terry of Operation Rescue.

18. Religious Coalition for Abortion Rights, informational brochure, undated.

19. Beverly LaHaye, Concerned Women for America, direct mail piece, undated.

20. National Abortion Rights Action League, informational brochure, undated.
21. National Right to Life Committee, direct mail piece, undated.
22. National Organization for Women, "Emergency Mobilization Bulletin," direct mail piece, undated.
23. Christian Action Council, "A Brief on Public Policy," 4 August 1988.
24. National Abortion Rights Action League, informational brochure, undated.
25. Beverly LaHaye, Concerned Women for America, direct mail piece, undated.
26. National Abortion Rights Action League, informational brochure, undated.
27. Judy Brown and Paul Brown, *Choices in Matters of Life and Death* (Avon, N.J.: Magnificat Press, 1987), p. 84.
28. Planned Parenthood Federation of America, "Caving In to the Extremists."
29. Judy and Paul Brown, *Choices in Matters of Life and Death*, p. 2.
30. Kate Michelman, National Abortion Rights Action League, direct mail piece, undated.
31. Guy Condon, "You Say Choice, I Say Murder," *Christianity Today*, 24 June 1991.
32. National Abortion Rights Action League, informational brochure, undated.
33. American United for Life, news release, July 1991.
34. Laurie Anne Ramsey, Americans United for Life, "Abortion and Moral Beliefs Survey," 12 April 1991.
35. Susan Kennedy, National Abortion Rights Action League, cited by Eloise Salholz, "Pro-Choice: A Sleeping Giant Awakes," *Newsweek*, 24 April 1989, pp. 30–40.
36. Beverly LaHaye, Concerned Women for America, direct mail piece, undated.
37. Illinois Pro-Choice Alliance Education Fund, "Memorandum from Betsy Brill, Executive Director," March 1991.
38. Virginia Organization to Keep Abortion Legal, promotional brochure, undated.
39. National Right to Life Committee, direct mail piece, undated.
40. Religious Coalition for Abortion Rights, informational brochure, undated.
41. Christian Action Council, direct mail piece, undated.
42. Planned Parenthood Federation of America, direct mail piece, undated.
43. Pro-life ad featured in the *Rocky Mountain News*, 25 August 1991.
44. National Abortion Rights Action League, "NARAL's Task for 1990," direct mail solicitation, undated.

45. Laurie Anne Ramsey, "Abortion and Moral Beliefs Survey."
46. Planned Parenthood Federation of America, full-page ad entitled "Would You Lie to a Pregnant Teenager?" 1989.
47. Ibid.
48. Randall Terry of Operation Rescue.
49. National Abortion Federation Fact Sheet, "What Is Abortion," April 1990.
50. Randall Terry of Operation Rescue.
51. Religious Coalition for Abortion Rights, "Words of Choice," Washington, D.C., 1991, p. 18.
52. Hayes Publishing Company, informational brochure, 1981.
53. Center for the Documentation of the American Holocaust, "The American Holocaust: The Chronology of the Weisberg Incident," Palm Springs, California, 1983.
54. Planned Parenthood Federation of America, full-page ad entitled: "One Step Closer to the Back-Alley," 1990.
55. *American Life League News,* Vol. 2, No. 23, October 3, 1986.
56. National Right to Life Education Trust Fund, full-page ad entitled: "If She Were Your Daughter, What Would You Do?" in *Time,* January 22, 1990.
57. National Abortion Rights Action League, Informational Packet: "Minors' Access to Abortion," undated.
58. Right to Life, Illinois, Two Page Pro-Life Ad, *Chicago Sun-Times,* Thursday, November 15, 1990.
59. Quotation from Amicus Curiae brief filed in *Webster v. Reproductive Health Services* by the American Medical Association, cited in "Pro-Life View Versus Medical View," FORUM Scrapbook, Tribune Media Services.
60. *Congressional Record,* vol. 129, no. 114, 4 August 1983 (reprinted from Tom Diaz, "Women Form WEBA to Fight Abortions," *Washington Times,* 3 August 1983.
61. Religious Coalition for Abortion Rights, "Words of Choice," citing N. Adler et al., "Psychological Responses After Abortion," *Science* 248 (1990), p. 41; M. Specter, "Psychiatric Panel Condemns Abortion Restrictions," *Washington Post,* 16 May 1990.
62. Right to Life Illinois, two-page ad in the *Chicago Sun-Times,* 15 November 1990, citing David C. Reardon, *Aborted Women: Silenced No More* (Chicago: Loyola University Press, 1987).
63. Ibid.
64. Kate Michelman, National Abortion Rights Action League, interviewed by Sharon Shahid, "Overturning 'Roe': Threat or Benefit to Women, Children?" *USA Today,* 7 January 1992.

65. Wanda Franz, National Right to Life, quoted ibid.
66. Planned Parenthood, direct mail piece, undated.
67. Judy and Paul Brown, *Choices in Matters of Life and Death,* p. 87.
68. Kate Michelman, National Abortion Rights Action League, quoted in "Overturning 'Roe': Threat or Benefit to Women, Children?"
69. Hayes Publishing Company, informational pamphlet, Ohio, 1981.
70. Kate Michelman, National Abortion Rights Action League, quoted in "Overturning 'Roe': Threat or Benefit to Women, Children?"
71. Planned Parenthood, direct mail piece, undated.
72. American Life League, one-page promotion, 1989.
73. Religious Coalition for Abortion Rights, information brochure, undated.
74. Headline taken from "The American Holocaust: The Chronology of the Weisberg Incident," produced by the Center for Documentation of the American Holocaust, Palm Spring, California, 1983.
75. From a speech by this title given at the University of Virginia Law School, 1992.
76. See *Culture Wars,* Chapter 6.
77. See Brigitte Berger and Peter Berger, "Goshtalk, Femspeak and the Battle of Language," in *The War Over the Family* (New York: Basic Books, 1984).
78. The statement is from Douglas Gould, former vice president for communications at Planned Parenthood of America, quoted in David Shaw, "Abortion Bias Seeps into News," *Los Angeles Times,* 1 July 1990, p. 2.

Chapter 3.

1. See Chapter Four.
2. Judy and Paul Brown, *Choices in Matters of Life and Death* (Avon, N.J.: Magnificat Press, 1987, p. 82).
3. This situation is exacerbated by the legal precedent established in *Planned Parenthood v. Danforth* (428 U.S. 52, 1976), in which the Court ruled that men had no rights to protect fetal life. Fatherhood is, for all practical purposes, denied until the moment of birth.
4. Daniel Callahan, "An Ethical Challenge to Pro-Choice Advocates: Abortion and the Pluralistic Proposition," *Commonweal,* 23 November 1990, pp. 681–687.
5. Catharine MacKinnon, "*Roe v. Wade:* A Study of Male Ideology," in *Abortion: Moral and Legal Perspectives,* edited by Jay L. Garfield and Patricia Hennessey (Amherst: University of Massachusetts Press,

1984), pp. 45–54. See also Judith Blake, "Abortion and Public Opinion: The 1960–1970 Decade," *Science* 171 (1971) pp. 540ff.

6. Mark Baker, "Men on Abortion," *Esquire* 113, no. 3, pp. 114–127.

7. Kathleen N. Franco, Marijo Tamburrino, Nancy Campbell, Judith Pentz, and Stephen Jurs, "Psychological Profile of Dysphoric Women Postabortion," *Journal of the American Medical Women's Association* 113 (July-August 1989).

8. See Mary K. Zimmerman, *Passage Through Abortion: The Personal and Social Reality of Women's Experiences* (New York: Praeger, 1977), p. 122.

9. See Carol Gilligan, *In a Different Voice* (Cambridge, Mass.: Harvard University Press, 1982). Of sixteen cases cited from her "Abortion Decision Study", six women noted the influence of men in their decisions: Denise (p. 81), Ellen (p. 89), Sarah (p. 91), Lisa (p. 123), and two other unnamed women (cited on p. 125). In Sarah's case, for example, Gilligan writes: "Although initially 'ecstatic' at the news [of being pregnant], her elation dissipated when her lover told her that he would leave if she chose to have the child" (p. 90). In Lisa's case, her boyfriend wanted her "not to murder his child," but then he left her, "ruin[ing] her life" (p. 123). Linda Bird Francke also notes that a pregnant woman often hopes her lover/husband will talk her out of the abortion and is resentful when he supports her decision. Francke, *The Ambivalence of Abortion* (New York: Random House, 1978), pp. 96, 100, 107.

10. This was Denise. See Gilligan, *In a Different Voice*, p. 81.

11. This logic has found its way into the courts as well, in a number of legal disputes. Some of these are amazingly bizarre. In one case, a surgeon impregnated his secretary during an affair, paid her more than twenty thousand dollars to have an abortion, and then sued her for breach of contract when she failed to comply. He also complained that the woman failed to return his money. After a paternity suit proved that he indeed was the father of the child, he asked the court for visitation rights and either custody or joint custody of the child. See Wolfson, "Lawsuit Raises Novel Questions in Abortion Case," *Louisville Courier-Journal*, 28 March 1991, p. 1.

12. This information is compiled in successive annual editions of the Foundation Grants Index, which lists grants of $5,000 or more awarded by the 100 largest American foundations and other private and community foundations that voluntarily report grants. The index is published by the Foundation Center in Washington, D.C. I drew here from the years 1986–1990.

13. Catharine MacKinnon, *Feminism Unmodified,* see Chapter 12, "'More Than Simply a Magazine': Playboy's Money," Cambridge: Harvard University Press, 1987.
14. Kolata, "Under Pressures and Stigma, More Doctors Shun Abortion," *New York Times,* January 8, 1990, p. 1.
15. See Mimi Swartz, "Abortion Street," *Texas Monthly,* April 1989, p. 68.
16. See Aida Torres and Jacqueline Darroch Forrest, "Why Do Women Have Abortions?" *Family Planning Perspectives* 20, no. 4 (1988), pp. 169–176.
17. Reported in *Family Planning Perspectives* of the Alan Guttmacher Institute, January-February 1987.
18. Americans United for Life, "The Half-Truths and Lies of Planned Parenthood Ads," 21 May 1990.
19. It publishes an extensive booklet, entitled "Standards for Abortion Clinics," that delineates obligatory standards for all NAF member facilities.
20. One's confidence in these numbers should not be without some reservation, however, first because many states do not require clinics to report abortion-related complications, and second because many abortion providers never see patients a second time and thus are rarely aware of any complications. For this reason, some individuals estimate the number of abortion-related complications to be much higher. In the end, though, any sense of the actual safety of the procedure will be speculative.
21. See Debbie Sontag, "Do Not Enter," *Miami Herald,* 17 September 1989, pp. 9–22.
22. See the *Chicago Sun-Times* series on "The Abortion Profiteers," published in the fall of 1978, for a series of articles on highly suspect abortion clinics operating in Chicago.
23. A listing of many of these situations can be found in Paige Comstock Cunningham and Clarke Forsythe, "Is Abortion the 'First Right' for Women?: Some Consequences of Legal Abortion," in *Abortion, Medicine and the Law,* 4th ed., edited by J. Douglas Butler and David B. Walbert (New York: Facts on File, 1992), pp. 100–158 (pp. 130–140 especially).
24. CBS News, "60 Minutes," vol. 23, no. 31, transcript 2332, 21 April 1991.
25. See Sontag, "Do Not Enter," p. 22.
26. Ibid., p. 14.
27. See, for example, Stanley Henshaw, Nancy Binkin, Ellen Blaine, and Jack C. Smith, "A Portrait of American Women Who Obtain Abortions," *Family Planning Perspectives* 17, no. 2 (1985), pp. 90–96.

28. Mike Snider, "Outcry Delays Study of Teen Sex," *USA Today,* 22 July 1991.
29. Mitchell Locin, "Bush's Stance on Women's Health Bill Is Criticized," *Chicago Tribune,* 25 July 1991, section 1, p. 12.
30. I explore the competing interests involved in the church-state conflict in J. D. Hunter, "Religion and the State: The Problem of Modern Pluralism," *Brookings Review,* Spring 1990, pp. 20–27.

Chapter 4.

1. Most of what we know of public opinion on abortion is from just a scant few questions added on to larger "omnibus" surveys in which pollsters ask dozens of questions dealing with everything from the popularity of a brand of toothpaste to the public's attitudes toward nuclear policy. This is how pollsters make their money. In-depth survey research on a particular subject is very rare. As a consequence, very few questions on any one subject are ever asked. This is true of survey research on abortion as well.
2. The survey was based on in-person interviews with 2,174 adults, aged eighteen and older, in more than 360 locations across the nation during the period of May 4–20, 1990. As is standard for the Gallup Organization, the sampling procedure for the survey was designed to produce an approximation of the adult civilian population eighteen years and older living in the United States, except those in institutions such as prisons or hospitals. This sample base, or "universe," approximates 169 million persons. All sample surveys are subject to sampling error—that is, the extent to which the results may differ from those that would be obtained if the whole population had been interviewed. In this survey, the sampling error was plus or minus 2.5 percent. The survey instrument was designed by myself and Dr. Carl Bowman (Bridgewater College), in consultation with Dr. Robert Wuthnow (Princeton University) and Dr. Harry Cotugno (of the Gallup Organization). As contractually required, the Gallup Organization, through Dr. Cotugno and his staff, had final say over questionnaire wording and sequence. Beyond this, the Gallup Organization conducted the survey interviews and did the initial tabulation of findings. The project was commissioned and underwritten by Americans United for Life. Neither the Gallup Organization nor AUL played any part in selecting the questions to be asked in the survey, nor in the analysis, interpretation, or reporting of the findings here.
3. All of the patterns reported here in this chapter are statistically significant at least at the .01 level of probability, using a chi-square test of independence. We did not report any patterns that were significant at any lesser degree.

4. See note 3 in Chapter One.

5. Poll of 1,200 registered voters conducted during the spring of 1990 by the public affairs division of Tarrance & Associates, a subsidiary of the Gallup Organization.

6. In a national study conducted by the Wirthlin Group during July 1990, 47 percent of Americans estimated the number of abortions performed annually in the United States to be less than 500,000 per year, while another 17 percent would not even venture a guess. The actual number of abortions performed annually is approximately 1.5 million (Wirthlin, "Abortion Survey" 1990: 48–49).

7. Curiously, the most confident in their misinformation about abortion law generally, and *Roe v. Wade* in particular, were those most hostile to the pro-life cause. Those who viewed themselves as moderately or strongly pro-choice (who were also disproportionately college educated), for example, were nearly 50 percent more likely than the national average to say that *Roe* only permits legal abortion in the first three months. Fifty-five percent of the moderately pro-choice and 58 percent of the strongly pro-choice believed that *Roe v. Wade* limits abortion to the first three months, compared to 45 percent of the moderately pro-life and 36 percent of the strongly pro-life; the national average was 41 percent. The strongly pro-life were more than twice as likely as the strongly pro-choice to say they had no idea about the meaning of *Roe v. Wade*.

8. Wirthlin, "Abortion Survey" p. 1.

9. One-half of those who said they would withdraw their support from a candidate over the abortion issue identified themselves as pro-life, compared to only 30 percent who were pro-choice.

10. This is based upon a percentage distribution of whether or not they would vote for a candidate whose abortion position they opposed, cross-tabulated by self-identification as pro-life or pro-choice.

11. Twelve percent of those who were moderately pro-life said they had drifted closer to a pro-choice position, while only 1 percent of those who were moderately pro-choice said they had drifted closer to a pro-life position. All in all, 20 percent of our subjects said they had drifted closer to a pro-choice view, compared to 16 percent who had drifted closer to a pro-life position.

12. National Abortion Rights Action League, promotional material, undated. Even Roger Rosenblatt says that "73 percent of all Americans favor choice." See Roger Rosenblatt, "How to End the Abortion War," *New York Times Magazine*, 19 January 1992, p. 56.

13. Life Choices Survey, 1990. These figures are based upon women's self-identification as pro-life or pro-choice.

14. Thirty-three percent of blacks in the sample considered themselves pro-life, compared to 27 percent who identified themselves as pro-choice (unweighted data). This moderate finding comports with other survey research showing that blacks are consistently more conservative on the abortion question, regardless of the circumstances. See Michael Combs and Susan Welch, "Blacks, Whites and Attitudes Toward Abortion," *Public Opinion Quarterly* 46, no. 4 (1982), pp. 510–520; Elaine Hall and Myra Ferree, "Race Differences in Abortion Attitudes," *Public Opinion Quarterly* 50, no. 2 (1986), pp. 193–207.

15. Of those who knew someone else who had had an abortion, they were evenly divided among those who believed it was the right decision and those who believed it was the wrong decision. Not in all cases, but in most, how one identifies oneself on the issue (pro-life or pro-choice) shapes one's moral judgment about the decision in that person's life.

16. Fifty-six percent of all women who had personally considered an abortion said they were pro-choice, compared to only 29 percent of those who had not considered an abortion.

17. Alas, the concept of humankind as *homo laborans* or *homo sentients* rings hollow even in an era of therapeutic materialism.

18. The remaining 10 percent are uncertain.

19. The actual figures were 86 percent strongly pro-life, and 22 percent strongly pro-choice. A word of elaboration: Americans who view personhood as a divine attribute are overwhelmingly inclined to date its beginning at conception. Those who define personhood, on the other hand, in terms of human rationality are more than four times as likely to date its beginning at the point of fetal viability or the moment of birth. Seventy-four percent of those who said that the most important thing distinguishing humans is "the fact that they were created by God in his own image" believed that personhood begins at conception, compared to only 46 percent of those who said the "ability to think and reason" is what distinguishes humans. Thirty-one percent of the latter said that personhood begins at or after the moment of fetal viability, compared to only 7 percent of the former.

20. The figures were 77 percent strongly pro-life, and 9 percent strongly pro-choice.

21. Forty-nine percent of the strongly pro-choice held this view.

22. What is more, one's assessment of the beginning of personhood is a direct window upon one's ethical evaluation of abortion. Seventy percent of those who saw personhood beginning at conception were prepared to label abortion as murder. This compares with only one out of every ten who see personhood beginning at, or after, the point of fetal viability. Those who said that abortion is "as bad as killing someone

who has already been born" were virtually unanimous in the belief that personhood begins at conception. There is almost as solid a consensus that it does not begin at conception, however, among those who see abortion as simply a surgical procedure. Eighty-six percent of those who believed abortion is "as bad as killing someone who has already been born" said that personhood begins at conception, while seventy-nine percent of those who saw abortion as a surgical procedure said that personhood begins sometime after conception. In light of this tight linkage, it is easy to understand why so much public debate has centered on the question of when human life really begins.

23. In circumstances involving rape, 52 percent viewed abortion as unacceptable; involving incest, 51 percent found it unacceptable; and involving a child with a strong chance of a serious deformity, 66 percent viewed it as unacceptable.

24. The figures read as follows: when the purpose is to relieve a family with a very low income of a heavy financial burden, 73 percent of the strong pro-choice supporters approved; in a situation involving a teenager whose pregnancy would require her to drop out of school, 65 percent of the strong pro-choice supporters approved; in circumstances where pregnancy would interrupt a professional woman's career, 56 percent approved; and in a situation where the father of the unborn child abandons the pregnant woman, 68 percent of the strong pro-choice supporters approved.

25. The proportion of strong pro-life supporters approving of abortion *after* the first three months of pregnancy in the circumstances involving rape was 19 percent; involving incest, 24 percent; involving a threat to the life of the mother, 32 percent; and where there is a strong chance of a serious deformity in the developing baby, 17 percent.

26. Three-quarters of those American Protestants who called themselves strongly pro-life, for example, took a more conservative, evangelical theological position; while three-quarters of those who said they were strongly pro-choice took a more liberal, mainline stance. Similarly, evangelical Protestants were more than twice as likely as their mainline counterparts to identify themselves as pro-life. In fact, knowing whether two Protestant individuals are evangelical or mainline in their religious orientation improves our ability to predict which is most pro-life by more than 50 percent (Goodman-Kruskal gamma = .522).

27. Respondents who met the following criteria were classified as participating in conservative communities of moral conversation: those (1) who believed that "there is a God," (2) who did not describe their religious outlook as "liberal," and (3) who met two of these three conditions: (a) reported that they had a "personal relationship" with God,

(b) believed the Bible is the actual word of God and is to be taken literally, and (c) reported that they pray daily. All Protestants who met these conditions were classified as evangelical, and all Catholics who met them as conservative. All remaining Protestants were classified as mainline and all remaining Catholics as liberal. Thus one's "community of moral conversation" was defined in terms of the language invoked to depict one's personal religious orientation, rather than in terms of denominational affiliation or membership.

28. The identification used here draws from the cluster analysis displayed in Figure 4–10 and described in note 33 below. Fifty-two percent of all evangelicals and 55 percent of all conservative Catholics were consistently pro-life.

29. A plurality of secularists (44 percent) would fit the consistently pro-choice position, more than twice the percentage as any other moral community mentioned here (evangelical, 4 percent; orthodox Catholic, 4 percent; mainline Protestant, 19 percent; and progressive Catholic, 16 percent).

30. The moral compass that directs the consistently pro-life is altogether unique. When asked what was most important in resolving situations of moral ambiguity, six out of ten (61 percent) responded, "doing what God or Scripture tells you is right," compared to only 23 percent of the privately pro-life, 25 percent of the conveniently pro-life, and approximately 10 percent of the various pro-choice coalitions. Every group except the consistently pro-life overwhelmingly cited "doing what would be best for everyone involved" as their primary ethical guideline. In this light, it is not surprising that 81 percent of the consistently pro-life say their religious beliefs are "very important" to them, compared to half or less of all of the other pro-life and pro-choice coalitions. On matters of sexual morality, the consistently pro-life similarly depart from national norms—only 19 percent agree that "homosexual relations are okay, if that is the person's choice," compared to 36 percent of the conveniently pro-life, 45 percent of the secretly pro-life, 49 percent of the reticent pro-choice, 54 percent of the personally opposed pro-choice, and 67 percent of the consistently pro-choice. Fifty-three percent of the conveniently pro-life are willing to concede that "sex before marriage is okay if a couple loves each other," as are 57 percent of the secretly pro-life, 69 percent of the reticent pro-choice, 71 percent of the personally opposed pro-choice, and 81 percent of the consistently pro-choice. Yet only 27 percent of the consistently pro-life say it is okay, while 71 percent *reject* the idea. Two-thirds or more of every group except the consistently pro-life believe that methods of birth control should be available to teenagers even if their parents dis-

approve; only four out of every ten among the consistently pro-life sanction the idea.

31. Three-quarters (75 percent) of those who identified themselves as strongly pro-choice said they favor the death penalty for persons convicted of murder, compared to 68 percent of the strongly pro-life.

32. Fifty-two percent of those who were neutral said that personhood begins at conception, yet less than half of these said that abortion is full-fledged murder.

33. Focusing upon those between the strongly pro-life and strongly pro-choice extremes, only 40 percent of those who say that personhood begins at conception believe that abortion is just as serious as killing someone who has already been born. A full 33 percent of this group believes that abortion should not be called murder even though it does involve the taking of human life.

34. SPSSX's Quick Cluster procedure was used to isolate six relatively discrete moral viewpoints on the abortion issue. These clusterings of opinion were based upon responses to variables measuring (1) willingness to personally consider the abortion alternative, (2) the number of circumstances under which abortion is deemed to be morally acceptable, (3) self-identification as pro-life or pro-choice, (4) assessments of the moral gravity of abortion (e.g., whether it can be considered "murder"), (5) assumptions about the ontological status of the human fetus, and (6) assessments of the moral priority of a woman's right to choose versus the fetus's right to life at various stages of the pregnancy.

    The Quick Cluster procedure maximizes the differences in patterns of response *between* clusters on the input variables, and similarities of responses *within* clusters, using squared Euclidean distances as the measure of similarity. Since this measure is highly sensitive to a variable's unit of measurement, the six variables were first transformed to equalize units of measurement, assigning them similar weights in the cluster analysis. Since a cluster analysis can maximize between-cluster differences on designated variables for any number of clusters, the number of clusters must be based upon heuristic as well as empirical criteria. Setting the number of clusters too small will yield large, relatively heterogeneous groupings and fail to discern meaningful differences in patterns of response on the variables in question. Setting the number too large, on the other hand, will yield empirically distinct, homogeneous groupings that are too numerous to be meaningfully interpreted. After exploring cluster solutions that yielded both smaller and larger numbers of clusters, six was settled upon as a number that yielded relatively homogeneous groupings that were few enough to be meaningfully presented and interpreted. An analysis of variance of mean differences between the six clusters on the six variables identified above yielded the following results:

Variable	Cluster MS	DF	Error MS	DF	F	Prob
1	522.8298	5	.4802	1862.0	1088.8416	.000
2	607.9921	5	.7356	2168.0	826.4814	.000
3	591,5358	5	.6846	2109.0	864.0290	.000
4	338.6640	5	.5202	2018.0	651.0823	.000
5	263.5212	5	.4002	2022.0	658.4509	.000
6	243.9760	5	.3916	1935.0	623.0712	.000

35. These findings are based upon an analysis of percentage differences in a multi-way cross-tabulation of abortion opinions by religious orientation and church attendance.

36. Naturally the pro-choice would like to make hay out of this, suggesting that opposition to abortion is mere sectarianism. Yet given the fact that most Americans still believe in God and, moreover, have at least some attachments to religious institutions, such arguments are spurious. Rather, religious sensibility is the very strength of the pro-life movement.

37. Only those who identified themselves as strongly pro-life were inclined to view pro-life Americans as more concerned about women and concerned about poverty than pro-choice Americans. Roughly thirty percent (29 percent) of those in the middle (who say they are neither strongly pro-life nor strongly pro-choice) tended to see pro-choice Americans as more concerned about poverty than pro-life Americans, compared to only 10 percent who saw it the other way around. Similarly, a third of those in the middle (33 percent) saw pro-choice Americans as more concerned about women, compared to 10 percent who saw pro-life Americans as more concerned. Yet when negative images were presented, this same middle group tended to finger pro-life Americans as more extremist (26 percent), violent (20 percent), and intolerant (23 percent) than pro-choice Americans. Only 12 percent, 13 percent, and 13 percent, respectively, saw it the other way around. Even though these figures indicate a pro-life image problem, it is significant that approximately a quarter of those in the middle consistently rated pro-choice and pro-life Americans the same on these characteristics, and approximately 40 percent do not even venture to guess whether the labels apply. In the middle, images of what it means to be pro-life and pro-choice are much more nebulous than often suggested.

Chapter 5.

1. The sample of individuals interviewed for this chapter was chosen purposively. Insofar as the culture war is waged primarily among the white

middle class, and insofar as the abortion issue in particular is one of primary relevance to men and women in their twenties, thirties, and forties, our sample was framed accordingly. In particular, our objective was to speak to men and women from various regions of the country and various occupations who were primarily from the age range noted above but who were not paid activists for either side of this controversy. A breakdown of the individuals interviewed is as follows:

Name	Age	Race	Gender	Marital Status	Occupation	Region
Susan Alder	30	W	F	S	Manager	West
Scott Allen	25	W	M	D	Computer analyst	East
Paul Archer	45	W	M	D	Architect	East
Kate Beck	56	W	F	M	Nurse	Midwest
Rich Carver	33	W	M	M	Writer	West
Barbara Cohen	42	W	F	M	Attorney/ mother	South
Sarah Cooper	27	W	F	S	Teacher	Midwest
Rebecca Darmin	32	W	F	M	Therapist	South
Saundra Ferris	31	W	F	S	Graduate student	Midwest
Mark Fielder	33	W	M	S	Manager	West
Glenda Goetz	25	W	F	S	Computer analyst	East
Kelly Gorman	27	W	F	S	Unemployed	East
Sam Hawkins	62	W	M	M	Pastor	Midwest
Alice Horning	64	W	F	M	Retired teacher	South
Julie Howard	35	W	F	M	Homemaker	South
Gary Jones	35	W	M	M	Executive	East
Betsy McRae	32	W	F	S	Actress	West
Melissa Michaels	60	W	F	M	Retired nurse	East
Karen Pentalla	27	W	F	M	Social worker	East
Ann Plotz	31	W	F	M	Homemaker	Midwest
Lisa Rodriguez	40	H	F	M	Accountant	South

Name	Age	Race	Gender	Marital Status	Occupation	Region
David Ronfeldt	28	W	M	M	Insurance sales	South
Louise Schaeffer	26	W	F	S	Graduate student	West
Mimi Smith	42	W	F	M	Sales	East
Marie Tagliano	29	W	F	M	Homemaker	East
Amy Taylor	33	W	F	M	Homemaker	Midwest
Chris Thomas	28	W	F	S	Business	West
Sylvia Turner	29	W	F	S	Actress	West
Nelson Vinte	26	W	M	S	Graduate student	East
Barry Walker	48	B	M	D	Photographer	Midwest
Sue Whittle	20	W	F	S	Student	Midwest
Robin Wysocki	30	W	F	S	Youth minister	East

In sum, of the 32 individuals we interviewed, 11 were from eastern states, 6 were from southern states, 8 were from midwestern states, and 7 were from western states; 23 were women and 9 were men; 15 were married, 13 were single, and 4 were currently divorced; 12 were in their twenties, 11 in their thirties, 5 in their forties, and 4 in their fifties and sixties.

2. It is not just the law, either. As noted in the last chapter, most Americans underestimate the number of abortions, too. Scott Allen, a computer technician from Boston, Massachusetts, was distinctive only in his understated humor. When asked about how many abortions take place each year, he guessed "somewhere around fifty thousand—I don't know, educate me." The interviewer responded by saying roughly a million and a half. Scott replied, "In the millions? See, here I'm at fifty thousand. I was off by a few."

3. It is worth noting that compassion does not necessarily involve an identification. Compassion toward others can be rooted in the obligations one has, by virtue of membership in a community, to care for others. The obligation in classical Christianity to "love one's enemy," for example, is a moral obligation that does not necessarily involve such feelings of empathy.

4. Another pro-life citizen spoke candidly of these tensions as hypocrisies: "At one level I believe that a child is a child before birth or after birth. But this is why I feel like a hypocrite a lot of times. If I *really* believed that these children are children, I should be doing more than I am."

5. Reflecting on the hypothetical single black mother with many children and one more on the way, Alice Horning said in a similar vein: "I think the government or someone should have her tubes tied. I really do. This overpopulation is a very big problem, and the fact that these children are born, they are not taken care of. This mother might love them, but she's turning her responsibility over to welfare to feed them and to clothe them and to take care of them. She can give love, I'm not denying that, but it's not just love. There are other responsibilities, and I don't think all of that should go to someone else."

Chapter 6.

1. Quoted in Thomas Jefferson, *Democracy,* edited by Saul K. Padover (New York: D. Appleton-Century, 1939), p. 135.
2. Quoted ibid., p. 134.
3. These words are those of John Stuart Mill, but they were echoed by many other of his contemporaries. D. R. Bhandari, *History of European Political Philosophy* (Bangalore, India: Bangalore Publishing Co., 1963), p. 451.
4. Quoted in Jefferson, *Democracy,* p. 57.
5. One need not dig far into the historical record to be convinced of this. Several old histories are quite good on this. See, for example, James Melvin Lee, *History of American Journalism* (Boston: Houghton Mifflin, 1923); and Frank Luther Mott, *American Journalism: A History of Newspapers in the United States Through 250 Years* (New York: Macmillan, 1941). More recently, see Marion Tuttle Marzolf, *Civilizing Voices: American Press Criticism, 1880–1950* (New York: Longman, 1991); and J. Carey, *Communication as Culture: Essays on Media and Society* (Boston: Unwin Hyman, 1989).
6. See Christopher Lasch's persuasive argument in "The Lost Art of Political Argument," *Harper's,* September 1990, pp. 17–22. Lasch takes the most positive construction of these affairs by arguing that nineteenth-century journalism served as an extension of the town meeting, not only reporting controversies but participating in them and, in so doing, compelling its readers to do the same.
7. Walter Lippmann, *Liberty and the News* (New York: Harcourt, Brace and Howe, 1920), p. 98ff.
8. Ibid., p. 47.
9. This series of quotes also comes from Lippmann's *Liberty and the News,* pp. 70, 99, 100.
10. One need only read Lippmann's *Public Opinion,* published two years after *Liberty and the News,* to see how far his mind had changed on this count. Ronald Steel's wonderful biography of Lippmann, *Walter*

Lippmann and the American Century (New York: Vintage, 1981) summarizes this cogently. (See pp. 180–185).

11. Political talk-television shows on public television stations (like "The McLaughlin Group," "Firing Line," and "One on One"), the left is quick to point out, all have big corporate funders who at least indirectly shape the content, form, and personnel of the shows. The major network news programs, they contend, also depend upon advertising from major corporations. The net effect is a presentation of public affairs that never strays far from a moderately conservative to far right-wing party line. More insidiously, they claim, the politics of commercialism sets the agenda for the press (its unwritten epigraph: never be too controversial). See, for example, Edward Herman and Noam Chomsky, *Manufacturing Consent: The Political Economy of the Mass Media* (New York: Pantheon, 1988).

12. To document this, they point to polls that show that the nation's media elite are, compared to the average American, distinctively secular, politically liberal (taking an adversarial posture toward the free market and a benevolent position toward the welfare state) and culturally progressive (hostile toward the traditional norms surrounding the family, gender, and sexuality).

13. An illustration of first-rate journalism of this kind is Cynthia Gorney's portrayal of the National Right to Life's John Wilke. See Cynthia Gorney, "The Dispassion of John C. Wilke," *Washington Post Magazine,* 22 April 1990, pp. 21–42.

14. David Shaw, "Abortion Bias Seeps into News," *Los Angeles Times,* 1 July 1990, p. 10f.

15. Jane Gross, "Patricia Ireland, President of NOW: Does She Speak for Today's Women?" *New York Times Magazine,* 1 March 1992, pp. 16–54.

16. Gary Wills, "Evangels of Abortion," *New York Times Review of Books,* 15 June 1989, pp. 15ff.

17. Francis Wilkinson, "The Gospel According to Randall Terry," *Rolling Stone,* 5 October 1989, pp. 85–92.

18. Walt Harrington, "Judie Brown, Sex, Politics and Religion in the Anti-Abortion Crusade," *Washington Post Magazine,* 5 January 1986, pp. 11–23.

19. Eileen McNamara of the *Boston Globe,* quoted in Shaw, "Abortion Bias," p. 11. It is worth noting that from the vantage point of the pro-life, this tendency is just typical of the double standard the media establishment uses on this issue.

20. Shaw, "Abortion Bias," p. 1. His analysis involved an examination of press coverage over a period of eighteen months. Along with this were interviews he conducted with more than 100 journalists and activists.

21. Ibid., p. 2.
22. Shaw makes this point in his series ("Abortion Bias," p. 13), but the quote here is taken from a statement he made at the Ethics and Public Policy Center conference "Abortion and the Media," 19 November 1991, Washington, D.C.
23. Shaw, "Abortion Bias," p. 1.
24. These two are recounted in James Burtchael, "Travesty at Wichita," *Christianity Today*, 11 November 1991, pp. 20–21.
25. The significant exception to this was offered by John Leo of *U.S. News and World Report*. See his essays "One Watchdog Missing in Action," *U.S. News and World Report*, 5 November 1990, p. 23; and "Score One for Operation Rescue," *U.S. News and World Report*, 26 August 1991, p. 21.
26. The silence extends to the way in which the Racketeer-Influenced and Corrupt Organizations (RICO) statute has been applied to prosecute many abortion protesters. Originally designed to fight the Mafia and other organized crime operations, RICO was applied to white-collar criminals in the realm of high finance during the late 1980s. In response to this, editors at most of the major newspapers questioned whether it was an appropriate use of the statute. The *Los Angeles Times* went further, saying that the RICO act was out of control and ought to be repealed. Civil libertarians agree that had RICO been applied to the desegregation efforts of Martin Luther King, his work might have been destroyed. But as this same statute has been invoked against Operation Rescue, the media has been all but silent. See David Shaw, "Abortion Bias," pp. 11–12ff.
27. Center for Media and Public Affairs, "Roe v. Webster: Media Coverage of the Abortion Debate," *Media Monitor* 3, no. 8 (October 1989).
28. Ibid. As mentioned earlier, the study included 118 stories on the ABC, CBS, and NBC evening news shows (seven hours, nineteen minutes of airtime) and 179 news stories and 36 opinion pieces in the *New York Times* and *Washington Post*. Pro-choice advocates were cited 538 times, or 26 percent of the total; pro-life advocates were cited 331 times, or 16 percent of the total.
29. There were two follow-up analyses. One was conducted by the Center for Media and Public Affairs (CMPA; published as "Abortion Rights and Wrongs: Media Coverage of the Abortion Debate, 1991–1992," *Media Monitor* 6, no. 6 (June-July 1992:) as a follow-up to its own 1989 analysis. Unlike the first treatment (which covered the period between January 1 and August 31, 1989), the time period covered in this second analysis was between May 1 and May 31, 1992. It included the stories from three major newsmagazines, but nothing in the major newspapers. For a more direct comparison with the 1989 study, a re-

search assistant and I examined all articles (254) and editorials (108) published in the *New York Times* and the *Washington Post* between January 1 and August 31, 1992. Differences in methodology notwithstanding, these two follow-ups were roughly comparable in their conclusions. In the content analysis of the *Times* and the *Post,* 42 percent of all sources quoted were pro-choice advocates, compared to 30 percent who were pro-life advocates.

30. Of the pro-life groups, for example, Operation Rescue representatives were quoted 144 times, compared to 28 times for representatives of the National Right to Life, 22 times for representatives of the National Conference of Bishops, and 2 times for representatives of Americans United for Life. Among pro-choice groups, Planned Parenthood was quoted 54 times, the ACLU 22 times, NARAL 24 times, NOW 16 times, and Republicans for Choice 10 times. The CMPA study found the same general distribution.

31. Seventy percent of the time reporters used either *abortion rights* or *anti-abortion.* Twenty percent of the time they used the terms *pro-choice* and *pro-life,* but from this 13 percent of the time they used the term *pro-choice* compared to 7 percent of the time they used the term *pro-life.*

32. From the CMPA study in 1992, reporters in these media used the term *anti-abortion* 68 percent of the time, *pro-life* 28 percent of the time, and *right to life* 4 percent of the time; while they used *abortion-rights* 51 percent of the time, *pro-choice* 47 percent of the time, and *pro-abortion* 2 percent of the time.

33. Of the 108 opinion columns and editorials examined, 66 were pro choice, 29 were neutral, and 13 were pro-life.

34. This activist was quoted by Shaw at the Ethics and Public Policy Center conference "Abortion and the Media." Shaw reflected about his series this way: "Although I received a number of nice calls and letters from journalists—and was, alas, virtually nominated for sainthood by abortion opponents from coast to coast—I was most surprised by the reaction I didn't receive. I heard virtually nothing from abortion-rights supporters, neither individually nor collectively. The leaders of one group did come in to meet with my editor, and a liberal group in Washington did issue a press release criticizing my story, but that was about it. My self-serving analysis of this silence was that abortion-rights advocates knew I was right, and they were media-wise enough to realize that if they protested too loudly, it would only give longer life to my findings."

35. Quoted in Shaw, "Abortion Bias."

36. Quoted in Fred Graham, *Happy Talk: Confessions of a TV Newsman* (New York: Norton, 1990), pp. 206ff.

37. See Christopher Georges, "Mock the Vote," *Washington Monthly*, May 1993, pp. 30–35.

38. The observation of a *Washington Post* reporter in 1993 that evangelical Christians were poorly educated and easy to manipulate is just one illustration of this brand of ethnocentrism. The calamity in Waco, Texas, later that year provides a more disastrous illustration of the same thing. As Neal Stephenson, writing on the op-ed page of the *New York Times*, put it, "No three cultures could be more mutually incomprehensible than the trinity at Waco: Branch Davidians, G-men and the media" ("Blind Secularism," 23 April 1993).

39. That the culture of the newsroom assumes the legitimacy of the pro-choice position is not entirely surprising, since the majority of media elites (between 80 and 90 percent, according to most surveys) are pro-choice in their personal convictions. This shared worldview is related to the social background common within the profession: disproportionately white, middle- and upper-middle class, highly educated, and urban—all features that typify Americans who hold a liberal, modernist worldview. The cultural predispositions toward the pro-choice perspective are even more salient among women journalists. According to the Lichter study, women reporters quoted supporters of abortion rights twice as often as they quoted abortion opponents in their stories, whereas in stories reported by men there was a rough balance in the sources quoted. In the print media, for example, pro-choice views predominated in articles written by women at a ratio of nearly three to one (74 percent to 26 percent) where in stories written by men, the pro-choice views predominated at only 55 percent to 45 percent. Center for Media and Public Affairs, "Roe v. Webster", p. 6.

   The sense that this cultural predisposition is especially strong among women journalists was observed by Shaw as well. One network news executive he spoke to put it bluntly: "The problem [with abortion coverage], pure and simple, is that the media's loaded with women who are strongly pro-choice" (Shaw, "Abortion Bias," p. 19.) From a strictly sociological perspective, the pressures (if not predilection) to report and write in a way that even implicitly favors the pro-choice view of the controversy is not shocking. Clearly journalists—especially women journalists—share much the same social characteristics of the typical pro-choice advocate (as described by Luker). They make similar claims upon public life; they have similar interests at stake.

40. These statements were made at the Ethics and Public Policy Center conference "Abortion and the Media."

41. Ethan Bronner of the *Boston Globe,* quoted in Shaw, "Abortion Bias," p. 9.

42. Steinfels is quoted from the Ethics and Public Policy Center conference "Abortion and the Media." It would be failure of mine not to note that Steinfel's own weekly column represents one of the few distinct exceptions to the rule on this point.

43. Carl Bernstein, "The Idiot Culture," *New Republic,* 8 June 1992, pp. 22–28.

44. Ibid., pp. 24–25.

45. Ibid., p. 24.

46. Karen Tumulty of the *Los Angeles Times,* quoted in Shaw, "Abortion Bias," p. 23.

47. George Gallup, Sr., "Public Opinion in a Democracy," Stafford Little Lectures, Princeton University, New Jersey, 1939, p. 15.

48. See Kristin Luker, *Abortion and the Politics of Motherhood* (Berkeley: University of California Press, 1984), pp. 142–143.

49. Nancy D. Holt, "ABA Faces Divisive Abortion Issue," *Chicago Lawyer,* August 1990, p. 20.

50. Reported by Christi Harlan and Wade Lambert, "Texas Bar Threatens to Withdraw From ABA over Abortion Stand," *Wall Street Journal,* February 20, 1990, B 8:3.

51. Gail Diane Cox, "Storm Abates over ABA Abortion Stance," *National Law Journal,* 5 March 1990, p. 43.

52. Quoted from Holt, "ABA Faces Divisive Abortion Issue," p. 20.

53. Freddrenna Lyle, cited in Holt, "ABA Faces Divisive Abortion Issue," p. 21.

54. Sara-Ann Determan of the ABA's Individual Rights and Responsibilities Committee is quoted in David Margolick, "Bar Group Votes Neutrality on Abortion," *New York Times,* Midwest edition, 7 August 1990, p. 42.

55. Then incoming president of the ABA John Curtin, quoted in Holt, "ABA Faces Divisive Abortion Issue," p. 22.

56. The statement is made by Darrell Jordan of the Texas Bar Association. See Holt, "ABA Faces Divisive Abortion Issue," p. 22.

57. The resolution read, "The ABA supports state and federal legislation which protects the right of a woman to choose to terminate a pregnancy before fetal viability or thereafter, if such a termination is necessary to protect the life or health of the woman."

58. Sylvia Law, Jane Larson, and Clyde Spillenger, "Brief of 281 American Historians as *Amici Curiae* Supporting Appellees," filed in *Webster v. Reproductive Health Services, Inc.* (1989), p. 1.

59. Ibid.

60. Jane E. Larson and Clyde Spillenger, "That's Not History: The Boundaries of Advocacy and Scholarship," *Public Historian* 12, no. 3 (Summer 1990), p. 34.

61. Law et al., "Brief of 281 American Historians," p. 4ff.
62. Ibid., p. 6.
63. Ibid., p. 13.
64. Ibid., p. 25.
65. Ibid.
66. Sylvia Law, "Conversations Between Historians and the Constitution," *Public Historian* 12, no. 3 (Summer 1990), p. 14.
67. Law et al., "Brief of 281 American Historians," p. 30.
68. Ibid., p. 29.
69. The first feature of the brief one will notice is its method. The brief concentrates much of its attention on the social history of abortion rather than its legal history.

    In searching our nation's history for evidence of our society's basic beliefs, practices, and understandings, statutes are neither the only source nor the best ones. As legal historian Hendrik Hartog has pointed out, "[i]n defining law as the command of the sovereign we ordinarily deny the legitimacy of interpretative stances other than those . . . which have the benefit of formal authoritativeness." In any calculus of traditions and "fundamental" values, the moral beliefs and practices of ordinary people are entitled to consideration. (Ibid., p. 4)

    Social history, of course, is an entirely legitimate approach to understanding the past, and its inclusion would be essential to understanding our "history and traditions." The special focus on the social history of abortion practice, however, permitted the authors to downplay the disposition of institutions, not least legal institutions, toward abortion.
70. See Joseph Dellapenna, "Brief of the American Academy of Medical Ethics as *Amicus Curiae* in Support of Respondents and Cross-Petitioners Robert P. Casey et al.," filed in *Planned Parenthood of Southeastern Pennsylvania v. Casey* 6 April 1992. Dellapenna summarizes the legal commentary and case law on this point. The case law was split on whether pre-quickening abortion was a common-law crime, (see note 59, page 24).
71. James Mohr, *Abortion in America: The Origins and Evolution of National Policy, 1800–1900* (New York: Oxford University Press, 1978, pp. 164–165.
72. "Nineteenth century physicians knew categorically that quickening had no special significance as a stage in gestation. Hence it is not difficult to grant the genuineness of their uneasiness over the continued use of what they regarded as an unimportant, almost incidental, occurrence during pregnancy to distinguish between legal life and legal non-existence in cases of assault against a fetus. The next step beyond the denial of quickening as an appropriate distinction between being and non-being was the conclusion that no single occurrence dur-

ing gestation could be pinpointed as the moment at which a fetus in utero became more 'alive' than it had been a moment before. Logically, then, if a child could legally exist in utero at some stage of gestation, say at eight months, when the law recognized it as a victim, it just as logically existed at all other stages of gestation." Ibid., p. 165.

73. These terms were used in various nineteenth-century feminist publications, not least Susan B. Anthony's and Elizabeth Cady Stanton's journal, *The Revolution.* As historian Carl Degler has noted, the feminist defense of pre-natal life "was in line with a number of movements to reduce cruelty and to expand the concept of the sanctity of life . . . the elimination of the death penalty, the peace movement, the abolition of torture and whipping in connections with crimes. . . . The prohibition of abortion was but the most recent effort in that larger concern." See Carl Degler, *At Odds: Women and Family in America from the Revolution to the Present* (New York: Oxford University Press, 1980), p. 247.

74. Law, "Conversations," p. 15.

75. Estelle Freedman, "Historical Interpretation and Legal Advocacy: Rethinking the *Webster Amicus* Brief," *Public Historian* 12, no. 3 (Summer 1990), p. 28.

76. Ibid., p. 30.

77. Ibid., p. 31. Freedman does not stop here. The greatest problem, it would seem, is the way the brief tries to force the historical argument into a modern political language. "By having to argue for abortion as a right of privacy, the brief necessarily oversimplifies a range of theoretical (and practical) justifications for abortion and neglects a range of related political issues. It adopts a liberal feminist politics, emphasizing rights without reconsidering the larger social system that makes reproduction problematic for women in the first place" (p. 32).

78. James C. Mohr, "Historically Based Legal Briefs: Observations of a Participant in the Webster Process," *Public Historian* 12, no. 3 (Summer 1990), p. 25.

79. Law, "Conversations," p. 16.

80. Freedman, "Historical Interpretation," p. 32.

81. Larson and Spillenger, "That's Not History," p. 38.

82. We called Mohr about his reasons, but he refused to comment for the record. (Phone conversation between Carol Sargeant and James Mohr, 25 June 1992.)

83. Mohr, "Historically Based Legal Briefs," p. 25.

84. For example, the APA testified before the U.S. House of Representatives on the subject of the psychological consequences of abortion. After summarizing the scientific weaknesses in the research, it made the following conclusions:

The available research does, however, demonstrate some repeated findings. Unwanted pregnancies are stressful experiences for most women. Research tends to agree that, at some level, abortion is also a stressful experience for most women. For the vast majority of women, however, abortion relieves the stress of an unplanned pregnancy. It is common for women to report both emotions of relief as well as feelings of regret and guilt after an abortion. These feelings and other psychological sequelae are usually mild and tend to diminish rapidly over time without adversely affecting the woman's ability to function. Temporary guilt, regret, and sadness are not unusual after difficult decisions and, more importantly, are not psychological disorders. There is no research documenting the existence of "Post-Abortion Syndrome" and this "syndrome" is not a scientifically or medically recognized psychological disorder. (*Summary of APA's Testimony on the Psychological Consequences of Abortion*, Washington, D.C.: American Psychological Association, 1989)

85. The National Education Association (NEA) is one illustration of this. The main legislation initiatives of this teacher's union focus, unsurprisingly, upon federal education policy. For instance, it opposes federally mandated standardized achievement testing from preschool through high school; it opposes teacher evaluation (at least to the degree that it is linked to merit pay); it favors compulsory busing and the vigorous enforcement of affirmative action quotas; it favors bilingual education that uses a student's primary language as the principal medium of instruction in a bicultural setting; it opposes vouchers and tuition tax credits for parents sending their children to private schools; it opposes prayer in schools; and so on.

    It also makes resolutions on a wide range of issues that may or may not have an indirect tie to education policy. Through the 1980s, for example, the NEA supported a negotiation of a bilateral nuclear weapons freeze and the observance of all previously negotiated international arms agreements; opposed aid to Reagan-backed governments in Guatemala and El Salvador; supported the Equal Rights Amendment; opposed any discrimination against homosexuals; and, as NEA lobbyist Michael Pons put it, supported "reproductive freedom without government intervention" (telephone conversation, 3 June 1992).

86. Laurence Tribe, *Abortion: The Clash of Absolutes* (New York: Norton, 1990), pp. 82–83.

87. "NEA Inaugurates Prayer and Voter Registration Campaign," press release, 3 March 1992. All quotes in this paragraph are taken from this statement.

88. From a letter by Pat Hoffman, Worcester County, Massachusetts, coordinator of Christian Coalition, dated 23 September 1992. Immediately preceding this description is a salutation: "Greetings in the name of our Lord Jesus Christ."

89. All of this was taken from statements made at the Hartford Seminary Foundation conference "Lessons from 20 Years of Church Activism," 4 October 1991.
90. "Political Responsibility: Revitalizing American Democracy" (Washington, D.C.: United States Catholic Conference, 1992).
91. Ibid., p. 3.
92. See Richard Neuhaus, "The Catholic Church as Interest Group," *First Things,* January 1992, pp. 55–56 for ironic commentary on this document.
93. See Allen D. Hertzke, *Representing God in Washington: The Role of Religious Lobbies in American Polity* (Knoxville: University of Tennessee Press, 1988), p. 5.
94. See Nancy Tatom Ammerman, *Baptist Battles* (New Brunswick, N.J.: Rutgers University Press, 1990).
95. See James Davison Hunter, *Culture Wars* (New York: Basic Books, 1991), chapter 3.
96. See Hertzke, *Representing God,* p. 128.
97. Policy formation in many religious bodies (particularly Protestant denominations) is, in fact, democratic in nature. Yet these same bodies voice positions arrived at not through the participation of the laity in a democratic process, but through the fiat of its leaders.
98. Hertzke's study also acknowledges this as a problem. Hertzke, *Representing God,* p. 207.

Chapter 7.

1. See the section on multiculturalism in chapter 8 of my book *Culture Wars* (New York: Basic Books, 1991) for a summary of the political dimensions of this issue.
2. Donald D. Sharpes, "Residence and Race in Education: Conflict in Courts and Communities," *Journal of Teacher Education,* Winter 1973, p. 292.
3. James B. Macdonald, "Living Democratically in Schools: Cultural Pluralism," in *Multicultural Education: Commitments, Issues, and Applications,* edited by Carl A. Grant (Washington, D.C.: Association for Supervision and Curriculum Development, 1977), p. 13.
4. Frances Kellor, "What Is Americanization?" *Yale Review* 8 (1919), pp. 282–299.
5. Robert A. Carlson, *The Quest for Conformity: Americanization Through Education,* New York: John Wiley and Sons, Inc., 1975, p. 126.
6. Ibid., p. 128.
7. Ibid., p. 123.

8. See the review by Howard Hill, "The Americanization Movement," *American Journal of Sociology* 24, no. 6, p. 630.
9. Quotation from the National Americanization Committee, cited ibid.
10. Kellor, "What Is Americanization?" p. 285.
11. See, for example, Stephan Brumberg, *Going to America, Going to School: The Jewish Immigrant Public School Encounters in Turn-of-the-Century New York City* (New York: Praeger, 1986).
12. Even at the time the movement was in full operation, observers doubted its success. Robert A. Carlson, "Americanization as an Early Twentieth-Century Adult Education Movement," *History of Education Quarterly* 10 (1970), pp. 440–464. Contemporary historians hold the same judgment. See, for example, John F. McClymer, "The Americanization Movement and the Education of the Foreign-Born Adult." In *American Education and European Immigrant: 1840–1940,* edited by Bernard J. Weiss (Urbana: University of Illinois Press, 1982).
13. See the review by Hill, "The Americanization Movement," pp. 609–642.
14. Ibid.
15. I draw extensively from Michael R. Olneck's insightful work in this section. See his "Americanization and the Education of Immigrants, 1900–1925: An Analysis of Symbolic Action," *American Journal of Education* 97 (1989), pp. 398–423. His work on the general matter of pluralism and education is the most impressive I have seen. My debt to him is evident throughout.
16. Quotation from the National Americanization Committee, cited in Hill, "The Americanization Movement," p. 630.
17. Frances Kellor, quoted in Olneck, "Americanization and the Education of Immigrants," p. 402.
18. President Wilson, quoted ibid.
19. Unsigned article in the Bureau of Education's *Americanization Bulletin,* quoted ibid.
20. Ibid., p. 403.
21. Kellor, "What Is Americanization?" p. 285.
22. Olneck, "Americanization and the Education of Immigrants," pp. 403–404.
23. Secretary of the Interior Franklin Lane, quoted ibid., pp. 398–411.
24. Frances Kellor, "What Is Americanization?" p. 287.
25. Michael Olneck, "The Recurring Dream: Symbolism and Ideology in Intercultural and Multicultural Education," *American Journal of Education* 98 (1990), pp. 147–170.
26. "What a Teacher Might Say to Her Students," from "A Sample Homeroom Discussion" (1934–1935), Rachel Davis DeBois papers.

27. Olneck summarizes this as follows: despite some tendencies within intercultural education to affirm distinctive cultural identities, the predominant emphasis within the rhetoric, symbolism, and practices of intercultural education was to mute the salience of differences, to harmonize social relationships among diverse individuals, and to circumscribe the representation and the reach of collective ethnic identity in America, while extending the reach of a shared mainstream.

28. As with Americanization and interculturalism, multiculturalism is not a single, unitary theory or set of policies toward pluralism. Rather, the term refers to a range of curricular, pedagogical, and organizational ideas, policies and practices directed toward addressing social and cultural diversity in American schools (primary, secondary and university). In their details, these are highly contentious, to say the least, not only among the theorists and apologists of multiculturalism but among its practitioners as well.

29. Albert Shanker, "Multiculturalism and Global Education—Value Free?" *New York Times* advertisement, 1991.

30. Quoted ibid.

31. District of Columbia Board of Education, "Final Report: Commission of Values-Centered Goals for the District of Columbia Public Schools," September 1988, p. 15.

32. California Task Force to Promote Self-Esteem and Personal and Social Responsibility, *Toward a State of Esteem* (Sacramento: California State Department of Education, 1990), pp. 31–32. The sentiment is ubiquitous. In its advice to teachers, one popular guide to curriculum insisted that teachers "must validate the traditions and values of each child's background and strengthen the child's respect for the customs of his or her culture." See *Supporting Young Adolescents: A Guide to Leading Parent Meetings* (Granville, Ohio: Quest International, 1987), p. 15.

33. Appropriately, they have been both well received but thoroughly institutionalized by the educational establishment in what some have called a "quiet revolution" (Arthur Levine and Neanette Cureton, "The Quiet Revolution: Eleven Facts About Multiculturalism and the Curriculum," *Change* 24, no. 1; [January-February 1992], pp. 25–29). "The National Education Association, for example, fully embraces the multiculturalist ideals. . . . They have been established in colleges and universities as well. More than a third of all American colleges and universities have a multicultural general education requirement; more than a third of these institutions offer courses in women's studies, African-American studies, Native-American studies and the like; more than half of these schools have included multicultural elements into their departmental course offerings; and half of all colleges and universities have multicultural advising programs." (Levine and Cureton,

"The Quiet Revolution," pp. 25–29.) So too have these concerns and ideals been embraced by professional academic societies. At the 1990 annual meeting of the American Philosophical Association, about 10 percent of the papers delivered dealt with matters of gender and race, compared to none in 1970. At the 1990 meeting of the Modern Language Association, 30 percent of the papers were on these topics, compared to 20 percent in 1970. (Johnnella Butler and Betty Schmitz, "Ethnic Studies, Women's Studies and Multiculturalism," *Change* 24, no. 1 [January-February 1992:, p. 39.]

34. This commitment was reflected in a proposal of the District of Columbia Board of Education: "The commission recommends that the D.C. Public Schools develop curricular and extracurricular programs that are multicultural in approach, to help students avoid egocentric and judgmental attitudes toward people who are different from themselves. These programs should emphasize the pluralism of contemporary America and help students appreciate the contributions of various minority and ethnic groups." ("Final Report," p. 15.)

35. Quoted in Olneck, "The Recurring Dream," p. 158.

36. "Encouraging Multicultural Education: A Statement of the ASCE Multicultural Education Commission," in *Multicultural Education: Commitments, Issues, and Applications*, edited by Carl A. Grant (Washington, D.C.: Association for Supervision and Curriculum Development, 1977), p. 1.

37. See Molefi Kete Asante, "The Afrocentric Idea in Education," *Journal of Negro Education* 60 (1991), pp. 170–180; and Molefi Asante and Diane Ravitch, "Multiculturalism: An Exchange," *American Scholar* 60 (1991), pp. 267–276.

38. See Michael Olneck, "Redefining Equality: Multiculturalism in American Education," unpublished paper, University of Wisconsin, Madison, 1992, p. 41.

39. See ibid., p. 28. For an illustration of how this is implemented at the school board level, consider the District of Columbia Board of Education worded this need:

African-American students must become the subject of their own history and not the object of others' history. Despite the fact that the D.C. Public Schools are staffed with predominantly African-American teachers and staff and attended by predominantly African-American students, informal studies reveal that African-American high school seniors in our school system know little or nothing about American slavery, the civil rights movement or the enormous contributions that African-Americans have made to this country and to the world. *The Commission cannot stress emphatically enough its conviction that African-American history is an absolutely essential course of study in the D.C. public schools.* ("Final Report," p. 15, emphasis in original)

40. The tensions between these two ideas about diversity are illustrated in the controversy surrounding California's adoption of a new multigrade series of multicultural textbooks. The textbooks embraced the former vision, providing a "warts and all" history of the nation, being careful to show the full range of diversity of experience in American life—including the often cruel treatment of native Americans through the Spanish missions system and the experiences of slaves, as well as histories of African and Islamic peoples. Its critics, however, insisted that the portraits of minorities and their histories were insensitive, stereotyped, and distorted. See Robert Reinhold, "Class Struggle," *New York Times Magazine,* Sept. 29, 1991, 6, 26:2.

41. This observation is not simply derived from a review of multiculturalist materials. It is theoretically propounded as well. One theorist identified five "vital components of culture" that educators "must recognize and accept while working with multicultural student populations. . . . Culture, in the context of cultural pluralism, would include commonality among individuals within any given group in: (1) language, (2) diet, (3) costuming, (4) social patterns, and (5) ethics." John Aragon, "An Impediment to Cultural Pluralism: Culturally Deficient Educators Attempting to Teach Culturally Different Children," *Cultural Pluralism in Education: A Mandate for Change* (New York: Appleton-Century-Croft, 1973), p. 78.

42. Frances Schoonmaker Bolin, *Growing Up Caring* (Lake Forest, Ill.: Glencoe, 1990), p. 65.

43. See "Encouraging Multicultural Education," p. 2.

44. James Macdonald, "Living Democratically in Schools: Cultural Pluralism," in *Multicultural Education: Commitments, Issues, and Applications,* edited by Carl Grant (Washington, D.C.: Association for Supervision and Curriculum Development, 1977), p. 8.

45. Donna M. Gollnick, Frank Klassen, and Joost Yff, "Multicultural Education and Ethnic Studies in the United States" (Washington, D.C.: American Association of Colleges for Teacher Education, 1976), p. 13, emphasis added.

46. Michael Sandel, "Freedom of Conscience or Freedom of Choice?" in J. D. Hunter and Os Guinness, *Articles of Faith, Articles of Peace: The Religious Liberty Clauses and the American Public Philosophy* (Washington, D.C.: Brookings Institution, 1990), p. 75.

47. "Understanding Diversity," unpublished position paper, Charlottesville City Schools, 1992, p. 2.

48. Bolin, *Growing Up Caring,* p. 108.

49. Ibid., p. 26.

50. Ibid., p. 360.

51. Ibid., p. 327.

52. "Understanding Diversity," p. 2.
53. Shanker, "Multicultural and Global Education."
54. As Cathy Young put it, "The central premise of the multiculturalist credo, after all, is that all cultures are created equal. To judge other cultures by Western standards is unforgivably ethnocentric." Equal Cultures—or Equality," *Washington Post*, 29 March 1992, p. C5. *Time* observed this as well: "It is an article of faith among most multiculturalists that no one system of values is innately superior to any others; all cultures are created equal." "Whose America," *Time*, 8 July 1991, pp. 12–17 (quote on p. 16).
55. William Hunter, ed., *Multicultural Education Through Competency-Based Teacher Education* (Washington, D.C.: American Association of Colleges for Teacher Education, 1974), p. 12.
56. The derivation is both implicit and explicit. See, for example, Carl A. Grant, "Anthropological Foundations of Education That Is Multicultural," in *Multicultural Education: Commitments, Issues, and Applications,* edited by Carl A. Grant (Washington, D.C.: Association for Supervision and Curriculum Development, 1977).
57. Ralph Linton, "Universal Ethical Principles: An Anthropological View," in *Moral Principles of Action,* edited by Ruth N. Anshen (New York: Harper and Row, 1952), p. 646.
58. Writing in 1945, George Murdock was explicit about this: "The assumption that all peoples now living or of whom we possess substantial historical records, irrespective of differences in geography and physique, are essentially alike in their basic psychological equipment and mechanism, and that cultural differences between them reflect only the different responses of essentially similar organisms to unlike stimuli or conditions." See G. P. Murdock, "The Common Denominator of Cultures," in *The Science of Man in the World Crisis,* edited by Ralph Linton (New York: Columbia University Press, 1945), p. 125. Clyde Kluckhohn also concurred: "The mere existence of universals after so many millennia of culture history and in such diverse environments suggest that they correspond to something extremely deep in man's nature and/or are necessary conditions to social life." See his "Education, Values, and Anthropological Relativity," *Culture and Behavior,* edited by Richard Kluckhohn (New York: Free Press, 1962), p. 296.
59. Kluckhohn put it this way: "Cultural differences, real and important though they are, are still so many variations on themes supplied by raw human nature. The common understandings between men of different cultures are very broad, very general, and very easily obscured by language and many other observable symbols. True universals or near-universals are apparently few in number. But they seem to be as

deep-going as they are rare. Anthropology's facts attest that the phrase 'A common humanity' is in no sense meaningless." "Education, Values, and Anthropological Relativity," p. 294.

60. Paul Rabinow, "Humanism as Nihilism: The Bracketing of Truth and Seriousness in American Cultural Anthropology," in Norma Haan et al., *Social Science as Moral Inquiry* (New York: Columbia University Press, 1983), p. 59–60.

61. Multiculturalism (and contemporary anthropology) take this position even further, arguing that since all knowledge and perceptions of the world are social constructions, then there is no such thing as Impartiality, Objectivity or Truth. Knowledge has no correspondence with Reality. There is only knowledge and truth from the particular realities that people inhabit which serve their particular interests. It is from this that multicultural theorists derive the cliché that "all knowledge is political."

62. California Task Force, *Toward a State of Esteem*, pp. 31–32 (emphasis added).

63. "Encouraging Multicultural Education," p. 2.

64. Thomas Sobol is quoted in Chester Finn, "Narcissus Goes to School," *Commentary*, June 1990, p. 40.

65. See Charles Taylor, *Multiculturalism and "The Politics of Recognition"* (Princeton, N.J.: Princeton University Press, 1992).

66. Whether the theory holds any scientific credibility or not is beside the point. The theory builds upon a dubious application of the insights of developmental psychology. Developmental psychologists have found that those who perform well in school have high levels of self-esteem. Developmentalists then conflate self-esteem with educational policy, arguing that since these two variables are correlated, by increasing the latter one will increase the former. Studies reviewed in a forthcoming work show the policy is misguided.

67. I might add that politicizing culture only makes matters worse. When power—either its acquisition or its maintenance—is the objective, the "mutual understanding of differences," which is the purported goal of multiculturalism, merely becomes a device by which legitimacy is established. Thus, to *require* children, adolescents, and college students to understand what makes a culture different is to imply that what makes that culture different is worth understanding. In this, the legitimacy of other "values" and cultural practices is the objective, not understanding for its own sake.

68. Quoted in Chester E. Finn, Jr., "Teacher Politics," *Commentary*, February 1983, pp. 30–31. This is also, in part, what is behind multiculturalist admonitions to teachers to be sensitive to "different learning

styles" that are "influenced by [the student's] cultural and linguistic backgrounds." *Skills for Growing,* (Granville, OH: Quest International, 1990), p. 38.

69. In all of the multicultural literature I have seen, abortion and the underlying cultural differences that are involved in this dispute are ignored completely.

70. The same problem exists in trying to defend justice, another central end to multiculturalism. The very idea of justice requires a moral foundation for it presupposes standards of right and wrong, good and bad. To *do* justice one must know the difference. The trivialization and relativization of culture implicit in multiculturalism deny the possibility of the establishment of any standards by which one can measure just from unjust. The de facto result is a therapeutic definition of justice—i.e. the feeling of appreciation, the feeling of inclusion, the feeling of respect. This point is elaborated by S. D. Gaede in *When Tolerance Is No Virtue*, Downers Grove, Ill.: Intervarsity Press, 1993.

Chapter 8.

1. Fred Barnes, "No Womb for Debate," *New Republic*, 27 July 1992, pp. 36–37.

2. Ibid., p. 37.

3. Ibid., p. 36.

4. David Von Drehle, "A Celebration by Religious Right as Platform Panel Sees the Light," *Washington Post*, 18 August 1992, p. A15.

5. Cited in Helen Dewar, "Frustrated Rudman to Leave Senate," *Washington Post*, 25 March 1992, pp. A1, A4.

6. On this point, Justice Scalia (in his dissenting opinion from the majority on *Casey*) is correct: "The court foreclos[es] all democratic outlet for the deep passions this issue arouses." Cited in *Casey v. Planned Parenthood* (1992).

7. Here I rely greatly on Benjamin Barber's discussion in *Strong Democracy* (Berkeley and Los Angeles: University of California Press, 1984). I quickly summarize points that Barber deals with more adequately in that text.

8. Barber shows that an anti-populism exists both on the right and on the left. See chapter 1, note 5 and chapter 7, note 16 in *Strong Democracy*.

9. Barber, *Strong Democracy*, pp. 154–155.

10. As Barber argues, representative government is not supplanted, but rather supplemented. *Strong Democracy*, p. 262.

11. Barber, *Strong Democracy*, p. xiii.

12. Barber, *Strong Democracy*, p. xvi.

Chapter 9.

1. Kennan suggests that the nation might be divided into nine relatively autonomous republics. See George Kennan, *Around the Cragged Hill* (New York: Norton, 1993), pp, 149ff.
2. For example, libertarian economist James Buchanan, a Nobel Prize winner in 1986, also recommends radical decentralization. He argues that there is no sense of a national community left in the United States except in periods of war. In this light he raises the possibility of political secession by region.
3. Consider, again, Adam Seligman's argument in *The Idea of Civil Society* (New York: Free Press, 1992).
4. In darker moods, I am inclined to agree with Eliot's observation (in his essay, "Notes Toward a Definition of Culture,") that one cannot put on a new culture ready made. "You must wait for the grass to grow to feed the sheep to give the wool out of which your new coat will be made. You must pass through many centuries of barbarism. We should not live to see the new culture, nor would our great-great-great-grandchildren: and if we did, not one of us would be happy in it." T. S. Eliot, *Christianity and Culture,* New York: Harcourt Brace Jovanovich, 1977, p. 200.
5. Bell is, in fact, summarizing the observations of Van Wyck Brooks and Perry Miller, among others. See Daniel Bell, *The Cultural Contradictions of Capitalism* (New York: Basic Books, 1976), p. 56.
6. The phrase is Max Weber's. See Max Weber, "Politics as a Vocation," in Hans Gerth and C. W. Mills, *On Max Weber* (New York: Oxford University Press, 1967), p. 122.
7. The ethic of ultimate ends apparently must go to pieces on the problem of the justification of means by ends. As a matter of fact, logically it has only the possibility of rejecting all action that employs morally dangerous means—in theory! In the world of realities, as a rule, we encounter the ever-renewed experience that the adherent of an ethic of ultimate ends suddenly turns into a chiliastic prophet. See Weber, "Politics as a Vocation."
8. See the Williamsburg Charter, in J. D. Hunter and Os Guinness, *Articles of Faith, Articles of Peace: The First Amendment Religious Liberty Clauses and the American Public Philosophy* (Washington, D.C.: Brookings Institution, 1991).
9. Weber, "Politics as a Vocation," p. 117.
10. Tamar Lewin, "In Bitter Abortion Debate, Opponents Learn to Reach for Common Ground," *New York Times*, 17 February 1992, p. A10.
11. Ibid.
12. Loretto Wagner, quoted in ibid.

13. Ibid.
14. See Alissa Rubin, "Project Rachel: Regretting Abortions," *Alicia Patterson Foundation Reporter* 15, no. 2 (1992), pp. 40–47 for a more extensive report on this initiative and its place in the larger scheme of abortion politics in Connecticut. Project Rachel can be found in eighty other dioceses in forty states.
15. Ibid.
16. Lewin, "In Bitter Abortion Debate."
17. Ibid.
18. Ibid.
19. The statement was made by Charlotte Taft of the Routh Street Women's Clinic in Dallas, mentioned in Chapter Four. She is also quoted in Lewin, "In Bitter Abortion Debate."
20. This statement was adopted by a more than two-thirds majority vote. "A Social Statement on Abortion," Evangelical Lutheran Church in America, adopted at the second biennial Churchwide Assembly, Orlando, Florida, August 28–September 4, 1991.
21. Ibid., pp. 10–11.
22. See Bill Wolfe, "Abortion Regulation Supported," *Washington Post,* 15 February 1992, p. B7.
23. Walter Lippmann, *The Public Philosophy* (Boston: Little, Brown and Company, 1955), pp. 126–127.
24. For more details on the Williamsburg Charter, see Hunter and Guinness, *Articles of Faith.*
25. Quoted in Os Guinness, *The American Hour* (New York: Free Press, 1992), pp. 213–214.
26. This document was republished under the same title in the journal *First Things,* November 1992, pp. 43–45.
27. Albert R. Jonsen and Stephen Toulmin, *The Abuse of Casuistry: A History of Moral Reasoning* (Berkeley and Los Angeles: University of California Press, 1988), p. 9.
28. Lippmann, *The Public Philosophy,* p. 130.
29. Ibid.
30. Again, see Benjamin Barber, *Strong Democracy* (Berkeley and Los Angeles: University of California Press, 1984), pp. 119, 129, 136, 151.

SELECTED BIBLIOGRAPHY

Ammerman, Nancy Tatom. *Baptist Battles.* New Brunswick, N.J.: Rutgers University Press, 1990.

Aragon, John. "An Impediment to Cultural Pluralism: Culturally Deficient Educators Attempting to Teach Culturally Different Children." *Cultural Pluralism in Education: A Mandate for Change.* New York: Appleton-Century-Croft, 1973.

Asante, Molefi Kete. "The Afrocentric Idea in Education." *Journal of Negro Education* 60 (1991).

Asante, Molefi Kete and Diane Ravitch. "Multiculturalism: An Exchange." *American Scholar* 60 (1991).

Barber, Benjamin. *Strong Democracy.* Berkeley and Los Angeles: University of California Press, 1984.

Bell, Daniel. "American Exceptionalism Revisited: The Role of Civil Society." *Public Interest* 95 (1989), pp. 38–56.

Bell, Daniel. *The Cultural Contradictions of Capitalism.* New York: Basic Books, 1976.

Bennett, Stephen Earl. *Apathy in America, 1960–1984: Causes and Consequences of Citizen Political Indifference.* Dobbs Ferry, N.Y.: Transnational Publishers, 1986.

Berger, Brigitte and Peter Berger. "Goshtalk, Femspeak and the Battle of Language." In *The War over the Family.* New York: Basic Books, 1984.

Berger, Peter L. and Richard John Neuhaus. *To Empower People: The Role of Mediating Structures in Public Policy.* Washington, D.C.: American Enterprise Institute for Public Policy Research, 1977.

Bernstein, Carl. "The Idiot Culture." *New Republic,* 8 June 1992, pp. 22–28.

Bhandari, D. R. *History of European Political Philosophy.* Bangalore, India: Bangalore Publishing Co., 1963.

Bourdieu, Pierre. "On Interest and the Relative Autonomy of Symbolic Power." Working papers and proceedings of the Center for Psychosocial Studies, Chicago, 1988.

Bourdieu, Pierre. "Symbolic Power." *Critique of Anthropology* 4 (1979), pp. 77–85.

Brumberg, Stephan. *Going to America, Going to School: The Jewish Immigrant Public School Encounters in Turn-of-the-Century New York City.* New York: Praeger, 1986.

Butler, Johnella and Betty Schmitz. "Ethnic Studies, Women's Studies and Multiculturalism." *Change* 24, no. 1 (January/February 1992).

Callahan, Daniel. "An Ethical Challenge to Pro-Choice Advocates: Abortion and the Pluralistic Proposition." *Commonweal,* 23 November 1990, pp. 681–687.

Carey, J. *Communication as Culture: Essays on Media and Society.* Boston: Unwin Hyman, 1989.

Carlson, Robert A. "Americanization as an Early Twentieth-Century Adult Education Movement." *History of Education Quarterly* 10 (1970), pp. 440–464.

Carlson, Robert A. *The Quest for Conformity: Americanization through Education.* New York: John Wiley and Sons, 1975.

Cover, Robert. "Nomos and Narrative." *Harvard Law Review* 9714 (1982).

Cox, Gail Diane. "Storm Abates over ABA Abortion Stance." *National Law Journal,* 5 March 1990, p. 43.

Cunningham, Paige Comstock and Clarke D. Forsythe. "Is Abortion the 'First Right' for Women? Some Consequences of Legal Abortion." In *Abortion, Medicine and the Law,* 4th ed., edited by J. Douglas Butler and David F. Walbert. New York: Facts on File, 1992.

Degler, Carl. *At Odds: Women and Family in America from the Revolution to the Present.* New York: Oxford University Press, 1980.

Dellapenna, Joseph. "Brief of the American Academy of Medical Ethics as *Amicus Curiae* in Support of Respondents and Cross-Petitioners Robert P. Casey et al." filed in *Planned Parenthood v. Casey,* 6 April 1992.

Finn, Chester. "Narcissus Goes to School." *Commentary,* June 1990, p. 40.

Foucault, Michel. *The History of Sexuality, Volume I.* New York: Vintage, 1990.

Franco, Kathleen N., Marijo Tamburrino, Nancy Campbell, Judith Pentz, and Stephen Jurs. "Psychological Profile of Dysphoric Women Postabortion." 44, *Journal of the American Medical Women's Association 113* (July/August 1989).

Freedman, Estelle. "Historical Interpretation and Legal Advocacy: Rethinking the *Webster Amicus* Brief." *Public Historian* 12, no. 3 (Summer 1990).

Gallup, George, Sr. "Public Opinion in a Democracy." Stafford Little Lectures, Princeton University, New Jersey, 1939.

Gerth, Hans and C. W. Mills. *On Max Weber.* New York: Oxford University Press, 1967.

Gilligan, Carol. *In a Different Voice.* Cambridge, Mass.: Harvard University Press, 1982.

Glendon, Mary Ann. *Abortion and Divorce in Western Law.* Cambridge, Mass.: Harvard University Press, 1987.

Gollnick, Donna M., Frank Klassen, and Joost Yff. *Multicultural Education and Ethnic Studies in the United States.* Washington, D.C.: American Association of Colleges for Teacher Education, 1976.

Graebner, Norman. "Government Without Consensus." *Virginia Quarterly Review* Vol. 54 (1978), pp. 648–664.

Grant, Carl A. "Anthropological Foundations of Education That is Multicultural." In *Multicultural Education: Commitments, Issues, and Applications.* Washington, D.C.: Association for Supervision and Curriculum Development, 1977.

Grant, Carl A. "Encouraging Multicultural Education: A Statement of the ASCE Multicultural Education Commission." In *Multicultural Education: Commitments, Issues, and Applications.* Washington, D.C.: Association for Supervision and Curriculum Development, 1977.

Guinness, Os. *The American Hour.* New York: Free Press, 1992.

Habermas, Jurgen. *Legitimation Crisis.* Boston: Beacon Press, 1975.

Habermas, Jurgen. "On Systematically Distorted Communication." *Inquiry* 13, no. 3 (Autumn 1970), pp. 205–218.

Habermas, Jurgen. "The Public Square." *New German Critique* 1, no. 3 (Fall, 1974), pp. 49–55.

Habermas, Jurgen. *Toward a Rational Society: Student Protest, Science and Politics.* Boston: Beacon Press, 1970.

Habermas, Jurgen. "Towards a Theory of Communicative Competence." *Inquiry* 13, no. 4 (Winter 1970), pp. 360–375.

Henshaw, Stanley, Nancy Binkin, Ellen Blaine, and Jack C. Smith. "A Portrait of American Women Who Obtain Abortions." *Family Planning Perspectives* 17, no. 2 (1985), pp. 90–96.

Herman, Edward and Noam Chomsky. *Manufacturing Consent: The Political Economy of the Mass Media.* New York: Pantheon, 1988.

Hertzke, Allen D. *Representing God in Washington: The Role of Religious Lobbies in the American Polity.* Knoxville: University of Tennessee Press, 1988.

Hill, Howard. "The Americanization Movement." *American Journal of Sociology* 24, no. 6 (May 1919), pp. 609–642.

Holt, Nancy D. "ABA Faces Divisive Abortion Issue." *Chicago Lawyer,* August 1990, p. 20.

Hunter, James Davison. *Culture Wars: The Struggle to Define America.* New York: Basic Books, 1991.

Hunter, James Davison. "Religion and the State: The Problem of Modern Pluralism." *Brookings Review,* Spring 1990, pp. 20–27.

Hunter, James Davison and Os Guinness. *Articles of Faith, Articles of Peace: The Religious Liberty Clauses and the American Public Philosophy.* Washington, D.C.: Brookings Institution, 1990.

Hunter, William, ed. *Multicultural Education Through Competency-Based Teacher Education.* Washington, D.C.: American Association of Colleges for Teacher Education, 1974.

Imber, Jonathan. "Abortion Policy and Medical Practice." *Society* 27, no. 5 (July/August 1990).

Jonsen, Albert R. and Stephen Toulmin. *The Abuse of Casuistry: A History of Moral Reasoning.* Berkeley and Los Angeles: University of California Press, 1988.

Kellor, Frances. "What is Americanization?" *Yale Review* 8 (1919), pp. 282–299.

Kennan, George. *Around the Cragged Hill.* New York: Norton, 1993.

Kluckhohn, Clyde. "Education, Values, and Anthropological Relativity." In *Culture and Behavior,* edited by Richard Kluckhohn. New York: Free Press, 1962.

Lamont, Michele and Annette Lareau. "Cultural Capital: Allusions, Gaps and Glissandos." *Recent Theoretical Developments in Sociological Theory* 6, no. 2 (Fall 1988), pp. 153–159.

Larson, Jane E. and Clyde Spillenger. "That's Not History: The Boundaries of Advocacy and Scholarship." *Public Historian* 12, no. 3 (Summer 1990).

Lasch, Christopher. "The Lost Art of Political Argument." *Harper's,* September 1990, pp. 17–22.

Law, Sylvia. "Conversations Between Historians and the Constitution." *Public Historian* 12, no. 3 (Summer 1990).

Lee, James Melvin. *History of American Journalism.* Boston: Houghton Mifflin, 1923.

Levine, Arthur and Neanette Cureton. "The Quiet Revolution: Eleven Facts About Multiculturalism and the Curriculum." *Change* 24, no. 1 (January/February 1992), pp. 25–29.

Linton, Ralph. "Universal Ethical Principles: An Anthropological View." In *Moral Principles of Action,* edited by Ruth N. Anshen. New York: Harper and Row, 1952.

Lippmann, Walter. *Liberty and the News.* New York: Harcourt, Brace and Howe, 1920.

Lippmann, Walter. *The Public Philosophy.* Boston: Little, Brown and Company, 1955.

Lipset, S. M. and William Schneider. *The Confidence Gap.* Baltimore: Johns Hopkins University Press, 1987.

Luker, Kristin. *Abortion and the Politics of Motherhood.* Berkeley: University of California Press, 1984.

Lukes, Stephen. *Power: A Radical View.* London: Macmillan Education Ltd., 1974.

Macdonald, James B. "Living Democratically in Schools: Cultural Pluralism." In *Multicultural Education: Commitments, Issues, and Applications,* edited by Carl A. Grant. Washington, D.C.: Association for Supervision and Curriculum Development, 1977.

MacKinnon, Catherine. *Feminism Unmodified.* Cambridge, Mass.: Harvard University Press, 1987.

MacKinnon, Catherine. "Roe v. Wade: A Study of Male Ideology." In *Abortion: Moral and Legal Perspectives,* edited by Jay L. Garfield and Patricia Hennessey. Amherst: University of Massachusetts Press, 1984.

Marzolf, Marion Tuttle. *Civilizing Voices: American Press Criticism, 1880–1950.* New York: Longman, 1991.

McClymer, John F. "The Americanization Movement and the Education of the Foreign-Born Adult." In *American Education and European Immigrants: 1840–1940,* edited by Bernard J. Weiss. Urbana: University of Illinois Press, 1982.

McConnell, Michael W. "How Not to Promote Serious Deliberation About Abortion." *University of Chicago Law Review* 58, no. 3 (Summer 1991), pp. 1181–1202.

Miller, James. *The Passion of Michel Foucault.* New York: Simon and Schuster, 1993.

Mohr, James. *Abortion in America: The Origins and Evolution of National Policy, 1800–1900.* New York: Oxford University Press, 1978.

Mohr, James C. "Historically Based Legal Briefs: Observations of a Participant in the Webster Process." *Public Historian* 12, no. 3 (Summer 1990).

Mott, Frank Luther. *American Journalism: A History of Newspapers in the United States Through 250 Years.* New York: Macmillan, 1941.

Murdock, George P. "The Common Denominator of Cultures." In *The Science of Man in the World Crisis,* edited by Ralph Linton. New York: Columbia University Press, 1945.

Olneck, Michael R. "Americanization and the Education of Immigrants, 1900–1925: An Analysis of Symbolic Action." *American Journal of Education* 97 (1989).

Olneck, Michael R. "The Recurring Dream: Symbolism and Ideology in Intercultural and Multicultural Education." *American Journal of Education* 98 (1990).

Olneck, Michael R. "Redefining Equality: Multiculturalism in American Education." Unpublished paper, University of Wisconsin, Madison, 1992.

Padover, Saul K., ed. *Democracy,* by Thomas Jefferson. New York: D. Appleton-Century, 1939.

Pangle, Thomas. *Ennobling Democracy.* Baltimore: Johns Hopkins University Press, 1992.

Percy, Walker. *Signposts in a Strange Land,* edited by Patrick Samway. New York: Noonday Press, 1991.

Rabinow, Paul. "Humanism as Nihilism: The Bracketing of Truth and Seriousness in American Cultural Anthropology." In *Social Science as Moral Inquiry,* by Norma Haan et al. New York: Columbia University Press, 1983.

Rieff, Philip. "The New Noises of War in the Second Culture Camp: Notes on Professor Burt's Legal Fictions." *Yale Journal of Law and the Humanities* 3, no. 2 (Summer 1991).

Rogers, James L., et al. "Impact of the Minnesota Parental Notification Law on Abortion and Birth." *American Journal of Public Health* 81, no. 3 (March 1991).

Rosenblatt, Roger. *Life Itself.* New York: Random House, 1992.

Sandel, Michael. "Freedom of Conscience or Freedom of Choice?" In *Articles of Faith, Articles of Peace: The Religious Liberty Clauses and the American Public Philosophy,* by J. D. Hunter and Os Guinness. Washington, D.C.: Brookings Institution, 1990.

Seligman, Adam, *The Idea of Civil Society.* New York: Free Press, 1992.

Sharpes, Donald D. "Residence and Race in Education: Conflict in Courts and Communities." *Journal of Teacher Education,* Winter 1973.

Sheldon, G. W. *The Political Philosophy of Thomas Jefferson.* Baltimore: Johns Hopkins University Press, 1991.

Sproul, R. C. *Abortion: A Rational Look at an Emotional Issue.* Colorado Springs, Colo.: NavPress, 1990.

Taylor, Charles. "Modes of Civil Society." *Public Culture* 3, no. 1 (Fall 1990), pp. 95–118.

Taylor, Charles. *Multiculturalism and "The Politics of Recognition."* Princeton, N.J.: Princeton University Press, 1992.

Tipton, Steven M. "The Church as a School for Virtue." *Daedalus* 117 (Spring 1988), pp. 163–175.

Tocqueville, Alexis De. *Democracy in America.* New York: Anchor-Doubleday, 1969.

Torres, Aida and Jacqueline Darroch Forrest. "Why Do Women Have Abortions?" *Family Planning Perspectives* 20, no. 4 (1988), pp. 169–177.

Tribe, Laurence. *Abortion: The Clash of Absolutes.* New York: Norton, 1990.

Waltzer, Michael. "The Idea of Civil Society." *Dissent,* Spring 1991, pp. 293–304.

Weigel, George. "The Requirements and Limits of Civility: How We Contend." Paper presented at the Williamsburg Charter Conference, "Commitment and Civility: The First Amendment Religion Clauses and American Public Life," Charlottesville, Virginia, April 11–14, 1988.

Zimmerman, Mary K. *Passage Through Abortion: The Personal and Social Reality of Women's Experiences.* New York: Praeger, 1977.

INDEX

301